Gastronomy of France

RAYMOND OLIVER

Gastronomy of France

Translated from the French by
CLAUDE DURRELL

The Wine and Food Society
in association with
World Publishing Company

A Publication of
The Wine and Food Society Limited
in association with
World Publishing Company
2231 West 110th Street, Cleveland, Ohio

This book was designed and produced by
George Rainbird Limited
2 Hyde Park Place, London w2

Phototypeset in Monophoto Bembo by
Oliver Burridge Filmsetting Limited, Crawley, Sussex, England

The book was printed and bound in Hungary by
Kossuth Nyomda, Budapest
House Editors: J. E. M. Hoare, Rosemary Joekes and Joy Law
Designer: Eric Hughes
The endpapers were drawn by Stewart Black

To my father, the anglophile of the family,
who taught me to love my work
To my mother, who helped me to accomplish it

Contents

Color Plates

Illustrations

10

Acknowledgements

The publishers and producers would like to thank the following publishers and individuals for permission to quote material from the sources given:

Librairie Larousse, *Larousse Gastronomique* by Prosper Montagné with the collaboration of Dr Gottschalk, Paris, 1938; Publications Françaises, *Recettes et Paysages*, Paris, 1950–52

Flammarion, *Gastronomie Pratique* by Ali Bab, Paris, 1928; Pellet, *La Cuisine de Monsieur Momo Celibataire*, Paris, 1930; Nilson, *L'Art du Bien Manger*, edited by Richardin; Jabillard, *Dictionnaire Universel de Cuisine Pratique* by Joseph Fabre; Pelletan, *Régimes Vegetariens* by Mmes. Coquelet and Tissier.

Maisons et Jardins, Paris, for permission to reproduce the colour plate on page 219

Editions Tiranty, for permission to reproduce the colour plate on page 167 from *La Bouillabaisse* by Raymond Oliver

They would also like to thank those museums, galleries, agents and collectors who have courteously assisted them in obtaining the material for the illustrations reproduced in this volume. They would especially like to thank the following (the figures refer to the page numbers of the illustrations):

Alinari-Giraudon, 43, 45, 52, 59, 70

J. R. Freeman, 56, 71, 154

Giraudon, 17, 30, 33, 67, 68, 72, 73, 75, 78, 80, 81, 84, 87, 91, 93, 100, 101, 106, 107, 108, 113, 115, 116, 117, 121, 122, 123, 129, 131, 132, 150, 157, 158, 161, 168, 171, 173, 177, 190, 226, 238, 264, 280, 282

Horak, 49, 50, 104, 199, 201, 202, 219, 243, 255, 260, 263, 268, 269, 271, 272, 273, 274, 276, 277, 303–19

A. F. Kersting, 296, 308

Radio Times, Picture Post Library, 97, 152, 153, 179, 180, 205, 211, 214, 247, 248, 249, 250, 251, 253, 254, 257, 258, 262, 302

Derrick E. Witty, 256

Foreword

My friend Bernard Grasset wrote a book entitled *Les Chemins de l'Ecriture*. During his long career as a brilliant publisher he not only discovered many talented writers but he also helped those who had something to say but did not know how to say it. My excellent friend and neighbour, Emmanuel Berl, used to tell me that in order to write one must indeed have something to say.

This book is not written because I have something to say, but because I wish to set down an essence of human knowledge in one field distilled from the work of others.

The paths of cookery wind across civilizations, by way of the shepherd's hut, the fisherman's nets, the ploughshare, the baker's art and finally emerge via the schoolroom. How did our childhood affect our adolescence and our puberty prepare for our love affairs? What were the gastronomic associations with all the major acts of our lives? Several times in this book I shall voice my conviction that gastronomy is one of the humanities.

If one day I am lucky enough to be read by the young members of our profession, they will probably survive the experience only to wonder what contribution *ratatouille* can possibly have made to the progress of civilization. And yet, each ingredient of that dish has a history, often amazing, sometimes poetic, always profoundly human. Whether it be the aubergine, hailing from the Orient, the 'love apple' brought back by the Elizabethans, or the olive oil from the Mediterranean, home of the gods and cradle of Christianity, each contains the search for perfection and the desire for cultivation.

13

When I look at the books in my library, I can only feel deeply grateful to all those who have worked and suffered to improve the lives of their fellow-men. Since time began, taste has remained the sense which gives us the most joy for it is the only one rooted in irresistible need. I have set out to tell the story of the creator of the art connected with it – the cook.

1 Introduction

The Paths of Cookery

I find myself, as a gastronome, in a curious situation. I am to start with, a cook, in my case of necessity. I have become a gastronome by definition and have consequently spent a lot of time with cooks, loved and hated them in turn, and ended by esteeming them highly. My father was a cook and believed wholeheartedly that his profession was the finest in the world and that to feed one's neighbour superbly was the greatest happiness. One can in fact turn an organic function, which may be commonplace or even unpleasant, into a genuine source of delight, and the pleasures of the table are those most likely to prepare for all others. Indeed, one may confidently assert that a meal has as much effect on a lover as it has on an athlete. For more than half a century, I have been in touch, in my professional capacity, with every kind of gastronome, wine lover and mere glutton. It is they who dictate this book, for it is they to whom we are in thrall.

Perhaps I should enlarge on this a little.

Who sets the fashion in Paris? Courrèges, Estérel, St Laurent? No doubt. Who wears their clothes? One is tempted to answer, nobody. Similarly, gastronomy of the highest order is no longer practised by more than a tiny number of restaurateurs, perhaps as few as the great couturiers. For both, the major problem is, and must continue to be, a problem of price. One has therefore to fall back on quantity. The great glory of French gastronomy is upheld by a handful of apostles though its roots lie far in the past.

French cookery is still the only one in the world which, taken as a whole, is

15

one of intention. Cookery of intention is woman's cookery and thus would appear to be outside our terms of reference. But I don't think so. If men are more brilliant, more inventive and bolder, women are the Vestals of traditional gastronomy.

It was generally assumed that when women went out to work and deserted the hearth for extraneous activities, the old habits would disappear. In fact, this was not so, for we were mistaken about the origin and constitution of these habits. Certainly the big cities have absorbed a high proportion of our rural population, and girls raised on the farm in the most classical family tradition have given up the thick steaming soup of the evening for the sandwich and half-pint, but they revert to the old customs the moment they marry and settle down. This is true of everything connected with food and drink, which continue to be governed by laws apparently impervious to logic.

Many people alive today will remember the serious riots which have often followed a rise in the price of bread. I myself have an autographed and unpublished letter of Napoleon III in which he mentions the problem and wonders if some artificial process might not be found to solve it. Today, the government's problem is the price of steak. This leads me to my first principle, of capital importance: apparent gastronomy is not real gastronomy.

If truffles and foie gras come from Périgord, local family tradition only very rarely allows their use. Of course peasants from the region conceive of a good meal as influenced by the truffle, but they hardly ever eat one.

There has been a more literary than practical form of gastronomic snobbery to which nearly everyone has at some time subscribed. Brillat-Savarin, influenced by Grimod de la Reynière, wrote *La Physiologie du Goût*, but its only real virtue is its pleasant and readable style. Marcel Rouff, in his *Life and Loves of Dodin-Bouffant, Gourmet*, exploited various types of ridiculous meal in order to urge a return to simplicity. Curnonsky combined a taste for the good and the simple with the wish to resume his old name of Maurice Saillant, to become once more just an Anjou lad.

One forgets easily, which is one of the ways our subconscious mind helps to make life easier.

'The Table' by Le Sidaner, late nineteenth century

However, in our folk gastronomy, the essentials reach us from the earliest time. Little by little, the number of foodstuffs has dwindled. It would be interesting to try and draw a diagram of these continuous disappearances. Probably the pace varied, with long periods when many products vanished, and others when there was a conscious, albeit quickly forgotten, search for our sources in the past. When spices were considered essential to cookery, those who could not afford them replaced them by the innumerable herbs which periodically come back into fashion. The reasons for this were curious. The periods when spices and herbs were in constant use were also those when meat was scarce, badly preserved and therefore always badly cooked. There is an old saying that 'good sauce washes down bad fish'. The cookery books of antiquity were written like chemical formulae, in a personal sort of code. I myself did not escape this influence in my early days at a time when, nevertheless, there was nothing to prevent my being clear and precise. But I fell into the trap and had to work hard to avoid becoming a mere echo of my father. To object to making sauces by reducing them by simmering and accept thickening them with flour may seem paradoxical but is not – for no amount of thickening is as bad as too much reduction. The rules for health laid down in early printed books seem pretty naive to us now, but dietetics learns to live amicably with greed.

In the face of all this, who could deny that cookery alters and develops age by age? Who can deny that people eat differently nowadays? An economist will give you the reasons: cultivation, distribution, methods of cooking, eight-hour working days, leisure, techniques. All this is true and it all permeates our daily lives. Even the staunchest gastronomes drink whisky or Coca-Cola, chew corn on the cob, or invent grilled meat and rosemary! I even know some who use Hickory salt, monosodium glutamate and put vitamin C in their asparagus sauce to increase the aphrodisiac virtue of that vegetable. But in spite of all this, French gastronomy based on cookery and wine not only survives but grows and indeed improves, as do all arts in a period of transition. The great crises of painting, whether impressionist, cubist, pointillist or abstract are simply stepping stones. There are paintings which reflect genius: those of Velasquez, Toulouse-Lautrec or Van Gogh. French cookery is analogous; it has had setbacks, periods of depression, moments of enthusiasm. It is an art and has its Muses, its admirers and its craftsmen.

There is no room for fashion or for snobbery. If the artist panders to contemporary taste (which is frequently the case), it simply adds to his experience, but to know what not to do is wisdom itself. I have seen a lot of very great cooks at work, and each has a style of his own. Jean Cocteau once said that a line, a simple line intended only to be more or less straight, betrayed its creator, and asserted that he could identify the artist whether Picasso, Dali or Mathieu. I think I could recognize a hollandaise sauce or a truffled omelette from the hands of a Marcel Laget, a Nello Decamp, a Humbert or a Bocuse. Each has something personal to say, and, more important still, each has style.

I don't intend to list all the famous French cooks. In any case, I should be certain to forget some of the best and probably some who are my friends.

But in gastronomy, cooks are only pieces - important ones, certainly - on the chessboard. Let us say they are the king. The queen, unquestionably, must be drink, which for the Frenchman means wine first and foremost, closely followed by spirits. Of course there are the other pieces too. The game is a thrilling one, but one must learn the rules: how to eat and drink. A proper education in both these subjects can greatly intensify the pleasures they have to offer - perhaps even prove a revelation.

What is the point of it all? It is searching for a memory. There are vague, imprecise childhood recollections, or tangible, material links with some place or person, or even lodged in the bloodcells and chromosomes, atavistic eating habits. If it takes tough training to appreciate that it never rains but it pours, it requires no less discipline to derive some enjoyment from eating a boiled leg of mutton sprinkled with mint sauce. However, this involves neither resignation nor withdrawal, and if it embodies any philosophy, it is obviously constructive.

Among the faults for which he is not usually blamed, the Frenchman may count the constant search for his normal home fare when abroad. He does not try to educate his palate to appreciate the subtlety of cod in lamb's kidney dripping. The dish doesn't exist in Toulouse, and it is only really delicious at Reykjavik. On the other hand, the most delicious mutton *cassoulet* at Reykjavik cannot compare with the meanest bean stew in Carcassonne.

19

Nonetheless French defects and French merits have added up to something quite considerable: French gastronomy. Of course there are wines which are not French; there are truffles which do not come from Souillac, but nowhere else is there such harmony. This harmony requires a conductor, an orchestra and soloists and, to justify it, an audience. Of course, not everyone is musically inclined. One probably needs natural talent to start with and then one must be educated. If all gypsies are musicians, then all Frenchmen are gastronomes. We often find it difficult when abroad to convince the inhabitants that we do not live entirely on frogs' legs, snails and songbirds. On the other hand, consider the recurrent problems of explaining to a Texan or an Australian the delicacy of an ortolan.

Obviously, I cannot hope, in a single volume, to cover every aspect of French cuisine, but I should like to expatiate upon the necessity for educating taste. As far as wine is concerned, the average Frenchman is more of a drinker than a critic. Among the upper class (whether by birth or fortune) we find roughly the same principles as in other countries. The Englishman who drinks wine is probably the most demanding and best-informed of all wine lovers; not, mind you, that I go all the way with him.

Neither do I agree with the time-honoured order of serving wines. First of all, white wine should not be iced (and never put in a refrigerator). Red wine should not be brought to room temperature either; it should be served at cellar temperature after being decanted in the cellar into a cool decanter. Wine has no drinking age unless it threatens to die on you; it is logical to drink it before it is too late. Personally, I feel one can increase one's enjoyment of wine if one follows its development step by step, especially since it will have been chosen to comply with certain criteria which endear it to us. All enthusiasts do not have the same tastes, and moreover these, too, alter over the years: a man who adored blondes may go wild about brunettes once he has discovered them. We often tend to confuse taste and good taste, and it is common knowledge that good taste is one's own and bad taste that of others. The star appeals to the majority by definition, but often for prosaic qualities.

I should like to doff my hat with a flourish to certain apostles of wine of whom the leader is undoubtedly André Simon. Their virtues, his in particular, have something oracular about them. Yet again, this is what lends weight to experience. Obviously these specialists are born talented, but their judgment is based on such an enormous range of knowledge that we owe them the greatest respect.

It is generally conceded that only wine-growing countries, with the exception of Belgium, have a developing gastronomy. This is quite a thought, although as a generalization it fails since there are so many exceptions to it. We must always beware of a single isolated sense; that of taste, in particular, is subject to many influences. Sight, smell and touch set off a whole range of processes which must automatically affect it. In the east, the problem has been partly solved by the use of a saliva-provoking excitant of the tastebuds – monosodium glutamate. Pavlov before his time, as it were. Insofar as it concerns infantile motivation, it is disturbing that children are not aware of taste at an early age. A child only notices sweet flavours and then only at the tip of his tongue. For him, other flavours are confused and bitterness is only apparent after swallowing.

In terms of wine-tasting, there is a well-known expression which defines the essential qualities of a vintage: the characteristic of lingering on the palate. In Sauternes, they go further still and ascribe to certain exceptional wines a 'second wind' of taste. It is simply an example of heightened gustatory perception, rather like the green ray left on the retina at sunset. I do not wish to attack popular misconceptions, but the palate plays absolutely no part in tasting. In fact tasting and the assessing of wine is done by the nose and the taste buds of the tongue. Pleasant though it may be to roll the wine around in one's mouth and oxygenate it, it does not alter any of its basic qualities and is merely disagreeable to one's neighbour. But this does not prevent us from saying that a wine-taster has a 'nose'; a colourful and meaningful phrase.

Wine has two vocations: in the kitchen, to be part of a dish and, at table, to accompany it. It is not absurd to match a dish with a wine, although it is usually the other way round; apart from a few rare and gross mistakes there are few wines and dishes which really do not marry. One should be wary of 'little' wines with highly-seasoned dishes, but that is fairly obvious anyway: fire and water are bad mixers. Generally speaking, if you have a 'little' wine, no matter how impressive its label, serve it cold and by itself and you will not need to apologise for it. I have always thought it foolish to insist on rigid pairings and codified lists. I am just as happy with one wine per course as with a single one throughout a meal. But that is not the point; I like a wine to be presented in a given context: the vintage of a friend's year of birth, a shared memory, an anniversary or some such reason. Then the wine becomes a symbol whose value lies outside the accepted canon. But for goodness' sake, let us not deprive ourselves of such pleasures by bowing to some Draconian law. Drinking and eating should be pleasurable, and, without being vulgar, easy-going.

Wine plays a big part in cookery and was of even greater importance in the ancient world; the widespread use of vinegar was originally an attempt to replace rare or costly wines. Thickening and evaporation produced much the same results and so its use has survived.

The main point I want to make here is that most nutritional customs have endured almost unchanged throughout the ages. Technical variants occur only with industrial processes; the difference between bought and home-made bread, even if made with identical flour, is remarkable. In the French countryside, prehistoric methods are still current; I shall try to describe how they came down to us.

2　The Historical Background

From Prehistoric times to the Roman era

Since nourishment is an absolute necessity, one could say that gastronomy and the world were twins – born simultaneously. But eating alone is not enough to create gastronomy which requires the exercise of choice. Although animals are seldom credited with intelligence, it is clear that they have preferences and that many of them are greedy. Perhaps choice arises from organic needs, and these are more demanding than the deficiencies which provoke them are acute. For a good number of us many childish motivations had no apparent reason for existence.

Since man has eaten from his first appearance, I propose to start with paleolithic gastronomy. Thus I shall try to evaluate the entire period from those early days to those of Curnonsky and Escoffier. How, and by what means, did France become the uncontested world centre of gastronomy? By what devious or obvious ways, as a result of what upheavals or refutals did the civilization of the table set up its dominion between Nice and Brest, between Bayonne and Lille? I am only concerned with the pleasures of the table. Some of the reasons are obviously religious or political, and there has been fluctuation between decadence and renaissance, but that is not what I am dealing with; it is not that I do not believe they exist, I just think they have nothing to do with the cook.

In his preface to *La Vie de Jésus*, François Mauriac asserts that the Biblical commentator is ill-fitted to talk about God. To date, very few cooks have talked about their gods. They have mostly written recipe books which the more inspired among them have tried to versify. They have described daily life in terms of their own private surroundings but they have never tried to analyse their professional lives in the context of their civilization. It is not so long since the cook was considered a mere servant and kept in his place. The middle classes, and to an even greater degree, the wealthy, treated them as lackeys, while the working class, aware that the services of such people were not for them, excluded them from their own circles. The job was no sinecure; occasionally an individual white-capped performer would be praised but without much conviction and only on a full stomach. Even the 'white bonnet' of the trade came in for criticism, especially when allied to a misguided propensity to chains, medals and ribbons. And yet, that is not what we mean by a cook. He is, alas, frequently uneducated – a fault due to inadequate methods of recruitment. I still feel depressed when I remember the Austrian court ruling whereby a cook's evidence was unacceptable, as if he were an old lag. This ostracism was a survival from pagan times when a decent person might not in any circumstances cook for strangers. Cooking, if it is not home cooking nor centred on the family hearth, takes on a pagan quality at once. The cook becomes confused with the priest and his work-table with the altar; he may only serve the initiated. It is hard to untangle these notions of popular belief, especially when the symbols mingle and superimpose themselves. All religions have been deeply concerned about food and the technique of its preparation. At the very start, it was necessary to preserve food and it is here that paleolithic cookery began. Man had few or no weapons and although there were larger numbers of less savage animals about, the problem of butchering and preserving a diplodochus in midsummer remained. Man went fishing, collected snails or hedgehogs which could not run away, ate fruit and berries and drank water, which was easy enough for most months of the year. He could also, like squirrels, fatten up in the summer and then hibernate. Gastronomy was born of the need to keep stocks. It was from early attempts to preserve fruit and berries that the first fermented beverages appeared.

Fire has always been known to man: the difficulty was to produce it at will, to keep it going and to revive it. Fire was worshipped and at a later date confided to the Vestal virgins, and the respect in which they were held bears witness to the importance of their functions.

24

Sunlight and flat stones, whereby meat was cured, became also the first infra-red cookers, and thereafter all grilling problems were solved. This remained the cooking method for thousands of years during the paleolithic era and in certain parts of the world survived the neolithic period too. Variations were rare and imagination the perquisite of only a few. It is thought that the staple diet for the whole of this epoch was a cereal cake eaten either cooked or raw. It was during the paleolithic age that people made their first attempts at communal living, before the foundation of a society based on the family, when they were prompted to share their food on specific occasions, either through need or glut.

We should be more puzzled about the nature of our earliest ancestors' feasts were we not acquainted with the behaviour of the aborigine in Australia where there are still some tribes utterly ignorant of our civilization, or indeed of any. They live exactly as did prehistoric man. Let us observe them in exceptional circumstances, such as at the beaching of a whale. These primitive people are faced with a mountain of flesh, weak and wounded, but still very much alive. Men, women and children literally hurl themselves upon the creature, and using limbs and teeth enlarge the wound until they are inside it. They eat as they go, covered in blood and excreta, drunk with the banquet. Each of them will eat twenty pounds of meat with no other tools than his teeth. This is no exaggeration; the event still takes place. I could describe many other eating habits of the Kanaka and Papuans which would serve as well.

Scholars have taken little interest in what man ate and how he ate. And yet, of all human functions, feeding and eating give rise to a humanism whose scope and magnitude dominates all other philosophies, even, indeed, all religions. The earliest civilizations, however primitive and simple, were deeply concerned with food from the outset. Man fed in groups, like animals, male and female battling for the survival of the child, but with a certain selflessness which inspired Musset's lyrical flight of fancy – 'lorsque le pélican . . .'* Family life, and the entire political and economic complex which grew out of the family, were built around the table. The table itself and its function could only have resulted from abundance; there had to be more

*Alfred de Musset, *La Nuit de Mai*.

than enough food so that it could be eaten in common. Conversely, when people stop eating together, one can assume scarcity. The periods in which men started to share their meals varied according to the latitudes in which they lived. All over the world, no matter how isolated one civilization from another, each has followed the same nutritional path. There are still wide variations in man's eating habits but banquets for celebrations and family festivities are universal.

The history of the table goes back to the fourth millennium in Egypt as in China. The Phoenicians, supreme pedlars of the ancient world, spread both ideas and culinary techniques. It is certain that for over two thousand years only a wide knowledge of food and how people eat made possible the engineering feats of antiquity. Cereals were the staple, but even so there remained the problems of distribution. How, for example, were the slaves who built the pyramids fed? The legend, generally believed, has it that as human lives were held in scant esteem by the Pharaohs, slaves responded better to the whip than to the sugar-lump. No one doubted that each of the pyramids cost several thousand human lives; nonetheless the men had to be fit to work, and therefore decently fed, though maltreated. That epidemics were relatively mild among them and took a light toll tends to prove this. What then did they eat, and how did they get it? There were some 100,000 men to be fed over a period of thirty years. The blunt answers are pemmican and self-service; there was nothing new under Ra! But where did it come from? Shipping sailed the Nile; if the building materials were delivered to the site by raft, presumably so was the food. We must rule out the notion that cattle were slaughtered locally. The only animals eaten were those which died on the job or were killed because they were wounded. These would have been sufficient for the privileged few, whereas there were 100,000 people to be fed with sufficient calories to keep the ropes pulled and the carts pushed.

The Phoenicians too stayed at sea for months and indeed even years on end. We know they distilled sea water – so much for drink. But what about food? They probably fished for it. In their early days on long journeys they followed the coastline and could therefore provision themselves in the traditional manner. Later they sailed further out to sea both for safety and to gain time. They crossed oceans and sailed in the Atlantic, in vessels with little protection and certainly no decent storage space. And yet they did not starve. They had tried and tested methods now lost to us and Dr Bombard's experiments confirm our conviction that man is not suited to the ocean's hardships.

When was agriculture invented? Never, according to some who think that man glided imperceptibly from picking nature's fruits to growing them. But it is generally accepted that husbandry of the soil led to civilization by allowing men to stay long enough in one place to start a family, a group and eventually a community. This is why gods and goddesses were created. The oldest effigies of goddesses are in the form of pregnant women, protectors of the harvest.

Fishing and hunting continued to be parallel sources of food. Cattle raising must have begun at the same time as agriculture and trade. Once this evolutionary phase was completed, man became a farmer and stayed so for thousands of years. Naturally, he was also his own cook. He felt that a share of his well-being was due to the gods even though it only consisted of daily bread. Consequently for centuries he considered that every animal he killed was in fact a sacrifice; we have inherited this notion. Sacrifices were not limited to creatures which had been killed, but could also consist of fruit or vegetables, and, exceptionally, fish. Anything that came from the sea was always curiously privileged. The sea was the beginning, the mother. The Egyptians would not eat certain fish, which were sacred, as was pork. But on certain feast-days the god they worshipped took upon himself the burden of their sins and it was then possible to eat forbidden food; the sacrifice purified the intention and thus absolved the sinner.

Food remained a basic preoccupation. Later, much later, some people wished to minimize its importance and there were many who considered any concern with eating vulgar. Yet there is no more imperative need.

The Egyptians consulted the stars on gastronomic matters as on those of strategy or love, and found in them an answer to every problem. Were they less demanding than we are, or more conversant with the magical signs? We know that their recipes included *Kphy*, or astral scent, as well as spices and honey and the Phoenicians who were more sophisticated and had a greater range of foodstuffs made use of it. They travelled to the land of Punt, that land of spices, and sailed to England in search of tin, used above all for making cooking utensils. Tyre withstood sieges of seven years' duration and no doubt the inhabitants survived on something more than love and cold water.

Solomon, that great repository of wisdom, after having formed an alliance with Tyre, flirted with the Queen of Sheba and taking as a first wife a daughter of Pharaoh, had the Temple built and thenceforward his kitchens were filled with enough spices to do honour to his guests. Thus was born the earliest gastronomy of the Mediterranean basin. A thousand years before Christ, Solomon gathered thousands of guests together for lavish ritual banquets. The laws governing food were respected in the same way as those governing reproduction, with the corollary that a failure to do so would unleash passions such as jealousy, envy, love or hate. But before obedience came cleanliness. One had to be pure to cook, to eat, to procreate, and if one became soiled during the sacrifice, it was not enough simply to wash. One had also to be purified, either by fasting or abstinence. From the earliest civilizations there have been rules for proper eating, many of which survive to this day, although in many cases the symbols or their meaning or their power have vanished. We can still glimpse some of them faintly, like water-marks. When the Jews eat Kosher they obey a law 5,000 years old which, like a prayer, is atavistic. Jews observe the Kosher law as Christians observe the Lenten fast. The strictness of Kosher law can be compared to that of certain fiscal laws which are basically aimed at the fraudulent. We shall see how the Jewish influence permeated the entire Mediterranean basin and one must admit that there is a great deal to be said for it. In the first place, from the point of view of hygiene, what now seems a minimum was then essential. We know of similar customs among the Chinese and Incas involving the annual purification of the kitchens. Is the Bible then the first cookery book? Certainly; one can quote examples ranging from Adam's apple through Esau's mess of pottage to Esther's banquets. Cain killed Abel through jealousy: all he could offer up were humble roots while the smoke of sheeps' entrails rose from his brother's sacrifice to Jehovah, to the shepherd's greater glory.

Alexander the Great, scorning Spartan gruel, set out to conquer new worlds, though not because of the detestable cooking of Greeks and Macedonians. From his encounter with Darius he learned to make caviar and botarga.*

*Mullet or tunny roe, salted and compressed.

28

Treading out the wheat: from the tomb of Menna, Thebes, Egypt

Though it seems unbelievable nowadays, the Mediterranean peoples ate relatively little fish until quite recently. Indeed, France today is a low fish consumer, a curious reflection.

On the other hand, the Greeks and Egyptians, pooling their knowledge, had a variety of bread-making and baking methods which would have made a Renaissance baker pale with envy. Egyptian civilization was based on wheat and was consequently totally un-African in its nature. One might say Africa began at the Sudanese border. To understand the objections of the King of Kings, the Emperor of Ethiopia, descended from the Queen of Sheba, to all Negro princes, one must realize that Ethiopian eating traditions are much closer to those of the Mediterranean than to those of the Congo. By and large history owes a great deal to the table – I am convinced of it.

What did men in antiquity eat? Were bread, honey and beer enough? Were sumptuary laws proclaimed for the protection of the race, of man from

Offerings: Egyptian painting

himself, or simply to serve as examples? The Greeks are portrayed cup in hand and when we speak of Roman orgies we lick our lips enviously. We must remember that mead, wine and resinated wine were only available in quantity for the privileged few and feasts were as infrequent as solar eclipses.

30

We know for certain that the *far* of Brittany is exactly the same as the staple diet of the Phoenicians and indeed of all the Mediterranean peoples of the period, with bread in second place and eaten only by organized sedentary communities.

What is *far*? A dough made of buckwheat or spelt, lightly greased or oiled and cooked in water. The best method is to cook it in a pudding cloth; it is then called *far en sac*. During the last fifty years it has undergone numerous transformations involving the addition of sugar, honey, fats and flavourings. In the south-west, at the beginning of this century, they still used a recipe for millet dumplings. In Guyenne we say *mil* but it is still the same cereal. In fact, it is a survival of neolithic agriculture. It is easy to understand why some neolithic varieties were abandoned. Why grow buckwheat when one can grow wheat? Throughout the ages the trend has been towards rejection. The same is true of hunting, which was supplanted by cattle raising; although now, to close the circle, we breed game. The neolithic age was one where food was guaranteed by rational means. One might almost say it was the last hump before the problems of storing and, above all, preserving food became the major ones. It was this concern which led to new methods and created gastronomy by so doing. We shall try to retrace its progress.

In attempting to establish the route travelled by gastronomy throughout the ages, one must take note of the links between the great periods, although differences of longitude and latitude have created variables. Different areas of the globe have not evolved simultaneously. This is true of Egypt compared with Australia, or of Canada with Mexico, and, less obvious but still perceptible, of the Gauls and the peoples of the Mediterranean. It is of course the latter who interest us most. It is not necessary to lard this book with figures, since we have knowledge of only 6,000 years, whereas we ought to think in terms of millions of years and a certain deliberate confusion is relevant to our point – the overlapping of the paleolithic and neolithic ages. So it seems sensible to eschew figures, for we shall have to reach our own day before the common denominator has any meaning.

There can be no question of comparing Brittany in the third millennium with the Chinese and Egyptian civilizations of the same period. And yet there are more traces of Celtic than of Roman culture in the Breton tradition. The Roman colonizers, though they brought with them the whole culture of the Mediterranean, never succeeded in popularizing *garum* (see page 58). This is an observation of prime importance, for throughout the ages one can observe consumer-resistance to every innovation, a resistance the more stubborn as novelty is automatically suspect.

It is interesting to note that the snail, which according to all the evidence was one of the commonest of neolithic foods, has not left the same gastronomic mark everywhere. It was necessary to resuscitate the recipe in order to rekindle interest in it. Instinct, the prime motivation, has now completely vanished; the more primitive a people, the more familiar it is with nature. Primitive peoples did not poison themselves with mushrooms. Safety was the first consideration of paleolithic man and as with all other living creatures it determined his choice of a home. The instinct of self-preservation seldom allowed him far from his cave or the shelter he had created. His habits arose directly from his geographical location. He did not eat whatever nature in her bounty provided at various seasons, but only what he could reach without compromising his own safety. At first, he ate raw. If by chance he came upon an animal cooked by a forest fire, he did not at first dare to taste it. One day he happened to, but did he like it any better? It seems doubtful. His jaws and teeth were those of a wild animal. He had no examples to copy; animals ate raw, and fire was a cruel god. His appetite was undisciplined. In a word, he had every reason for hesitating. It would be futile to imagine him sniffing the scent of a wild boar roasting in a bush fire; it was need and not taste which led him to cook his food. His first problem was how to keep meat. He had to dry, cure or smoke it. At first, he used the sun and a flat stone, but if the stone was always available, the sun was not. Fire was a piece of sun, and like it, shone and gave heat; it was sun to order. It was not easy to obtain but, incomparable treasure, it was by its very nature easy to keep. Like all treasures, it was jealously guarded. The first step was taken, and mistakes, impatience and accidents surrounded the first experiments. For a recipe to become established involves repeating, from memory, an identical gesture in identical circumstances. It is a symbolic act.

The first cooking experiments were not necessarily limited to grilling. The

Polynesians do not grill, nor do the Icelanders. Both these peoples live near volcanoes and are familiar with fire. There were also volcanoes and far more hot springs than exist today in Europe. Woodfires and direct-heat cookery are so attractive that we should easily be inclined to assume the contrary. 'Our ancestors the Gauls . . .' Man was acquainted with fire from the outset. At different stages of his development he used it for different purposes according to instinct and to need; and one can assume that the most pressing need was nourishment. If we say that the paleolithic period represents a purity resulting from innocence, then the cookery of that age can be summed up as a boiled egg. Toast fingers, rosy salt and fresh butter are decadent inventions. Throughout history, gastronomic progress is in direct ratio to standards of comfort, which can only exist in privileged civilizations. It was the appearance of a society settling down in luxury (which can be defined as the superfluous) which, by its excesses in eating, dressing, making love, and setting up idols or gods, released the evolutionary, and sometimes revolutionary, processes which were to affect every aspect of daily life.

Offerings: from an Egyptian stele and a wall painting

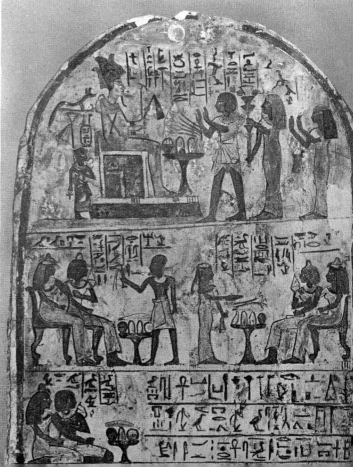

We know that the first luxury was baked clay or terracotta.

Before that there was the flat stone, and here are six paleolithic recipes which require virtually no cooking utensil. There are others which we shall find when we come to the neolithic recipes.

Vegetables baked in ashes

Coleseed, carrots and other root vegetables. Clean, scrape and wash them. Wrap in leaves, preferably hazel leaves, and fasten them with acacia thorns or small chips of wood, which can be stuck right into the vegetables. The layer of leaves must be thick. Make a good fire with large pieces of wood so as to obtain a good hot bed of ashes as soon as possible. Rake the ashes apart, put the vegetables in the middle, and cover them over with the ashes. Keep the fire going over them for an hour. Remove the ashes, take out the vegetables and open the leaves. Eat with a pinch of salt.

Eggs on a flat stone

Crush some hazelnuts with a round stone, either on a plane leaf or on chestnut leaves laid side by side. Heat the nuts quickly, shaping them into a circle with a higher outer edge. Break the eggs into the centre, salt, cover with the leaves on which the nuts were cracked, and allow to cook for 10 minutes. Use the leaves for picking up the eggs, by sliding between the eggs and the stone.

Fish on a flat stone

Find a large very smooth flat stone about 3 foot square. It may be set into the ground and impossible to carry away or it may be on a slope. This can be an advantage but must be taken into account. A stone that can be moved is easier to heat than the same expanse of rock. In any case, heating it is a long process. Settle the stone firmly with a slight slope if you wish. Light a big fire covering it. Keep the fire going for at least an hour. Prepare a broom of reeds or leaves. The fire must be kept up until you are ready; then, and only then, clean the stone. All fish and meat can be grilled on it. The only thing that matters is to put the food on to a clean, hot surface. So you need only clear part of the stone, leaving the embers on the other half until it is needed. Food does not stick to the stone, so there is no need to add anything but salt. Large pieces of meat or fish require some skill as they are difficult to heat through, but sardines and mackerel are no trouble.

Burnt fish

Only large sea fish may be used. One should also bear in mind that they will be mainly destroyed by the flames. This is an expensive method only to be used rarely. Make a fire of small twigs and sticks and keep it going for a while. As soon as there is a good bed of very hot ash, put in the fish without having scaled or gutted it. Cover with small twigs and pine needles, etc., and keep a very hot fire going for at least half an hour. Then remove the fish which now looks like a great lump of coal. Wash it quickly in sea water, without letting it cool too much. Open it down the back and spoon the contents out with a spoon or sea shell.

Mussel terrée

Choose mussels of equal size. Clean them thoroughly and place in any vessel which is both fireproof and straight-sided (this is essential). Stand the mussels on end, hinge at the bottom, and wedge them closely together in the dish which one should be able to turn upside down without their falling out. Put the vessel on the ground and cover with pine needles or twigs. Set fire to them and keep them blazing for about 10 minutes, constantly adding a few more pine-needles or twigs. Remove the dish, turn it upside down to get rid of the ashes. Wait a few minutes and take out the mussels one at a time. They will be open and cooked in their own juice. Eat at once.

Young wild boar roasted on gorse

First make a fork. Choose a long stiff branch. Do not look for an elegant shape but for solidity. It is bound to burn and you must therefore choose green sappy wood, and not peel the bark off. Your fork can have more than two tines. Skin the boar and gut it without damaging the belly-skin. Spit it with the fork, folding the belly-skin over. Secure the whole thing firmly with sharpened pegs. Add salt. Wait 15 minutes and begin cooking. The boar must be exposed to the fire and turned as soon as it begins to sizzle. You must never put down the fork. The job calls for great care and swift handling. Salt once or twice during the cooking. Halfway through, the boar may be smeared with honey. This is not difficult, but care must be taken to avoid burning the meat.

Neolithic broth

Scrub with dry hay or grass a hollow in a rock and fill it to a third of its capacity with spring or rain water. Allow a quart per person. By its side, where the wind cannot blow its ashes into the broth, light a very hot fire. Heat round stones, preferably balls of sandstone, in its centre. When they are very hot, take one and drop it into the water. Remove it and replace with another and so on until the water boils, Have a mat of twigs ready to cover it between operations. Prepare the vegetables: onions, beans, carrots, wild asparagus, beech nuts, peeled acorns, rue, nettles, dandelion, coleseed and herbs. Add these to the water with salt and wild rose petals. You may also add the hips. Continue with the stones until the vegetables are cooked. Then add grated animal fat (such as mutton tail or kidney fat) and add one last very hot stone to complete the blending of fat and liquid. Eat with a scallop shell held with a wooden fork.

All specialists and propagandists, not excluding the student of the sea, think and behave as if theirs was the only subject in the world, and to put French gastronomy in its proper context, we must take the Mediterranean as our starting point.

If we try today to analyse the cookery of the French Mediterranean coast, we find it little different from that of other provinces. This is because, from the Middle Ages onwards, communication was constant and only personal idiosyncracies introduced variety. On the other hand, new supplies considerably changed the staple diet. Even so, it is no less true that traditional food in the coastal regions is less influenced by the sea than one might suppose. Fish is not a basic food there, and in spite of occasional need, will not become so. A meat diet has gradually taken precedence since the twenties of this century (yes; only since then) and is evenly balanced by fish and preserved foods. So what, one may well ask, is the traditional basic food? Cereals and dried pulses in the first place, then green vegetables, with the addition of animal and vegetable fats – soup, bean stew, porridge, *far*.

Far was one of the main foods of the Mediterranean from the time of the Phoenicians onwards. About the fourth millennium this race sailed the Mediterranean, the Atlantic, the Red Sea and the Indian Ocean. In ships the size of the *Santa Maria de la Trinidad* or of the *Pelican*, they traded bronze for tin, went after amber, and ate *far*. Could they have taken it direct to Brittany where it is still an item of daily fare? The Phoenicians sailed to England for tin, to Scandinavia for amber, and to the Canaries, the garden of the Hesperides. True, *far* might have travelled overland, but if porridge was generally known throughout the area, *far* itself seems to have been less widely known.

36

Maize or Spanish wheat (in our patois *blat d'Espagne*) was only known after Columbus and became an important item of diet only in northern Italy and the south-west of France.

In the Middle Ages, when famine threatened Europe, herring was available in enormous quantities, but was regarded with suspicion as food.

Transport by sea was vital to the ancients as it has been to us for much of our era. It would appear that trade between distant ports was of greater importance than neighbouring sources of supply. The Phoceans were more influenced by Spain than was Roussillon, its neighbour.

Two thousand years B.C. the Phoenicians were exchanging spices against kitchen utensils. Recent excavations in East Africa reveal the Indian origins of these exchanges, and confirm that the bronze pot was contemporaneous with the first white-metal weapons.

As farming was slow to take over from gleaning, it is interesting to note that olive oil, which the Egyptians knew in the fourth millennium, was not

Bronze basin from Hallstadt: early Iron Age, c. 600 B.C.

imported into Italy until a few centuries before Christ. Its progress across the Mediterranean followed a zigzag course, and one must assume it arrived by sea.

Civilizations based on wheat, spelt, buckwheat and millet flourished all around the Mediterranean. While the Egyptians knew how to grind grain and bake bread, Europe at the same period was still crushing grain between two stones and boiling it unkneaded.

But progress can never be halted. Slowly, perhaps, but surely, a technique was established. Indeed, technique was all that the inhabitants of France then lacked, and one may legitimately wonder whether their epicurean destinies were not already rooted in its soil.

The vine which came from Turkey with the Roman legions found its ideal home in France. But before then, beer was already famous and mead highly rated. Pork and fowls were current farm produce before Caesar's day, and the cheeses of Cantal as old as their Biblical equivalents. French oysters were already the best, their coleseed the finest and their onions the strongest tasting. France was blessed by the gods who therefore had to exploit her.

From written evidence and the oral traditions which have reached us, it is certain that, as I must repeat at the risk of boring, the most important factors in the appreciation and use of local produce were the changes wrought by technique applied to food, although of course what I have already said on the subject only concerns cooking and wine, themselves of secondary importance. Obviously, the influence of technical innovations on agriculture, fishing, hunting and cattle raising must come before one can even start discussing cookery or indeed food preservation.

The preservation of food, since Nicolas Appert and Birdseye, has influenced French cookery and altered some of its most rooted prejudices, and Accelerated Freeze Drying (A.F.D.) is bound to make further changes of which we should be aware.

Technology has not always spread automatically from east to west, as is generally believed. Stemming from the east, as it undoubtedly did, its impact made itself felt at different moments and in distant places without any apparent order; which makes one think of the irregular appearances and movements of the truffle. A possible explanation might be the slow cooling of the earth's crust, but as far as I know, this would be too slow to be perceptible to us. There have been occasions when truffle beds have moved over nearly eighty miles within two or three generations. One can therefore assume that vegetable migrations take place without human intervention, aided by wind, rain, birds and flocks acting as vehicles. But on the whole they are due to deliberate action by man. If Lucullus had not imported the cherry tree, how many thousands of years would it have taken to reach France? Nonetheless, it would have arrived.

Time despises what is done without it, says the proverb. In matters of food, habits take root with difficulty, but are that much more difficult to eradicate once they have become part of our way of life. We already know the source of our basic gastronomic culture; it came from the east. How did it get to us? Greece and Italy were themselves the heirs of Egypt and the Persia of Darius. To go further and state categorically that the fountain-head was India is a step I should be unwilling to take despite the Tibetan mystery.

In terms of cookery, the neolithic age was the age of grilling and thenceforward nothing was to change in the application of this particular principle. For some time man made no distinction between weapons and tools, but kept a special instrument for cooking. The only means of survival was strength, and strength required food. Civilization came in with the cauldron.

The aborigine of Oceania exemplifies the link between paleolithic and neolithic man. The Kanaka oven is incontrovertibly paleolithic inasmuch as its use involves no instruments of any kind. In order to be quite clear, I must repeat that prehistoric man could only cook with the means nature provided, yet cook he did. In Oceania the vast number of volcanoes makes it likely that fire must have been commonly used, and the fact that it was thought to be divine adds to my conviction.

I still find it astonishing that Daniel Defoe showed so little imagination about cookery and did not allow Robinson Crusoe to recreate ancient methods. True, they were both English, and the Virgin Islands are not in the Pacific. At all events, there is no doubt that culinary progress has always been slow where foodstuffs are concerned and rapid in matters of technique.

We know that some of the most popular foods of the past have been abandoned, and that their number continues to dwindle. Paleolithic man was very close to nature, and the closer man is to the soil, the less vulnerable he is to its dangers. This is generally called instinct.

Nowadays, mushrooms are classified and listed. There are dozens of text-books and thousands of illustrations to show which are safe and which poisonous, yet the more books there are, the fewer varieties of mushroom people eat. Urban man by definition, and the intellectual by extension, are particularly sensitive to the dangers of the forest. It is fairly certain that if paleolithic man had been fond of *amanita phalloida* we should not be here to talk about it.

I thoroughly enjoyed a remark made in my presence by a peasant when a townsman informed him that some herb or other was poisonous. 'If it were,' replied the rustic, 'we'd know it.' A whole rural philosophy is encompassed in those few words.

Much the same applied to other vegetables as to mushrooms. Neolithic man, according to the latitudes in which he lived, must have behaved both as *homo sapiens* and as an Olympian god; he might have been King Chronos, or one of the giants who are said to sleep in the crypt of the Tibetan monastery at Lhasa.

The transition from gleaning to agriculture is an important milestone in human history. When God set man down in Eden he did not give him know-ledge, but limited him to a gastronomic experiment. Adam was not required to respect his spouse, but forbidden to bite into the apple. A symbol, you may say. But then why not Bluebeard's locked door, or the interdiction laid on Orpheus? Why forbid the eating of a fruit? I should like to imagine that fruit as generating erotic powers (I almost said erogeneous). It is also possible that God simply wished to insist upon the obedience of his creature. The abundance of apples made the temptation a constant one, and resistance therefore more worthy of merit. But this is taking a poor view of divine intentions. Ovid claimed that in the Golden Age man was a vegetarian, and it seems that Adam was too.

It is hard to imagine where Eden was and how the first couple spent their day. They ate the fruit in the garden. Therefore one must assume that God considered a frugal diet sufficient for man's happiness. If that was his plan, we are heading the wrong way for a re-conquest of Eden. The gods, by the intervention of their ministers, always saw that food was involved in the celebrations of their cults. And indeed, there was a certain confusion for a long time; sacrifices were intended for the gods both in spirit and symbolically, but in practice were also advantageous to men whose priests were the first to benefit therefrom.

When the Ark landed on Ararat, God took over from Bacchus. Turkey, the Pontus which Lucullus was to conquer, is the land of roses and fruit, and, it seems, the birthplace of the vine. Little was needed for wine to be invented; some wines fermented from fruits other than grapes and from cereals were already and still are popular. Saké is a typical example. Nonetheless, the grape is the source of the undeniably superior products which we call wines today, which again goes to show that gradually a number of beverages and foods have been abandoned in favour of those which are of better quality or easier to obtain. It is a fact that ten degree wine is easier to produce by simple fermentation than any other drink. A high degree of alcohol is most easily achieved by distilling grain; the opposite of wine is vodka.

The Bible is an absolute treasure house of culinary advice. Initially, it deals with sacrifices and lays down rules about food. It is strange to think that Christ ate Kosher, as did Paul and the early Christians who adhered to Jewish laws for a considerable time, especially in connection with eating blood, which was forbidden. Esau sold his birthright for a mess of pottage, and Solomon charmed the Queen of Sheba to start a trade in spices; Esther, in her book, gives a detailed description of the banquet she served to Ahasuerus. The Kabalists, or some of them at any rate, sought concealed meanings in the plainest passages of Holy Writ, and of course, a great many symbols may be concealed in food.

The most stringent rule of Kosher law, the one which is, so to speak, taken for granted, is 'thou shalt not eat the flesh of the kid in the milk of its mother', and forbids the consumption of a milk product and meat at the same meal. The other laws are mainly physical and only concern forbidden foods, such as fish without scales, all that creeps or walks askew, beasts with uncloven hooves, wounded animals and so on. The ban on pork goes back to Egyptian days when the boar was a totem whose protection was thus ensured. The theory of an impure animal is a much later one. In any case, in Egypt there were occasions when the ban was lifted. During votive or ritual feasts, sacrifices were offered to the totem itself which thereby took the sin upon itself. The stars and especially the moon played a great part in the choice of time for these rites.

Alexander the Great, in company with Solomon (who made no secret of his interest in gastronomy), the ancient Egyptians and the Phoenicians (who transmitted Eastern customs), was one of the founders of Mediterranean gastronomy. His conquest of what was then the whole world, including his sally into China, must have made a great change in eating habits.

The Greeks had a simple diet based upon bread, as did the Egyptians. By sharing their techniques they produced between them literally dozens of different kinds. Alexander began to learn what gastronomy was during his victorious campaigns in Persia against Darius; it was there that he discovered what a feast could be like. Plato's banquet where nobody ate anything because Socrates was holding forth was a mere snack, anyway, compared with the fare of Oriental princes. As they drew closer to the Indies, fruit and spices became more abundant; for a frugal Greek it must have been paradise. The Ptolemies organized their domestic lives along lines far more Egyptian or oriental than Greek, and the most famous member of the family, Cleopatra, was a renowned gastronome. While in Rome she had acquired a taste for luxury and wilful extravagance.

Lucullus was wealthier than Caesar, and made a point of publicizing what he spent on his table. The Caesars always announced the cost of their 'Triumphs', emphasizing that to be able to spend so freely one must first have earned the money. The immediately pre-Christian era, which was much influenced gastronomically by Lucullus, was a time of great and important events. Certainly it was a period of change and corresponded with an increase and advance in husbandry and cattle raising. The Romans, about whom we have such precise records, were the great exponents of taste in culinary matters. They borrowed new methods, which they did not understand, from far and wide and generally behaved as *nouveaux riches*. Luckily, the wealth of detail we have about their period allows us to recreate the most important stage in the gastronomic development of the Mediterranean basin.

To understand the structure of Roman gastronomy we must point out that

Etruscan banqueters: fresco from the tomb of the Leopards, Tarquinia

the Romans knew bread, wine and oil on the one hand, and the cauldron, the frying pan and the grill on the other. Therefore one may say that basic foods and cooking techniques have hardly altered since then. The vast majority ate very simply, and special meals were very few and far between. It is probable that for most people, marriages and births, the winter and summer solstices, and possibly the spring celebrations and the vintage festival were the only occasions for feasting; not very many banquets in a year. For the rich, whether senior officer, politician or big business man, it was different, but even so, they had very few of the facilities which today we take for granted.

During the whole period from the death of Alexander to the third century A.D., there were three, or occasionally, four meals a day. For the populace they consisted of bread or cereal cake each time. The better-off ate three

43

rather more elaborate meals. They started in the morning with bread dipped in wine (remember as you dip your croissant into your coffee that you are repeating Caesar's gesture). They also ate onions and cheese. At eleven they would have bread and fruit, more cheese, and water to drink. Their main meal was at about five or six o'clock according to the season, and was not unlike that which we eat today.

Cleopatra learned all this in Rome, and conformed to it while Antony lived with her. On one occasion, she boasted to her guests that the meal they were eating had cost as much as one given by Pompey. When a guest expressed doubt at the enormous sum she mentioned, she threw a pearl from her necklace into the salad as a make-weight. This anecdote has reached us so corrupted by time that it is said that she dissolved pearls in vinegar as an aphrodisiac. Just try! However, she was responsible for one of the most striking gastronomic gestures of all time. She had a wild boar set to roast at every hour of the day so that Antony should find one just ready at whatever time he returned to the palace.

Although I feel there would be little point in listing the dishes and foods that the Romans ate, I think I must give a careful description of their general habits.

We must first list our sources of information, and when discussing the first century, take into account those that preceded it. Our earlier references are from Plautus, and Cato, then from Cicero, Horace and Virgil; but our richest finds are in Apicius, Columella and Pliny the Elder. There are also, of course, Juvenal, Petronius, Seneca, Martial and others who have provided us with many interesting details.

Thus we start with the table and the status of the dining-room in the house. For at that time there was a dining-room, although it came and went at various periods, and in it was the *triclinium*. We know that the Romans ate in a reclining position, and had 'orgies'. This combination led to the popular misconception of Romans with rose-garlands askew on their heads, surrounded by naked women and lute-players, quaffing nectar from amphorae and gulping down the most elaborate sauces. The truth is very different indeed. In the first place, the number of guests at most Roman meals was limited to 'more than the Graces and fewer than the Muses'; that is, from four to nine people.

44

Roman banqueters: fresco from Herculaneum

Their customs were totally different from ours, and calling in courtesans was as commonplace as calling in geishas today in Tokyo. Like the geishas, the courtesans did not join in the meal, or at least, not as we would understand it. Geishas are allowed to drink with the guests, if not to eat, but the courtesans of Rome had neither specific rights nor restrictions of this sort.

The same was true of the hangers-on (also known as parasites) who were treated with a high-handedness that would shock us today, for our respect for human dignity would be offended by behaviour which they considered entirely correct.

Let us see what the meal known to us as an 'orgy' was like. There would be the host, four or five friends, the hostess and a relative. The meal began at five and was over by eight o'clock. The wife and relative then took their leave but the friends stayed on. Then the musicians, courtesans and hangers-on joined the party. There would be two or three musicians, seldom more than three courtesans, and as many hangers-on as there were guests; roughly twelve to fifteen people in all. (The hangers-on never reclined on the *triclinium*.)

The *triclinium* was a sort of U-shaped sofa; a cubist horse-shoe. On the middle sofa were the host, the guest of honour, and sometimes another guest; and at either side two or three more guests so that the total was usually below nine. They reclined, leaning on one elbow, and facing the hollow within which the table, laden with food, was placed by the servants. It was removed and replaced by another, equally ready, at each course. A cup-bearer served the wine from outside the *triclinium*, passing behind the guests.

There was no set rule about the number of courses or dishes or the balance of the menu. The order in which the courses were served was similar to that of today, although they began with fruit as one still does in Provence. Indeed, the Roman meal had great affinities with the traditional Provençal meal. The eating had to end before the party could begin. In the purest Roman tradition they then disposed of the first meal before undertaking another.

We have only a sketchy notion of the wine the Romans drank. They nearly always watered it down as it was undrinkable neat. It was often cooked to preserve it, and mingled with tars, resins and gums to thicken it. The flavour of the Greek and Corfiot resinated wines of today must have a great deal in common with the finest wines of ancient Rome. For myself, I rather like that turpentiny taste which reminds me of the waters off the resin pots in the forests of the Landes which we used to drink as children and which was considered strengthening and good for the lungs. Traces of wine have been found in sealed amphorae brought up from the sea but it is hard to appreciate the taste after two thousand years of immersion.

It was the second part of the meal which might be described as an orgy. But we must take a realistic view of this; we do not consider strip-tease as debauchery, nor the Folies Bergères or the Lido as perversions. The Romans who undressed the courtesans after dinner in order to prove their virility were only sacrificing to Aphrodite after having honoured Bacchus. The hangers-on were there to entertain the guests, like the troubadours at a later date and nowadays the *chansonniers*. They were paid for their work and departed with the leftovers of the meal just as did, indeed, the guests. It was customary to take one's own table linen and indeed a lighter, more comfortable, toga to enhance the pleasure of the meal. Hands and feet were washed before eating. Nowadays washing one's feet before dinner seems superfluous, but it was necessary then. The Romans walked barefoot in open sandals along muddy or dusty paths, hence the need for ablutions which we are spared by socks, shoes, tarmac and closed cars.

In general, Roman meal times differed from ours. This was mainly because they wished to avoid using artificial lighting whenever possible. Dining between five and seven o'clock obviated the need for lamps during some eight months of the year, and in any case, people lived by the sun, preferring to eat out of doors. When Kipling was asked how he had managed to depict the life of a Roman centurion in *Puck of Pook's Hill*, he replied that he simply observed the daily round of an adjutant on the frontier in India. We can do the same; a Neapolitan family in a working-class suburb is similar to that of a Roman family in the first century. That things should have changed so little in 2,000 years is not surprising when one remembers that the greatest changes have taken place in the last fifty years.

Now let us see what the Romans ate. First of all, we must classify foods, which I should like to do in order of appearance: fruit, cereals, eggs and milk products, meat, fish, fowls, snails, vegetables, pastries, drinks, condiments and other ingredients used in cookery.

Fruit: The fig is the most important of the various fruits which made a major contribution to the Mediterranean diet. It was easy to dry and kept perfectly which greatly added to its popularity, and there were more than three dozen varieties. It is very interesting to note that the Provençal tradition requires figs to be on the table at the beginning of the meal and for them to be consumed first. Actually the Romans ate figs, and at a later date, celery or shrimps, with bread, as we now do butter. At certain times of the year and for some labourers, figs and bread were the staple food. Workmen were normally given a ration of five pounds of bread per day per head which was cut down to four when there were plenty of figs.

Grapes were a close second to figs for the same reasons. Dried grapes or raisins, like figs, were produced in small quantities in Italy and mainly imported from Greece, Syria or Africa. Bread dipped in oil and rubbed with garlic seems to have been the traditional food of the vine grower since Noah's day, and it, together with raisins, seems to have been the eternal food of the Mediterranean. *Bagnat* bread, which Colette so loved and which she and I shared while chatting about the beach at Pampelonne where Cleopatra landed when she visited Gaul, is little more than a sophisticated variant of the garlic loaf.

Apples, those Biblical and universal fruit, were also very popular. They too, after being cut into quarters and dried in the sun on wicker trays, were stocked in jars or barrels. The pear tree was among the most carefully tended, and dried pears were considered a great delicacy. Apart from these, which were very common, the Romans knew more or less the same fruits as we do; peaches, apricots, cherries, wild cherries, quinces, plums, pomegranates, blackberries, citrons, carobs, medlars, elderberries, melons, water melons, mulberries, strawberries, blueberries, sloes, dates and many more.

Wild cherries had already been known for a long time, and cherries had been grown in Greece three centuries before Lucullus, who, indeed, brought them back from the Pontus after defeating Mithridates. One could easily elaborate on the importance of red fruits in their diet, and the cherry was among the most prized. Plums too were very popular, again because they

---

Orders for the dispatch of a barrel of wine, Coptic manuscript: Egypt, fifth century

Ensuit La nef de sãte
Auec le gouernail du
corps humain/ et la cõ
dãnaciõ des bãcquetz
A la louenge de diepte.
et sobriete Et le traictie des passions
de lame. Jmprime a paris en la Rue
neufue nostre dame A lescu de frãce

were easy to preserve. The *pruneau d'Agen* or Ante plum was well known and was grown in Rome as well as imported in large quantities from Spain.

The Romans served fruit as a main dish in its own right, whereas we serve it at the end of the meal. Some of their recipes remind us that duck with peaches is not a twentieth-century invention.

Cereals: Although barley was the first cereal to be grown on a large scale in Italy, in Lucullus' time wheat was the most widely consumed. Spelt was a hard grained wheat, one of the most popular varieties of which was *far*, which gave its name to the well known Breton preparation, and is also the root of the word *farine*. There was an immense Mediterranean trade in wheat during the first century which goes to prove its importance in daily consumption, and it was traded between Egypt, Italy, Gaul, Sicily and Sardinia.

Rye and oats even though regarded as poor stuff, were nevertheless quite popular. The Romans considered that both these cereals, as well as barley, were little better than weeds. Millet was equally despised, but it continues to be grown to this day and millet is still in favour in the south-west of France and other more Mediterranean regions. Rice was known but not cultivated; acorns were eaten – mostly grilled. It is not so long since (during the war years of 1939-45) that we made an *ersatz* coffee which consisted largely of roasted acorns.

Talking of grilling, the Romans were familiar with this method which served more than one purpose; it not only improved the flavour, but also purified sacrifices and therefore made them more acceptable to the gods.

Apparently the inhabitants of Chios invented starch. Their method of extracting it was extremely simple, and is still taught in primary schools. They softened the grain, then soaked it in constantly changing water, then crushed and pressed it. The resulting juice was put in the sun to evaporate. The starch residue was used for many purposes including, as today, the binding of sauces.

The Romans knew how to mill grain. They did not, however, disdain the mortar and pestle for producing semolina which is in some ways superior to flour, since it retains the living elements of the grain and is more easily

Title-page from 'La Nef de Santé', Paris, 1505

Roman meal, kitchen, bakery and buttery

digested. *Polenta* which is still in current use, comes from the root-word *pollen* or *polental*. Today of course it is made from maize flour which was totally unknown then.

The use of flours: First of all, bread. For a very long time bread-making was a cottage industry and it is therefore hard to say when it began. But we do know that, 200 years B.C., there were increasing numbers of professional bakers who knew about fermentation and used it in a variety of ways mainly to preserve the yeast. The different methods of salting and baking, the addition of herbs or of seeds (sunflower, sesame or cumin), and its separation into various shapes accounted for several dozen different types of bread which were known in the first century. Bread was still considered a luxury, but cereal cake and porridges continued to be common fare. It requires no exercise of imagination to guess what these porridges were like; *cruchade, polenta* and *gaudes* are survivals from that age, as well as *far*.

Eggs: Hens were favoured by the poultry farmers and their eggs were the most highly regarded. Then came the eggs of ducks, pigeons, pheasants,

52

partridges, and especially geese. Probably wild birds' eggs were also collected as they still are in Scandinavia and elsewhere.

Quail eggs are very popular today in France because for some time now these birds have been intensively raised throughout the country, but one must confess that hens' eggs are the easiest of all to use and that they give, say in binding a stuffing or making a cake, a more uniform result than any other.

Egg cookery was very similar to that of today; eggs in sauces, fried eggs, boiled, hard-boiled, poached, etc. Sweet omelettes, *ova spongia*, were very popular. Eggs were used in many dishes, either whole or separated into yolks and whites.

Milk and cheese: The Romans did not drink cow's milk. The milch-cow as we know her today did not exist; cows were beasts of burden and the little milk they gave was just enough to feed the very young calves.

Goats and ewes were more or less the same as today; their milk was used for cooking and especially for making cheese which in turn figured largely in many recipes. Asses' and mares' milk was also drunk, and more as a medicine than as a common beverage. It would seem that the fermented milk, the *koumys* of the barbarians, was unknown to the Romans although it was already consumed in other countries at that time.

Dairy produce was less popular than cheese. I mentioned the sweet omelette which contained milk and it is probable that the Roman *dulcia* was very similar to *dulche de leche*. A sort of brioche was already being baked and milk was also used with various porridges much as it is now added to a *polenta* or a soup.

During rationing in 1939–45, I decided to make cheese.

One of my friends had a few cows, and later I bought some goats, so I was able to make cheese throughout the Occupation. This is how I went about it. I measured out into a glazed pot the very slightly warmed milk to which I added rennet (a few drops per quart). I stood the pot away from the fire but in a warm place and left the milk to curdle. Then I heated it again (either on the oven door or before the fire, according to season) turning the pot round every now and again. When I thought it hot enough (but not too hot to dip one's hands in it) I removed it from the heat and set it on a table or a stool,

53

and breaking up the coagulated mass with my hands, kneaded it between my palms until it was a compact, homogeneous ball. Then I warmed the mixture for a few minutes and prepared the mould (which more often than not was an old strainer or a box with a lot of holes made with a big nail). When my hands could only just stand the temperature, I had to seize the ball which was in the whey, and transfer it with one swift, neat gesture into the mould I had prepared. It wasn't really acrobatic, but had to be done very quickly. There were several difficulties involved; the first was to create a single mass which absorbed absolutely all the solid elements, then to avoid letting holes or bubbles appear in it, and finally to get it out of the liquid without breaking it or letting it crumble. I pressed it down into the mould, neither too hard nor too lightly, and left it there for eight days. At the end of the week, I salted the exposed surface and turned the mould upside down on a straw mat, a process I repeated every four days, lightly salting it twice more. As soon as the crust had formed, the cheese was edible. It may surprise you in a chapter dealing with the first century that I should explain how I made cheese at Sauternes or in the *maquis* of l'Oisans twenty years ago, but in fact there is absolutely no difference between my method and that used by the Romans.

The cheeses I made differed very much from each other. The variety was not so great in my experiments at Sauternes when the quantities and quality of the milk were consistent. Moreover, I was new to the game, and was particularly careful to follow the rules an old Italian cook had given me. As I grew more skilful, so I became bolder and more confident. For instance, I stopped measuring the rennet, and warmed the milk on the stove before pouring it into the glazed pot. As time went on, I no longer used pure cows' milk, but a mixture of cows' and goats' milk in varying proportions. The results were picturesque in the extreme. There were some brilliant successes (a whole series of absolutely marvellous fermented cheeses of the Camembert type) and some pretty grim efforts of pale, crumbly plaster.

These experiments enabled me to imagine the slow progress of cheese-making techniques. I came up against all the beginners' problems. I should for instance have noted down what I did, as well as what quantities and temperatures I used. Had I done this, I should probably have obtained uniform results, for that is the way in which techniques are evolved. Leaves were used both to preserve cheeses and to scent them. The Romans also smoked their cheese more often than we do for they were very fond of a smoky flavour, which is still much liked in most Mediterranean countries.

It is thought that the barbarians did not make cheese, although they were pastoral peoples, but I am inclined to disagree, for the Romans readily alluded to the Gauls and the Huns as barbarians, although dairy farming there was far more advanced than among the Romans. One must admit that Italy has never produced superlative cheeses, whereas those of northern and mountain countries can rank with the best. The importance of cheese in first-century cooking is so great that one cannot ignore it, but it is a pity that the recipes involving milk and cheese give too little information about the quality of these ingredients.

Butter was brought from Gaul but was unknown in cookery, for it was only used in northern countries where cream-skimming was facilitated by low temperatures. At any rate, it was not used by the Roman cooks any more than cream, for which no word existed.

Meat: Butchers' meat was certainly known and eaten by the Romans, but again only by the few; even the prosperous seldom put it on their menu.

The period was still one in which religious taboos affected some meats. For instance, horse flesh was not eaten, out of respect for the animal nor was beef, which enjoyed an almost human immunity. Sacrificing a steer could lead to the death penalty or banishment. The practice of sacrifice was still current, though less so in Italy than elsewhere, and it generally consisted of cereals and flour.

When an animal was sacrificed, it was shared out and its sexual organs burned. This cremation was an important symbol since it represented the gods' share. The remainder was distributed; first to the priests, and then to the person offering the sacrifice. The rest was sold or given away. For centuries the only meat the Romans ate was that resulting from sacrifices.

Once the butchers' trade became as important as it is today, pork was preferred to all other meats. Pig farming was largely empirical, the quality of the meat depending entirely on the animals' diet. There were bean pigs, acorn pigs, chestnut pigs, much as today we have acacia or lavender honey. Sucking

55

A Roman pork butcher's shop

pigs were considered superior to pork, and, in general, all young animals were preferred to the full-grown; the feeding of cattle was erratic, so full-grown beasts tended to give tough meat. There was no comparison between the high esteem in which baby lamb was held and the contempt accorded to mutton. Veal then as now, tended to be red, stringy and tough, and was uneasily placed between lamb and beef.

The Romans were particularly fond of certain cuts of pork, among which sows' udders were rated as the greatest delicacy. The peasant raised pigs, goats and sheep, slaughtered them himself, and had to preserve some of the meat for future use. It was therefore logical that he should favour pigs which gave the best results for the same amount of trouble.

We must also mention donkey and dog. Puppy dog was eaten in Rome as it is today in China, and donkey was popular for *charcuterie*.

Game: The Romans frequently had wild boar and liked it as much as pork. Wild sows too were in great demand and prepared in the same way as domestic animals. There were also bears, whose meat was much enjoyed

56

except when the animals had fought in the arenas and were, as so often, gorged on human flesh; although the flavour may just as well have been spoilt because of the flow of adrenalin into the tissues when the animal was killed in combat.

Other big game included venison, fallow deer, stag, roe-deer and also the oryx, an antelope imported from Africa. There were also plenty of wild goats, wild sheep and *mouflon*, and probably *chamois* too, although these may have been included among the wild goats. The Romans also imported wild asses, but the locally raised farmyard animal, when young, was much more popular.

Apart from pheasant and rabbit, small game was much the same as it is now, although the breeds were probably different for since then many strains have been imported. Hares were also much the same and included the mountain hares which go white in winter.

Game breeding then was much as it was here fifty years ago, consisting mainly of establishing and enclosing reserves and putting down plenty of feed. Whortleberries were planted in selected spots for the game, just as today we plant elderberries and buckwheat.

The Romans were also very fond of birds such as the flamingo, the crane and the stork which have totally deserted our tables. Indeed, it is hard to understand their liking for foods which we should certainly replace with woodcock, grouse or partridge. We are also surprised at their custom of stitching swans' eyelids together to fatten them, although a similar operation performed on other birds existed not long ago in the Landes.

Fish: It is more difficult to draw the line between fact and legend on this subject than on any other concerning Roman eating habits. The Mediterranean provided then the same fish as now; those which were easiest to catch were the most popular. Roman taste differed from ours as did their cooking methods, but they were unanimous in favouring red mullet, still as popular today as ever.

Hence the famous story of the auction at which 8,000 sesterces were bid for one of these fish. Its liver was reckoned to possess exceptional properties, and rightly so in my opinion. Scomber, the best-known varieties of which are mackerel, tunny and *bonito* (Mediterranean tunny) seem to have been particularly appreciated. There were also *muraena*, sardine, conger-eel, *baudroie*, *danty*, *meron*, *loche*, scorpion-fish (*rascasse*), and all the many-coloured and delicious fauna of that sea. In that domain, nothing has altered. It is amusing to note in passing some picturesque names, such as for instance *mendole* for a variety of turbot (probably brill) whose shape is reminiscent of the Italian mandoline.

One could almost devote a chapter to *garum*. This was either a sauce or a condiment, whichever one prefers to assume about a preparation now extinct. Many people think it is simply a version of the present day Indochinese *muoc-mam*. The Roman recipes which have reached us are very incomplete since no one has succeeded in reconstituting any of them. This is easily explained by the fact that when there is an enormous consumption of a given product, whatever it may be, it is so well known that oral tradition suffices for its perpetuation. Moreover, *garum* was a base to which other elements were added, just as today we add either lemon juice, yellow wine or soy sauce to *muoc-mam*. *Garum* was therefore a substance to which could be added honey, vinegar, water, wine, fruit juice and so on.

Today our taste would probably rebel against what we would regard as heretical, a mixture of *garum* and red mullet liver, for example. One must however bear in mind that *garum* was a liquid, the colour and consistency of which we do not know, made from the putrefied innards of scomber or, occasionally, other fish. For some time it was generally agreed that certain fish (like thornback) were better eaten slightly high. This was even true of red mullet, which were known as sea-woodcock. Another reason for using this name is that neither mullet nor woodcock should be cleaned before cooking. This, rather than the high flavour of the bird, is the aspect which interests us here. Red mullet should be eaten fresh. For centuries it was taken for granted that it should not be scaled, because if the fish were to be grilled over embers, the delicate flesh and innards had to be protected from the fire. It was purely a safety precaution. Today, reasons which were valid even fifty years ago are obsolete.

Fish, crustaceans and shells: from a Roman mosaic

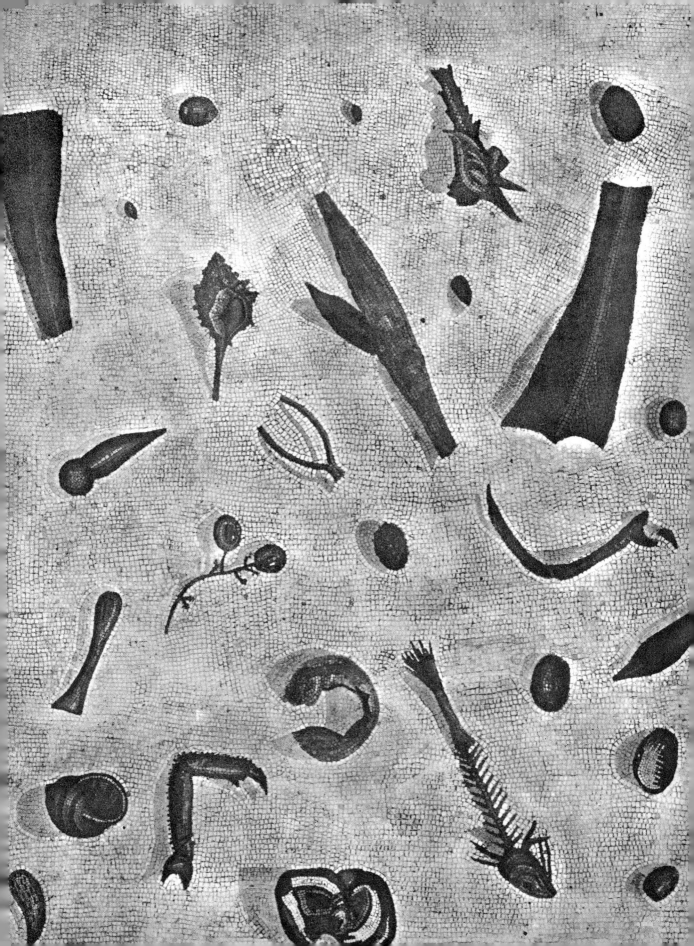

There are various reasons why the Romans ate few fish and which made those few very expensive. They disliked water, and were poor sailors and fishermen. It was perhaps because they were newcomers to the coast and because the Mediterranean, despite her smiling aspect, has always been a tricky sea.

The literary tradition which depicts the Romans as frugal is not accurate. Fish consumption has always been balanced between supply and demand – in Rome, demand controlled the market.

Fowls: Fowls were sold, live, in pairs, as they still are in some of our country markets. Indeed, only twenty-five years ago, fowls were all sold that way, and only retailers sold individual dead birds.

Wild and domestic duck existed in Italy long before chickens, although chickens had been known for three centuries, at the time of Lucullus. Though the Pharaohs did not know the breed, it was probably introduced to Egypt, though indirectly, by the Greeks. For a long time, chickens were known as 'birds of Persia', just as later *pintades* were known as Guinea fowl, or African or Numidian hens. There seems to have been little technical change in poultry raising and egg collecting, or in the relative popularity of fat or spring chickens, and stews of old cocks and hens. The Romans castrated most cocks, and capon was then as proud a dish as it is now.

Goose was much sought after. My friend Jacques Bourgeat tells a very amusing anecdote about geese. These birds used, he claims, to be walked all the way from Picardy to Rome; admittedly a long walk, but the only way. During the trip, the geese toughened up their legs and learned to put up with the strong smell of their Gaulish keepers. When, later, the Gauls tried surreptitiously to seize the Capitol, the geese locked up inside recognized the smell, and fearing a pedestrian return to Flanders, made a great fuss which, if it did not save them, at least made them famous.

Geese were fattened up, without, however, being forcibly fed. Some form of foie gras seems to have been known in Rome. Perhaps it has undergone the same transformation as champagne since Dom Pérignon. There must have been large and small livers, according to luck, and they were set to swell in milk with honey and spices. I don't think such a method would make them swell much. Legend has it that Metellus Scipio invented foie gras by using an improved version of a Greek recipe.

Pheasant was not game, but a farmyard bird, as was the peacock. The hoary legend of a peacock as the central dish of important banquets was based more upon the splendour of its plumage than the delicacy of its meat. I did cook some several years ago, but do not remember any of them as exceptional in any way.

Stories of flamingoes' and other birds' tongues, of parrots on the spit and herons' brains are legendary. However, eccentrics like Heliogabalus were, later it is true, producing dishes to make imagination boggle.

Pigeons were among the most popular birds. Several species were domesticated and kept in aviaries, as well as turtle-doves, and wood-pigeons. Their eggs were considered a great delicacy, and as we shall see, continued to be so for a long time.

Snails: Snails were known, but not nearly as popular as they are today. Here is an example of the gradual development of a liking for food not imposed by its nature but as a result of research. Probably snails cooked in clear broth and served with butter provided the basis for all subsequent recipes for serving this gastropod. At any rate, the Romans raised them as we do now, and already knew how to fatten them on flour. They were grilled or sautéd in oil; our little grey snail in ham sauce does not seem to have been one of the Caesars' delights.

Vegetables: Here at least we are on safe ground; the Romans have left us so much documentation on market gardening that we have a clear picture of their vegetarian diet. Indeed, with cereals, it formed the bulk of their food.

Once again we see the gradual jettisoning of one food in favour of another. Slowly, half the plants which were originally eaten were abandoned. I shall not list them all, and I do not wish to draw any particular conclusions from those that I do mention. One can simply note that the Romans grew a number of root vegetables (for instance taro, still eaten in Polynesia) which are no longer grown in Europe.

I still remember certain kitchen gardens in my part of the country where some edible and now forgotten plants grew. Sometimes their growers had themselves forgotten their use. Then they would come and find my father, carrying a basket covered with a clean white cloth which they would raise delicately to display some gnarled root which perplexed us all deeply. Gathered together around the basket, we tried to imagine what sauce could possibly enhance such a vegetable, and we generally came to the conclusion that it could not be very delicious if it was so little known. The potato alone has replaced dozens of varieties of coleseed. And yet coleseed and other root vegetables were highly esteemed; parsnips and turnips were items of daily fare. Although the word radish was used, the vegetable as we know it is the result of much cross-breeding, and did not exist. Horseradish was widely used both as a vegetable and as a condiment.

Onion and garlic were certainly the two most prized and widely used bulb vegetables. There are two schools of thought among writers; one which believes that because of the smell only the poor ate onion and garlic and the other which, like myself, is almost certain that everyone enjoyed both. Spring onions eaten with salt at breakfast seem to have delighted legionaries and peasants, but patricians no less.

Baiae braisé

Put finely chopped oysters in an earthenware pot, with marrowbones and sea-nettles. Add grilled and chopped fir-cones, rue, wild celery, pepper, coriander, cumin, raisin wine, *garum*, date wine and oil. Cook and serve.

Braise (embractium)

This Baiae stew had to be cooked until almost all the liquid had evaporated. We think it was eaten cold and jellied. No doubt it is to this dish that Seneca refers when he says (letter 95) that he 'once heard speak of a famous dish into which a glutton, determined on bankruptcy, threw pell-mell all the delicacies that would satisfy the most epicurean for a whole day: shells of Venus, marrowbones, oysters (the fringe trimmed off as they are not eaten); sea-urchins separate these layers of sea fruit; and beneath everything, red mullet finely chopped and boned'. (*Les Dix Livres de Cuisine d'Apicius* translated from the Latin by Bertrand Guégan, 1933)

62

A dish of roses

Take roses, remove their leaves and the calyx. Put them in a mortar and crush them. Pour over the roses a cup and a half of *garum* and sieve the mixture. Take 4 brains, remove all the nerves, then crush with 8 scruples of pepper. Pour this over the roses, and mix well. Then break 8 eggs into the mixture, moisten with a cup of wine, a cup of raisin wine and a little oil. Oil a dish generously, place it on hot embers and fill with the above composition. When the dish is cooked, dust with ground pepper and serve.

The *unguis* was removed from each petal before extracting the juice from the roses (cf. Pliny, XXI, 73). Aelius Verus, who often slept on flowers, would only have flowers prepared in this way on his bed (Aelius, *Spartianus*, ch. 4). 'Here is what I call a "pot of roses",' says a cook in *Athenaeus* (IX, 16); 'I prepared it in this manner that you might enjoy the sweet scent of garlands upon your head and within you, that your whole body might share the pleasure. After crushing the sweetest scented roses in a mortar, I threw in the brains of a great many birds and animals well boiled and from which I had removed the last tiny filaments. I added yolks of eggs, then oil, *garum*, pepper and wine. When I had thoroughly ground and mixed all these, I threw it into a new pot and gave it only regular gentle heat.'
(*Les Dix Livres de Cuisine d'Apicius* translated from the Latin by Bertrand Guégan, 1933)

Stuffed udders

Grind pepper, caraway and salted sea-urchins. Stuff a sow's belly with the mixture, sew up and cook. Eat the udders with *halec* and mustard.

Salted sea urchins

'In December, those who live near the sea will preserve in salt the flesh of sea-urchins, when the moon favours the operation, for it is then that this planet fattens animals and shellfish in the ocean's womb' (Palladius, XIII, 6). The Ancients believed in the moon's power over plants and animals: 'The Moon,' writes Aristotle (*Gen. anim.*, IV, 10), 'is, so to speak, a second small sun; that is why it contributes to the begetting and growth of all things, for heat and cold within certain limits induce generation, and afterwards, too, destruction.' *Halec* or *alex*: '*Alex*,' writes Pliny (XXXI, 44), 'is the sediment of *garum*, a coarse and badly-filtered lees.' However, one begins its preparation with a tiny little fish, which serves no purpose; this is the *apua* of the latins, the *aphye* of the Greeks, so named because it is engendered by rain. The inhabitants of Fréjus make *alex* with a fish which they call 'wolf' [it is the sea-perch]. *Alex* became a luxury product and was made in an infinity of varieties, which is how it came to include oysters, sea-urchins, lobsters, and the livers of red mullet. *Alex* cures mange in sheep – it is poured on to the skin which is incised; it is also good for sting-ray bites and is applied on lint.

To make mortadella

Take the pulp of a leg of veal and cut it up small with the fat from the calf and with bacon; crush marjoram and parsley; and with a knife or spoon beat the yolk of an egg with grated cheese, and sprinkle with spices and mix with spices and mingle the whole with the meat, making a mass. Cut a cloth or fat pork caul or veal caul into portions, and place within them the mixture wrapped like handsome little loaves the size of an egg. Finally spit them on small spits and cook softly that they be not too cooked, so they shall be sweeter and more pleasant to eat. And although they are slow to digest and cause obstruction, gravel and the stone, they help the heart and the liver.

(*Le Livre de l'Honneste Volupte* by Platina of Cremona, 1474)
(*La Fleur de la Cuisine Française* by Bertrand Guégan, 1934)

64

From the Dark Ages to the Renaissance

When the Romans conquered Gaul they found a higher level of gastronomy there than they brought with them. Certainly the Gauls were not very refined, but their larders were far richer than those of the Mediterranean peoples who were their unquestioned superiors in terms of culture and civilization. It is true that Roman influences in Gaul were quick to make themselves felt, and Roman notions of comfort which were new to the Gauls greatly affected their cookery.

I have already sketched the gastronomic picture of the period. One may perhaps take as the best example the smallest community, the family. It owned a kitchen garden, raised a few pigs and some chickens; its vegetable diet consisted largely of beans, mainly dried, coleseed and cereals – in short all the vegetables which were easy to preserve and were winter staples. Pork was mainly salted down, but also provided fats. Fowls, lending themselves to division into small portions, were ideal family fare.

Bread was consumed with cereals ranging from *far* to cereal cake throughout the year as staple food. Game was occasionally a welcome addition to the ordinary diet but could never be taken for granted.

Soup was the main dish up to and beyond the reign of Henri IV (1553–1610) who praised it so highly. The method of preparation was very simple. A huge cauldron, filled with water and permanently suspended over the fire, cooked everything. Until the time of Charlemagne (742–814) everything was indiscriminately lumped in together. Portions were ladled out, and replaced by other ingredients to keep the pot full. Sometimes even fish and meat were mixed together in the pot, for there was no rule against it; but this was rare, for food was not often available in great abundance or variety.

It is important to try and understand the peasant mentality, which has not altered so conspicuously since; the tiller of the soil has always been the slave of the seasons and their vagaries. Safety first is his motto, then organization.

Some historians have chosen to picture the Gauls as gluttons gathered around roaring fires on which they roasted game, fowls and pigs. The truth is perhaps less impressive. We are told the Gauls also drank and were fond of beer and mead. They used cow horns for cups, and even human skulls, but abandoned both in favour of the Roman metal goblet. Their favourite drink was the barley beer which the Phoenicians had brought from Egypt and which was made in the same way all over the country. It consisted of barley and yeast; the addition of honey was a throwback to the Greek habit of never drinking anything unmixed.

Salt was not scarce but it was expensive. As essential to life as it was to the preservation of food, it became the object of an enormous trade, against which only a few other commodities could be bartered. A salt merchant would not have dreamed of exchanging salt for lentils, the bulk and weight of which would have made transport costs prohibitive. Hence the difficulty in obtaining salt, and the expeditions in search of it organized by various communities.

The Roman occupation changed little in the Gauls' eating habits, apart from the cottage industries of baking and brewing. Julius Caesar took with him the vine which was soon planted almost everywhere in Gaul, and wine began to replace all other drinks. This was, so to speak, the first marriage of cheese and wine – for the Gauls already had cheese. From the Massif Central, cradle of a prehistoric civilization, came a cheese very similar to our modern Cantal, which would appear to be the oldest variety known. There was also a goats' or ewes' milk cheese which was the ancestor of all our blue cheeses from the *fourme* of Ambert to Roquefort. There were also plenty of fermented cheeses, but no set rules for making them.

Gallic feasts were probably much as we imagine them to have been, few and far between, but certainly Gargantuan. The company remained at table for hours and hours on end, eating and drinking prodigiously, probably because it would be a long time before another chance arose. The wood-cutter in his smoky hovel as an image is a nineteenth-century illustrator's fancy. Until the Romans introduced their architectural techniques, with central heating and kitchens half indoors and half out, everyone was in the

'Banquet' by L. de Caullery, 1600

same rather chilly boat, and the shared human warmth of a banquet was appreciated in the same way as the food. There were few winter festivals, and it was not until the fourth century that Pope Julius I decreed that Christmas should be celebrated on 25 December, thus providing an excuse for what soon became the traditional *réveillon* – an enormous midnight feast.

The Gauls became Franks, then Carolingians; if they had taught the Romans what to eat, it was certainly the Romans who taught them how to eat it, starting with a table, with seats around it, and all that was served on it. Of course, the first to enjoy these domestic improvements were, as always, the privileged minority. Kings and great lords were the only people to own plate, which they valued immensely. The anecdote of the vase of Soissons,★ so corrupted by time, boils down to a simple sordid story of broken crockery. Nevertheless, if one chooses, as I do, to regard gastronomy as one of the humanities, then the Carolingian period can fairly be regarded as one of fruitful transition.

Charlemagne prided himself on being a gastronome, and was the first sovereign of our era to rank as an epicure. This monarch 'of the flowering beard' had not a single hair on his chin, but a heavy, slightly drooping moustache. Tradition has it that he encouraged the exchange of recipes and local methods of preserving or distilling between regions and villages. This should be true, for it is eminently logical. The emperors were anxious to enhance their popularity by raising the standard of living of their subjects. They were all ambitious men, whereas a king by birth and divine right could allow himself to be a dyspeptic stay-at-home. Among the laws promulgated by Charlemagne, in his Capitularies, were several advising people to drink cider, to exchange recipes and to share local gastronomic secrets. Each village had by this time its own jealously-guarded formula for brewing barley beer or mead, passed on by word of mouth from one generation to the next. To advise the Palatinate to drink cider from Normandy was a first move towards a wider publicity. From a more human point of view, he was responsible for another

★The occasion when Clovis, the first Frankish King to become a Christian, punished the licentious soldiery for breaking a church vessel in the Cathedral of Soissons.

'Still Life with Wafer Biscuits' by Baugin, 1630

Christian love feast (Agape): *from a ninth-century pulpit*

great innovation that was to alter the very spirit of the meal; for the first time, women were allowed to sit down at table. Once again, a custom restricted to the upper classes and one which, though we take it for granted today, was very slow to be adopted in humbler homes. I have personally known families where it was still not practised.

Eating habits were still largely unchanged. Bread had acquired a great pre-eminence and replaced porridge and cereal cake to a great extent, but not entirely; for the old habits were still to endure for many centuries. However, the bread the Gauls ate at that time had only the faintest resemblance to our French or Vienna loaves. It was made with yeasts of greater or lesser raising power mixed with coarse and ill-sieved flour, and it was eaten like biscuit or hard tack, which, for anyone who has not tried it, I shall describe as it was twenty-five years ago. The soldiers were issued with a very large, immensely hard biscuit which could be slowly nibbled by someone with a tough jaw and strong teeth, but it had generally to be dipped into liquid before consumption. The Gallic loaf was very big, and each person took a slice which he put in the bottom of his dish. On to this slice he piled everything he was going to eat, cut it up, prepared it, and moistened it. The bread was usually the bulk of the meal. To do this of course meant that there was something to cut up (to slice, *trancher*) so the piece of bread became known as the trencher. All too often there was only dry bread on hand, hence the habit of moistening it with broth, so that the trencher changed its name with soup; 'one soaked the soup'.

70

Medieval husbandry: from the 'Livre de Prouffitz Champêtres', 1529 edition

Musicians at a feast: from a fourteenth-century manuscript by Guillaume de Machault

The broth which was eaten two or three times a day remained basic for many years.

I have used the word 'dish', but in many regions, especially in the mountains, there was no such thing; there were hollows simply scooped out of the wooden table, another custom which survived for a long time.

Charlemagne had fancied himself as a Roman Emperor but after him, gastronomy was involved in politics more than ever before. Although the Hundred Years' War was less murderous than 6 August 1945, it had disastrous effects upon gastronomic progress. Nor did the famines which descended upon the whole of Europe help matters, while at the same time, the Moors brought Mediterranean trade to a standstill. We must not be too hard on the

Middle Ages; they were certainly dark, but provided a solid platform for the brilliant evolution of the Renaissance.

We cannot help being amazed at the tastes of our early ancestors. One of the choicest medieval dishes, as it had been of the earlier period, was peacock, served in its feathers and surrounded by small chicks. I do not agree with those who say that peacock has no gastronomic value and while it is not as good as turkey hen, it is better than elderly pheasant. Moreover, it keeps particularly

The Grail appearing to the Knights of the Round Table: from a fourteenth-century manuscript

well and, for people who ate as frugally as they did in the tenth century, the sight of a great bird spitting flames on the table was an exciting spectacle.

Talking of flames, I have certain reservations about the popularity of that form of presentation and the fantastic recipes which have come down to us. Nowadays we sometimes serve birds in the same way, which we describe as 'in aviary'. It is not at all difficult, and Eleanor of Aquitaine's cooks certainly had the same means of doing it as we have. What is never mentioned is the erotic symbolism of the male bird adorned with its own feathers and surrounded by numerous small victims. Throughout history, the table, cookery, and everything connected with them, have been powerfully influenced by symbols and by deeply ingrained habits which have been hard to eradicate. For instance, during the famines of the Middle Ages it proved almost impossible to persuade starving people to eat herring; they would rather die of hunger than change their traditional eating habits. Five hundred years later, the same phenomenon occurred when Parmentier introduced the potato into France. This reluctance to accept new foods has always existed, and even today, the unfamiliar is condemned outright without a trial.

It is therefore safe to say that the consumer has always been readier to give up familiar foods than to accept new ones. What seems saddening in France is that people are more inclined to put up with privations in quantity than in quality. I don't know enough about other countries to say that this is true everywhere. But I do think that other people are more attached to traditional foods or dishes than we are. The lack of these would affect them far more than the lack of bread and wine would affect a Frenchman whose basic foods they are. Imagine an Asiatic deprived of rice, an American of corn, a Polynesian of taro, and Eskimo of seal meat, and so on. They would feel lost even if there were plenty of other foods, which played no part in their ordinary diet, but a Frenchman would soon have accustomed himself to the change. Indeed, together with the Chinese, the French are the people who have taken advantage of the widest range of foodstuffs, and although they do obey the universal rule of regularly discarding certain victuals, one must admit that this nearly always applies to luxuries.

Prince Zizim entertained by the Knights of Rhodes: from a fourteenth-century manuscript

Catherine de' Medici: medal by Germaine Pilon, sixteenth century

From the Renaissance to the Twentieth Century

Henri II's marriage to Catherine de' Medici in 1553 marked a significant stage in the development of French gastronomy. Most historians think it happened earlier, with the accession of the Valois dynasty. Their conviction is based upon a book by Messire Guillaume Tirel, called Taillevent, who was the Valois' cook. A manuscript is in the Vatican library, and as early as 1480 there was an edition of which only three copies still exist. I own what I believe to be the finest of them. There was a new edition in 1536, and then another modern one edited by Baron Pichon.

Catherine de' Medici brought her Florentine cooks to France with her. Marco Polo also travelled with his cooks and my theories about him are well known. On his return to Venice from China he brought, besides gunpowder (another use for saltpetre), the recipe for ices, and even more important, *pasta* in its definitive form. This was to alter the whole basis of Italian eating within a few decades. Such revolutions leave their mark. Better fed, and in a way which suited them permanently, the Italians began to flower. That the noodle should have given birth to the Quattrocento and encouraged the development of all the arts does not seem to me too fantastic, though of course this is only my personal opinion. Cooking always evolves more slowly than the other arts, and every attempt to alter eating habits is initially doomed to failure. It would be interesting today to compare the relative success of Charlemagne's widely-promulgated advice, and a television campaign in favour of the self-same apple juice. There is nothing new under the sun.

History has need of its references, and every time one tackles a serious gastronomic question, one comes up against great classical tirades. The Gauls ate wild boar, the Druids cut mistletoe, the Crusaders took the 'peacock's oath' and Montaigne made witticisms at the expense of cooks.

Monsieur Malraux has not put a limit to the price for a stained glass window

The Great Khan of China entertaining Marco Polo: from a fifteenth-century manuscript

by Chagall, but the exchequer sets the price for Claude Terrail's duck in blood sauce at the *Tour d'Argent* restaurant. Let us give Montaigne his due without ascribing to him an eclecticism which he probably lacked. As history

78

Light refreshments with music: from a sixteenth-century tapestry

always repeats itself, it is easy to place Renaissance cooks. They were part of their period, doing as much in their sphere as Michaelangelo did in his. Why should we discriminate against them?

Domestic scene: from 'La Maison de Repos', fifteenth century

Vatel did not commit suicide because the fish did not arrive, but because he felt misunderstood. Though jilted by one of the Princesse de Condé's ladies-in-waiting, he spared no effort to be certain that the Prince's banquet for Louis XIV should be successful. Unluckily, the roast ran short at a few tables where minor courtiers were seated and there was not enough fish. Nobody else noticed this. Nor, more important, did the King or Condé. However, Vatel, out of some kind of masochism, told Condé about it and

80

was brushed aside. His master's lack of interest in his art depressed Vatel even more than his unsuccessful love affair, and thus sparked off the impulse to suicide.

Though Montaigne in his *Essays* waxed ironic about the 'gift of the gab' of Italian cooks, there is no doubt that cooks already held and aired definite views not only on food, but on the artistic value of their profession. Of course,

Rôtisseur turning his spit: misericord from the abbey of St Lucien, c. 1500

from Montaigne's point of view it seemed shocking that cooks should discuss gastronomy as others discussed politics. Montaigne also lived to see the reign of Henri IV, a great king who also achieved fame in the world of gastronomy.

The Béarnais loved garlic and Henri hailed from the south-west of France which has always been the land of Cockayne, of geese, pigs and migratory game and fish. He himself had been simply brought up. Christened with wine from the Jurançon and his lips rubbed with garlic, he enjoyed rustic food. His marriage did not alter his attitude much; he was never greatly influenced by his wife or her courtiers though his court was, and the court set the tone.

We are all familiar with the highly-coloured sentimental lithograph of Henri IV with one hand tumbling the girls without bothering to court them and with the other raising the lid to peer into the pots into which he had put the famous chickens. Henri IV as a clown and Henri IV as a politician, a shepherd or a ploughman! All these are well known clichés, though it was Olivier de Serre who was the real creator of gastronomy at this period, yet Henri IV is said to have been far from disinterested. His slogan 'I want each of my peasants to have a chicken in his pot on Sunday' had no other end than the promotion of a political campaign for popularity. Gastronomically we must put his statement into its proper context. The pot was nearly always the cauldron which hung in the smoky fireplace on its famous *crémaillère* (hook); all season long it was filled and used without ever being entirely emptied. When the fire was out, the draught kept the contents of the pot in an excellent state of preservation. Every morning, more water, salt and vegetables were added, the fire was lighted and now and again a piece of bacon, a chicken, or a shin bone was put in to provide pot luck. The irregularity of these additions, and the Friday abstinence from meat which continued, willy-nilly during centuries, made Sunday the obvious day for festivity.

Historical records indicate that the story of the chicken in the pot is true but different. The good King Henri was asked by his guest, the Duke of Savoy, at a game of tennis in the Faubourg St Germain, what revenues France brought him in. Trying to evade the direct question, Henri replied, 'She is worth what I want.' When pressed to be more precise, he produced this parable: 'Yes, whatever I want, because if I have the heart of my people, I shall have what I want, and if God lets me live, I shall make sure that there is no labourer in my kingdom who cannot afford to put a chicken in his pot on Sunday.' This quotation comes from Péréfixe.

The age of coffee and croissants had not yet dawned. From Roman times onwards bread was dunked at breakfast time. Joan of Arc used wine, the French peasant, broth. There were spring onions eaten raw and fresh garlic with salt, and later, all the first fruits. Rustic man is susceptible to the call of nature, especially when it concerns him personally. He seeks what he needs instinctively. He is also closer to the earth, its pitfalls and its treasures. Peasants drink mallow tea, rub rheumatic limbs with nettles, cook chestnuts with fig-leaves; everything has its own reason for existence, and even if one does not know what it is, one knows it has to be.

We are told that the Medici cooks changed the face of French gastronomy during the Renaissance, but this only applied in their great houses. The new passion for ices led architects to plan special ice-stores in the castle cellars. The ice was collected in winter and stored against the warm season. In a 'good year' it could be used for months. . . . 'But where are the snows of yester-year?' Imports of crude ice from Norway proved more practical and less expensive than bringing it down from the Alps; the Caesars brought their ice from the Appenines, the kings of France from Sonnefjord.

Florentine gastronomy of the period is generally considered to have been more advanced and refined; it was gradually shedding the heaviness of medieval cookery. If we owe Hippocras to Guillaume Tirel, we can also see the Borgia influence spreading to the French court where wine was normally drunk. A modern Sherlock Holmes has uncovered the methods whereby the Borgias despatched those who had lost favour with them. Contrary to popular belief, they used neither a distillation of poisoned mushrooms nor compli-cated philtres, nor even poisoned rings. It was much simpler; the victim's cup was simply rubbed with a toxic solution, allowed to dry, and carefully identi-fied. It was then filled with the same harmless wine that was given to the other guests to remove the taste of bread. This seems a likely theory in that it was done in public and based on the habit of instantly draining a full beaker. The cup-bearers offered water as well as wine and draughts were small but frequent. Undiluted wine was seldom drunk.

These customs were soon adopted in France and popular story-tellers made

84

the most of the theme; the melodramas of Buridan or Isabeau of Bavaria lean heavily upon it for effect. Villon and Rabelais give us faithful descriptions of contemporary feasts. I fear that, though the former was not yet involved in it, the latter did not much care for Italianization. Of course, there is always an inevitable time-lag which must be taken into account. But it is all too easy to assume that these accounts of banquets resembled the daily fare of each period. Nothing could be further from the truth, and the diet of the populace during the reign of Catherine de' Medici was scanty. The nobles alone feasted, and sporadically at that, and they did their very best to prevent the masses from imitating them. Charles IX declared war on greed and promulgated the most stringent sumptuary edicts on 20 January 1563. These had no effect and had to be reissued two years later in February 1565. One of these laws forbade the consumption of lambs so that they might be allowed to grow to maturity. Similar to religious restrictions, they were mainly intended to protect breeding herds. Today it is still a rule in private shoots not to kill females, an understandable protective law.

The notion of allowing lambs to become sheep was not intended to produce more meat per animal, but to ensure that each beast would in turn procreate. For many years a flock was a symbol of wealth, and any beast taken from it was only for sacrifice. Laws forbidding the consumption of fish and meat at the same meal have much in common with the Hebrew prohibitions about eating the flesh of the kid in the milk of the mother. There were numerous Jewish communities in France and they undoubtedly influenced the French. If the 'cruel God' of the Jews and the 'Heavenly Father' of the Christians might have been one and the same, why should Mosaic law not be applied in certain circumstances?

The wide gap between the feast and daily fare continued to exist; certainly, nobody went breadless any more, but bread became more of a symbol as it became the basis of the daily meal.

An immense capacity for food was another attribute of this period and one which Rabelais allowed full rein in his heroes. This of course gave virility to his poetry, but also exalted abilities to which everyone aspired. I have known

Domestic scene: Capricorn, from the 'Almanach des Bergers', 1491

gluttons to whom over-eating gave no pleasure, but who insisted on keeping up their reputations by eating twenty-four hard-boiled eggs and twenty-four croissants after an enormous meal. A cousin of mine could eat a Gargantuan luncheon and then swallow twelve fried eggs and a pound of *dragées* in red wine eaten with a spoon. There have always been people to perform such prodigies and for sheer extravagance they only confirm character of an extra-ordinary kind as symbolized by Pantagruel and Gargantua.

It was about the time of Rabelais that maize came to France from Spain. It was mainly used as cattle food and only eaten by men in Gascony. At the same period Sir Walter Ralegh sent Queen Elizabeth I the first potato plants; they were a failure. Maize had no greater success; the eggs of chickens fed on maize were cheaper than others. Its popularity today is all the more startling.

Sir Walter Ralegh sent Queen Elizabeth the first potato plants with all the necessary information and detailed instructions on how to grow them. The Queen gave them to her chamberlain, told him what to do, and to get on with it. He obeyed to the letter and *solenaceae* were to be seen growing on the banks of the Thames. Harvesting at the appointed time, the chamberlain thought it would popularize the new vegetable if he invited the gentry to a banquet which would feature potatoes with every course. His only mistake was to serve the leaves and stems instead of the tuber in the soups, sauces and purées. When one knows that these are poisonous (though only mildly), one can easily imagine the stomach-aches that followed a disgusting meal, and why it took all the genius of Parmentier to rehabilitate the potato. The scandal caused by this banquet prevented the propagation of the tuber, for the publicity turned into a boomerang. Meanwhile, the Church, never dis-interested, gave the problem some attention. She had made great profits from importing chocolate and now tried to use the potato. There was not a convent or a parsonage kitchen garden without some of the precious roots. Indeed, from the sixteenth century onwards, a little curiosity would have sufficed to develop potato growing, but in fact the plant had to wait more than two hundred years to achieve any kind of popularity.

Trade in cocoa, maize and potatoes from that time went through the hands of the Spanish Church and the Conquistadors with their great white ships. A curious route, perhaps, but it was more profitable than that of gold. More-

Abstinence: from the 'Livre de Bonnes Moeurs', fifteenth century

over, the first explorations were not organized piracy or for plunder but a genuine search for spice routes.

For various reasons the sixteenth century saw a revolutionary development of gastronomy. It received as great a stimulus as did the arts; fruits brought back by the Crusaders were popularized; America was discovered and, lastly, there was peace for long enough to gather in and stock the harvests.

Although gastronomy was evolving quite fast at the time, it was still too slow to make much impact on daily life. But, if I may be forgiven the expression, 'the first shot had been fired'. The notion that progress cannot be arrested was already formulated.

We know how important spices were becoming. It is more than likely that their main purpose was to make stale fish palatable and cinnamon was at least as good as *asafoetida*. We find the cut-throat competition in spices over several generations hard to understand. I am now talking again of the Middle Ages, where once again legend overlays truth. It was the total destruction of Mediterranean trade with the Near East by Saracen pirates that caused the price of spices to rise in proportion to their scarcity. The overland routes, hardly safer than those of the sea, ended at Venice or Florence, where the Medici made their fortunes dealing in spices. The three balls on their family escutcheon do not represent, as is generally believed, an unusual generosity of nature towards its male members (though it seems that some of them did enjoy this privilege) but were the sign of spice merchants. Call them traders, ship owners, importers, what you will, it sounds more elegant than grocers and makes no difference now.

It is noteworthy that demand becomes greater in times of need. A cousin of mine had never smoked before 1940 when tobacco was rationed. Until then it had never occurred to her that she was entitled to smoke.

I shall not go into the whole story of spices and their important part in the national economy, but simply point out that they were included in the dowries of queens and great ladies, and that magistrates were commonly paid in cloves or cinnamon. In the chapter on erotic cookery I shall discuss spices at greater length.

One thing is certain; it was a period when spices were used in all kinds of cooking, sometimes even to excess, but both the sixteenth and seventeenth centuries were, above all, ages of transition. A slow transition in some ways; buckwheat, rice and sugar had been known since the days of the first crusades, but had never been grown in France. They were successfully introduced from Spain, although the usual meal at this period in country cottages was still porridge, and the children were fed on *pannade* or soaked bread.

A new bird arrived from America, actually from Mexico: the turkey.

Henri IV knew of it, but it did not become really popular until after his reign. It takes time for habits to develop. Its vogue was largely due to the fact that when plucked it looked like a peacock, and moreover, it had far more delicate meat. It was originally known as Indian Hen (*poule d'Inde*) before the name was corrupted and became *dinde, dindon*. Reaching maturity at the end of the year, as it did, it was an obvious choice for the main course of the Christmas meal, despite its pagan origins.

The evolution of wine is closely linked to that of eating habits. Henri III was interested in viticulture, and resurrected yet another of Charles IX's edicts which ordered the vines to be thinned out wherever they grew too thickly. Some wine was being fermented all over France. If today we should not think highly of its quality, we must remember that more than half of France was then harvesting wines incomparably superior to anything produced in Europe or the Near East for some 2,000 years before.

I am not a wine specialist. I know something about Sauternes because my family is native to the province. I know a little about the Bordeaux wines because I like them, just as I like all good wines. In fact, I have no prejudices about wine, nor any real preferences. It is to clarify my position as a cook that I shall discuss wines. They can simply not be dissociated from a culinary preparation, however modest this may be (though I should prefer it not to be too modest). I want to show the parallels which exist between the evolution of wine as a drink and part of daily life, and its influence upon cookery.

Changes in cooking are closely connected with the development of kitchen equipment. From the reign of François I onwards, cooking was no longer restricted to the hearth but was also done on primitive stoves or *potagers*. Cast-iron pots and cauldrons of every kind, soup-kettles and other cooking vessels were now available, and kitchen tools and tableware had also been vastly improved. The use of an individual knife, no longer brought by the guest but laid by his place at table, became general long before forks came in. Some historians think that one can tell the difference in customs between two countries simply by observing their respective attitudes to the knife. Thus, the Italians disliked lending theirs and were offended if asked to, whereas in France nobody minded if his neighbour borrowed his without asking. Ownership of a personal knife was already common in Switzerland.

I am reminded that, until the present day in Haute Provence or in the Cantal where tradition dies hard, the meal ended when the master closed his knife. Until he had done this, everyone could remain seated, nibbling or chatting, but all had to leap to their feet at the click of the Pradel or Opinel blade. Even today the peasant carries a single-bladed knife from which he is never parted, and which he has chosen with particular attention to the quality of blade and handle. The Frenchman of the nineteenth and twentieth centuries has always been reluctant to lend his personal knife and indeed, it is still best not to ask him to do so if one does not wish to annoy him. Notice how customs have changed in France and Italy. Of course, the sixteenth-century chroniclers do not say whether the Italians they referred to were Neapolitans or from Ventimiglia, which would lend added significance to the permanence of a given tradition in the same geographical region of the country.

On the other hand, Italy had adopted the fork, which was in common use there long before reaching France. It had been known from the earliest times; the Egyptians and the Romans used it, and cooks had always used it too, but then it was a slim sharp instrument, generally with two tines. The functional fork with four or five tines created a sensation; pamphleteers sneered a good deal at the first snobs who used it, especially for eating peas, beans or lentils.

If we can legitimately quote the age-old riddle of 'which came first, the chicken or the egg?' I can also say 'Why is Chinese food cut into small pieces? Is it to make the use of chopsticks easier? Or are chopsticks used because everything is cut up small?' If we don't know God's reasoning, we do know that the Chinese had only one knife per household because metal ore was scarce in the Celestial Empire.

Consider the changes wrought by the fork as a personal instrument, in methods of serving and in basic culinary techniques. Personal place laying, with spoon, knife and fork, eliminated the duties of the carving groom, that character who was not exactly a servant, but rather one of the pages who sliced from the joint the pieces his lord preferred. Carving in the kitchen was to come later when restaurant owners were forced for economic reasons to serve set portions. The differences between French and Chinese cookery were then far more marked than they are now. Louis XIV still ate mainly with his

Lutanist playing at a feast: fifteenth-century miniature

fingers. We know from various authors of different periods what rules existed
for good table manners, the most important of which was to have clean
fingers. One had to try and keep them clean without licking them too
greedily. Montaigne admits that when he was extremely hungry he sometimes bit his fingers in his haste.

Renaud de Montauban dining in his tent during a campaign: from a fifteenth-century manuscript

What might seem puzzling, however, is how the sauces were served. The sauce had to be thick enough to coat the solid food. There are two explanations which in fact come to the same thing. One method was to thicken the sauce by reducing it (hence the principles of concentrated meat essence and braising); the other consisted of thickening the sauce at the last moment with breadcrumbs. The automatic toaster having not yet been invented, young apprentices, whose job it was, would place two slices of bread on a most practical instrument which was then placed at an appropriate distance from the fire. When the bread was the right golden colour, they turned it over. A long two-pronged toasting fork was also used. The toasted bread was then crumbled into crumbs, and at the last moment, when the sauce was ready to leave the kitchen for the table, it was sprinkled with them and they absorbed so much of the liquid that they virtually solidified the sauce. This made serving much easier. The trencher was still in use, but the great slice of bread soaked in the juices of the various dishes which had made up the meal was no longer always eaten by the guest, and frequently given to the servants or the poor of the parish.

The wide use of the bakers' oven also contributed greatly to the progress of cookery at this time. There were collective professional, communal, and family ovens: in the first case people took their pâtés, tarts, roasts and so on to the baker or to the communal oven to be baked. The temperature of the oven was calculated with this secondary purpose in mind. There was even a second baking if there were too many dishes waiting to be cooked. The family oven was used in much the same way but was more flexible because it had fewer demands made on it. The vogue for pâtés, with or without pastry, owed less to a general taste for chopped or minced meat than to the ease and convenience of baking as a method of cooking. One should also remember that bread was not baked every day. This is a fairly recent custom and indeed was only at all common in towns.

The art of baking had a whole complicated technique of its own. However well built the oven, and however well heated, it contained zones of greater and lesser heat. The position of each dish had therefore to be carefully chosen, as to all intents and purposes, cooking times were equal. The quality of the wood burned to heat the oven was also important; certain scented types of wood were particularly sought after, and it was even said that cassoulet should be baked in an oven heated only by broom.

Again, it is amusing to compare the European with the Chinese oven. The Chinese, who did not have bread at all, had no reason to build horizontal

93

ovens. They therefore built vertical ones. Until modern times, these ovens had no metal parts for metal was scarce. However, the Chinese oven has one advantage over the western one; it can be heated while the food is cooking, although cooking cannot begin until the oven is already hot. The pieces to be cooked are hung up on hooks inside the oven. As in the case of our European ovens, the size of the piece to be cooked and the degree of cooking required have conditioned the length of the hook-shank (in other words, its position in the oven). Cooking times, as in the west, are pretty well uniform; a factor of major importance in both types of oven.

It is dangerous to open an oven for two reasons; the first, logically enough, is the loss of heat entailed by opening the door or lid. The second is the risk of a draught which causes some rising doughs to fall, never to rise again. This applied particularly to the canary bread and puff pastries so popular at the time.

Talking of puff pastry, gastronomes have argued for a long time about when and by whom it was invented. It is popularly believed to have been discovered by Claude Gellée, known as Claude Lorrain the painter, no one knows whether by accident or as a result of painstaking research. Claude was apparently employed by a pastry-cook who lived in the Rue St Honoré, and whose fortune he made. Two crimes are said to have been committed in order to obtain this jealously guarded formula. There is also a story of industrial espionage ahead of its time, where a certain *Commissaire* San Antonio, locked himself in a cupboard. The whole story is embellished and complicated by farcical Neapolitan adventures. However, there is no smoke without fire. Claude of course lived through the greater part of the seventeenth century, from 1600–82, but we know of a charter of Robert, Bishop of Amiens, dated 1311, in which it is mentioned; this, by being so much earlier, makes nonsense of the fable.

I vividly remember my father describing and miming the invention of puff pastry. His is probably the version nearest to the truth. Puff pastry in fact was already known; its origins were believed to be Arab, or more probably, Persian. A detailed recipe existed but in practice it was difficult to make and delicate to handle. Probably Claude found a way of overcoming these difficulties which his employer subsequently perfected.

94

Sixteenth-century silver sconce

Though proportions have changed because of different flour textures and different butters or fats, the process is the same the world over. Of course, tricks of the trade do exist, and some people think that they have the secret of making puff pastry rise perfectly but, in fact, success lies in the correct balance between the dough (flour kneaded with water), salt, milk, cream, lemon juice and butter or fat. The fat must not be blended with the dough

95

but must alternate with layers of it. It is easy to see how, at a time when dough could not be put into the refrigerator, an easy and practical technical method was regarded as a secret which could make its owners' fortune.

Pastry cookery cannot, to my mind, be separated from other cookery. If it was indeed Charlemagne who set the fashion for Brie cheese, he probably also launched the brioche. This word came from Brie cheese, one of its ingredients and the word *hocher*, meaning to shake or stir. Certainly, cheese was used in popular cake-making during the first centuries, long before butter. Throughout our era we find much the same traditional pastries, and well before the Middle Ages, there were already *flamiches*, tarts, *oublies*, *talmouses*, *gaufres*, gingerbread, *darioles* and other *gnieules*.

Not long ago I presided at the *gnieules* festival at Armentières; a survival of the feasts given by the nobles on their return from the Crusades. The etymology of pastry names is often picturesque. When we say that something is *croquignolet* we are associating the words *croquer* (to bite or chew something crackly) and the *gneules* or pastry. The word *gnioleux* in professional slang means a bad pastry-cook and certainly recalls the word *gnieule*. But it may have another association: the *niole* or *gnole* was the rotating cakestand on which the cake was set to be iced or decorated. This may be fanciful but is a deep-rooted tradition in the pastry-cook's world.

The second great basic period in the history of French gastronomy was the Renaissance.

'Those were the days' the Sun King's courtiers may well have said, remembering the hearty boozing of Villon and the gorging of Grandgousier.

Without running on too far ahead (we can always retrace our steps later) we should look at the gastronomy of the seventeenth century to get some idea of aristocratic tastes during the Renaissance. But it would be wrong to assume that the gastronomic habits of Louis XIV were general. He was a great worker, brimming over with energy, constantly purged and given enemas, whose appetite has remained legendary. But this applies only to him, and one must see things in perspective. The King ate three, or sometimes four, times a day. The meals were normally of average size for the times, and those which were the most memorable were the spectacular ones. The King usually ate in company, or while travelling, campaigning, or out hunting. The legend

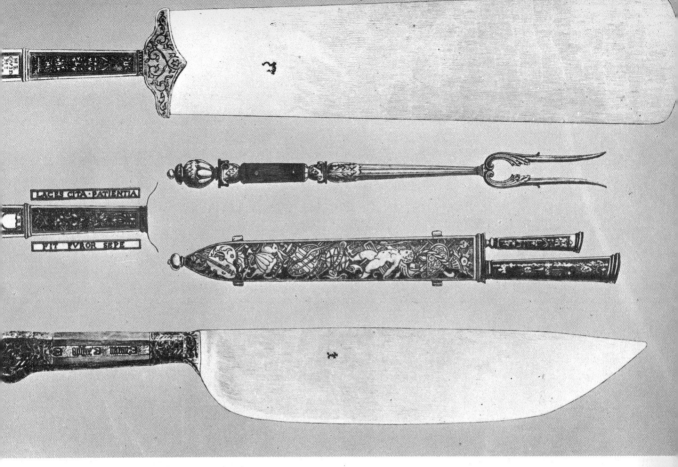

Designs for sixteenth-century cutlery

of his inviting Molière to eat alone with him seems most improbable. Sometimes during an amorous *tête-à-tête* he would order a fairly elaborate snack, but this involved no complicated table service and therefore no ceremonial. Usually, however, he ate in his room, served by courtiers who fought for the privilege.

I do not intend to go into details of the ceremonial. One thing however, was compulsory: the tasting. No food or drink could be served to the King without first having been tasted by a courtier. It was not, as today, a matter of checking the seasoning or seeing if a wine was corked, but a precaution against poison. The kings of France knew the wisdom of fearing arsenic. The table laid, the seals broken, the wine and water duly tested, the servants came in bearing eight courses, each of eight dishes, of most of which the King ate heartily. All these dishes had to be tasted, remember, and the King

97

generally ate three soups, five *entrées*, three fowls, two fish and vegetables, tasted the various roasts, nibbled a few shell-fish, returned to the *entremets*, ate some desserts and ended up cheerfully with a few hard-boiled eggs. Ouf! However, there was no question of separate courses as we understand them today, with co-ordination, change of plates and the individual presentation of each dish. A large number of dishes were simply placed on the table or the sideboard. Fish and game pies, stews, puff pastries, crayfish and desserts all lay side by side, equally tempting but in no special order. The order in which the dishes were intended to be consumed was shown only on the menu which gave the precise number of dishes and details of the courses to which each belonged.

I have mentioned *entremets*. The word, which requires no explanation in itself, has meant something quite different at different epochs. At first, it was really a sort of interval or recreation. The very slow pace of a banquet called for some diversions, music being the most lasting. But there were other *entremets* ranging from real music hall turns to wrestling, conjuring, juggling and sword-swallowing.

In this connection, it is generally accepted that one cannot enjoy more than one of the senses at a time. Monks who were doing penance, and eating little and badly, improved their meals by listening to one of their number reading Holy Writ aloud without any punctuation at all. Their hearing was thus kept on the alert, even subconsciously, and this to some extent compensated for the meagre fare. Some unkind people aver that it is for the same reason that certain restaurants play music at meal times and that the *Guide Michelin* is performing a service by mentioning it.

Between the fifteenth and sixteenth centuries, the vaudeville act was replaced by a dish which, if it had rather different qualities, at least created a diversion and in some cases whetted a flagging appetite. This was the water ice which is still thought of as an *entremet* and is still so from the point of view of digestion. In fact the intention and the effect are at variance. Water ices, like the *trou Normand* (a glass of fierce spirits swallowed in one gulp between courses) were supposed to assist the digestive process. Actually, alcohol and

Louis XIV (1638-1715) by Hyacinthe Rigaud

Grace at table: from 'l'Histoire du Protestantisme' by Abraham Bosse, seventeenth century

cold halt it. Nothing is worse than to continue eating once digestion has already begun. The Romans, who knew neither of the above methods, used a goose feather. The *entremet* found its proper place and justified its name in the seventeenth century. Later it became a dessert and is nowadays never taken to mean anything else. *Entremets* may be made by the cook or the pastry cooks, but in kitchen etymology, the *entremetier* is the man who deals with the vegetables. During the reign of Louis XIV, vegetable *entremets* were actually served. The green peas grown in the kitchen garden at Versailles, thanks to La Quintinie's methods, were among the most delicious of the early vegetables. So was asparagus, which had been known ever since it grew wild in the neolithic and paleolithic ages. Thus, after being a real performance at the time of the oath 'By the peacock!' (or the pheasant), the *entremet* finally became a mere dish like any other with which we end a meal today. It has steadily dwindled in importance.

The seventeenth century was above all a period which assimilated everything from preceding centuries, and we pass naturally to another age of

100

transition, that of the nineteenth century and the period of consolidation at the turn of the century. The pace has changed; progress in cultivation and equipment has accelerated faster in the last ten years than in the previous five hundred. The times we live in move faster than the historian. Louis XV, brought up in great luxury, had more refined tastes than his great-grand-father. But there is not much of a gulf between the Roi Soleil and Louis the Well-beloved although there were of course the Regent's 'little suppers' at which the guests did their own cooking in gold or silver utensils, a startling innovation. The pretty ladies, who did not care for servants to witness their lighter pastimes, competed for culinary honours.

If the Palais Royal had been equipped with bottled gas, what marvellous dishes might not have been prepared underneath its arches! But alas, it was not, and it is only of sausages fried in silver pans that we have an unforgettable memory.

The courtiers played at cookery, but in the cottages they still dunked bread in cabbage soup. Context is all, and one must beware of confounding the gastronomy of Louis XV with that of the eighteenth century. I do not mean that the influence of the court did not affect evolution in the kitchen, an evolution which did literally break out immediately after Thermidor. Louis

Family life by Abraham Bosse, seventeenth century

XVI was perpetually hungry. There are many stories about him of which three are regarded as historical facts: the pâté of Varennes, the Chaumette bun, and the last meal before his execution. He liked wine, and changed wines during a meal, a peculiarity which seems important to me for it reveals the gourmet in him, whereas he has generally been considered a detestable glutton. His family drank only water, which allowed him plenty of leeway, even when imprisoned in the Temple.

The records of the Temple prison reassure us about the food provided for the royal family. The Revolution abruptly stopped all gastronomic impulses, and if it had no need of a scientist such as Lavoisier, one might have hoped it would have made use of cooks. In fact it firmly discouraged imitation of the luxurious tastes of the *ci-devants*.

As in Occupied France and in London during the worst days of rationing lavish meals were clandestine ones; the type of gastronomy which seeks and enjoys only what is forbidden. No respecter of tradition ever runs a black-market restaurant.

If Bonaparte had been as great an epicure as were Barras, Cambacérès and Talleyrand, the already rapid progress of gastronomy would have been very considerably speeded up.

It is to Grimod de la Reynière (1758-1838) that we must look at this time. His influence upon the powerful and wealthy, and especially upon cooks and restaurateurs, was immense. There were many restaurants at the time, but they had not been in existence long. Many of them were new creations and though fashionable, lacked tradition. They were coining money, and customers flocked to their tables for fare they could not obtain at home.

Grimod, the son of a *Fermier-Général*,★ coddled by a mother who felt responsible for his being deformed, could boast of having received the finest possible gastronomic education. An anecdote tells of his father stopping at an inn where several handsome turkeys were roasting on the spit. He asked for some turkey and was refused on the grounds that a gentleman had ordered all five. The older man wished to meet such a doughty trencherman and was promptly introduced to his own son, who, when asked what on earth he intended to do with so much meat, replied, 'You taught me, sir, that the only

★ An official who had the right to farm out the tax collecting.

edible piece of turkey is the parson's nose, so you can see why I had to order all this, can't you? Anyway, we can now share it happily.'

Plenty of money and a good appetite are not, however, enough to make a gastronome. I think one cannot stress too much that in this context, knowledge comes through experience, and even more through experiments. I have sometimes had to refute the pronouncement of a guest about a dish when it was clear he wouldn't have liked it anyway. Then an opinion ceases to be a judgment and becomes a matter of personal taste. It is often difficult to enjoy tasting something quite new; classic examples are caviar and snails, both of which are an acquired taste. For example, Iceland shark, kept for three years in an open barrel on the quayside and then brought to table redolent of ammonia and literally phosphorescent is even more than a Mediterranean stomach can bear, yet it must have some value since it is produced and consumed.

Grimod, our gastronome, was born with tiny webbed hands which he covered with metal gloves. He was below average height and adopted a hunchback's stance. Stories and jokes about him, often in the worst possible taste, abounded, but did not prevent him from displaying a certain courageous indifference. As he was dedicated to gastronomy and professed the most profound contempt for politics, he passed unscathed, though not without need of circumspection, through the years of the Terror, dangerous times for an aristocrat and the son of a *Fermier-Général*. By the time of the Empire, his only concern was with eating and exploring the novel delights of fashionable restaurants. With a canny eye on publicity, he organized his 'Jury of Taste' whose impartiality was doubtful, but which was highly successful. He managed to combine in himself the qualities of two vastly different contemporaries of ours: Francis Amunatégui, always amiable and indulgent, finding an excuse for every mistake, and a compliment for each success, and Robert Courtine, master of witty criticism, fair but far from indulgent, whose comments have all the tang of sweet-and-sour sauce. Grimod was regarded as a scandalous character; his reputation was dubious and he made no secret of his liaison with a Mademoiselle Feuchère, of the Opéra, with whom he corresponded in tiny illegible spidery writing. But despite this, he left his mark. Brillat-Savarin (1755-1826) was one of the first to follow in his footsteps,

*Grimod de la Reynière
(1758–1838) by Dunan*

Dunan pinx.

Blanchard sc.

though he was less courageous. I do not blame Brillat-Savarin for wanting to save a life he had dedicated to fine eating. He posted up on the walls of Belley a declaration of his loyalty to the Convention, and fled the same day via Pontarlier to Switzerland with the help of a music-loving lady admirer. He lived in England for some time, mixing salads, and in America, playing the fiddle, occupations not calculated to strengthen his sense of civic duty. Admittedly the *Physiologie du Goût* became a success which, knowing its sources, he could hardly have expected. Though he had borrowed a great deal from Grimod, Grimod in his turn bowed to him and called him 'the Professor'. Brillat-Savarin shamelessly plagiarized the work of writers from Confucius to Moncelet, and did not dare sign his work; he had the courage

Title-page from 'Physiologie du Goût' by Brillat Savarin, 1826

104

PHYSIOLOGIE
DU GOUT,

OU

MÉDITATIONS DE GASTRONOMIE

TRANSCENDANTE;

OUVRAGE THÉORIQUE, HISTORIQUE ET A L'ORDRE DU JOUR,

Dédié aux Gastronomes parisiens,

PAR UN PROFESSEUR,

MEMBRE DE PLUSIEURS SOCIÉTÉS LITTÉRAIRES ET SAVANTES.

Dis-moi ce que tu manges, je te dirai qui tu es.
APHOR. DU PROF.

TOME PREMIER.

PARIS,

CHEZ A. SAUTELET ET Cie LIBRAIRES,

PLACE DE LA BOURSE, PRÈS LA RUE FEYDEAU.

1826.

Life in a rich and profligate household by Abraham Bosse, seventeenth century

neither to face his public nor to profess his lack of political convictions. He used the pseudonym of 'A Professor' which he hoped would be transparent, and hastened to send a copy of the book to Cussy. The Marquis made a number of corrections after the death of the former mayor of Belley, which he swore had met with the author's approval. However, none of these corrections ever appeared in the numerous later editions of the work. A few days after publication of the book, Brillat attended the anniversary memorial Mass for Louis XVI, and caught cold in the church of St Germain l'Auxerrois. He died soon after as elderly people then did of a 'fine winter bronchitis'.

Though Grimod was a writer of importance and produced *Les Manuels des Amphitryons* inspired by *Ecuyers Tranchants du Moyen Age*, calendars and the *Almanach des Gourmands*, he is practically unknown to the general public,

'Peasants' Meal' by Louis Le Nain, 1642

whereas if nobody has read *La Physiologie du Goût*, everyone knows who Brillat-Savarin was. He has been accepted as a philosopher and scholar, whereas it is Grimod the publicist who deserves the reputation. But a publicist is always suspect to the public which does not believe that one can earn money by telling the truth even when it agrees with one's own convictions.

The enormous success of gastronomic literature in the middle of the nineteenth century prepared public opinion for the remarkable developments in this field during the Second Empire. However, we should probably take a closer look at this period which survived the relative famine caused by the Revolution (itself, remember, originating in famine).

Bread was the staple food of the masses and it was poverty which caused rebellion. The more naive than caustic comments of Marie Antoinette, 'Let

Ladies dining by Abraham Bosse, seventeenth century

them eat cake,' was explosive in an already tense atmosphere. What the people wanted was bread, with all its symbolic implications. During the last war, I had saved some flour which I kept for occasional desserts. At Christmas 1943 I suggested that I bake my friends a fine cake, but they preferred white bread to any other delicacy. Bernardin de St Pierre, writing to his wife on 27 May 1795, thanks her for sending him bread, and remarks wryly that he is more often invited for the sake of the country loaf under his arm than for his talents as a moralist.

One finds the same obsession with bread from the Revolution to our own times when circumstances have been difficult; during the siege of Paris in 1870, during the 1914-18 war, and during that of 1939-45. I own a little paperweight made just after 1870 containing a piece of siege-bread. During the 1914-18 war, French propaganda and newspapers endlessly reported that German bread was blacker than ours which was small comfort.

There is a black bread in Germany called *pumpernickel* which was already popular before the French Revolution. Napoleon's groom when offered some, refused it, the story goes, saying it was only fit for the Emperor's horse, Nickel: '*C'est du pain pour Nickel*'. The name has stuck.

Bread always was and will be the barometer of famine. Though not at present very popular, we need only the slightest shortage to see what vital importance our stomachs attach to it.

Jean-Jacques Rousseau, who was not without responsibility for the French Revolution, pops up in an oddly gastronomic context in a manuscript which I own. Mme Dupin, mother of George Sand, employed Jean-Jacques as her secretary and noted her views on him in her kitchen accounts book amongst a list of grey shallots. You must agree that to find a comment on the behaviour and character of the author of the *Contrat Social* sharing a page with bottles of Malaga and goats' cheese is not without its spice!

Civic banquets were inaugurated just after the fall of the Bastille, and were started by an aristocrat, the Marquis de Villette. Later, Cambacérès went in for them a great deal, and there were more and more of them as time went on; there were 12,000 guests at the Mayor's Banquet in 1889, and 40,000 at one held on 5 November 1905 at the Champ de Mars.

To think that poor Grimod had feared that the three years of abstinence decreed by the 'vandals' would consign to oblivion even the simplest recipes, like chicken fricassée! In his *Almanach des Gourmands* he sings the praises of good restaurants and condemns bad ones with the same prejudice as can today be ascribed to the *Guide Juillard*. But one must remember that in troubled times, most people tend to go running to restaurants either because food supplies at home are difficult or because devalued currency seems less precious to those who have suffered or fear even worse to come.

The man who epitomizes the whole of nineteenth-century gastronomy was a young cook whose name is famous in the culinary world: Antonin Carême (1784-1833). The same miracle was to recur a century later with another gifted cook, Auguste Escoffier (1847-1935). It is unimportant whether or not Antonin Carême was the best cook of his time; possibly some equally talented performer in the field existed at the same time but remained totally unknown to the general public. Carême and Riquette were selected by Talleyrand, who gave French cookery a great name. From then on it became an export.

Up to that time, the Court and the great nobles had had foreign cooks. They were few, most of them Mediterraneans, with a sprinkling of Swiss and Austrians. It was only at the beginning of the nineteenth century that French cookery came into its own and assumed a national character. Carême admitted he had learned a great deal from Laguipière (d. 1812), and one day the Emperor went especially to talk to Carême in the kitchen, which was all the more extraordinary as Napoleon was never a gourmet. So little so, in fact, that his head cook, Dunand, was Swiss. He had, however, been trained in France, and copying Cleopatra on a slightly more modest scale, put, instead of a wild boar, a chicken on the spit every quarter of an hour so that there should always be one ready for 'the little corporal's' meal.

Though Napoleon was neither a gourmet nor greedy, he was wise enough to give gastronomy a free rein and indeed even to urge it on to his armies. Coffee became a popular drink during the Revolution and Corcelet, trading in the Palais Royal arcades in the very house where Colette spent her last years, was its great advocate. Bonaparte, knowing coffee to be a less dangerous stimulant than alcohol, made it the military beverage, and it was his armies who popularized the brew so dear to the heart of Joséphine de Beauharnais.

The Marquis de Cussy, intimate enemy of Brillat-Savarin, but a genuine gastronome, had the Emperor's support in organizing Imperial meals. If emperors feel it incumbent upon them to prove their valour in every field, not being, like kings, sovereigns by Divine Right, Louis XVIII tried to put history back by reverting to the complicated ceremonial of the court of Louis XIV. Though this attempt was doomed to failure, Louis XVIII was nonetheless the best trencherman in his kingdom. While he and his major domo, the Duc d'Escars, were demolishing a new dish they had jointly invented for a gastronomic competition, the Duke expired which prompted the King to remark, 'Poor d'Escars! So mine is the better stomach!'

The King's brother, the Comte d'Artois, was not particularly greedy, but when he acceded to the throne as Charles X, he tried not to discourage gastronomy and saw to it that court meals were lavish and elegant as befitted a King of France.

Louis-Philippe, the son of Philippe Egalité, must have remembered the feasts at the Palais Royal purely sentimentally, for he was the very antithesis of a gastronome. It is said that his father had set up his own cook, Jean Véfour in business in a building which he had himself had erected (and which was apparently the first speculative building). Yet he had his own meals sent in by a caterer. I have had the honour of cooking at the Louvre and at the Palais Cardinal, in other words at the Ministry of Cultural Affairs and the Ministry of Finance, and could not help remembering my famous predecessor who followed the path between palace and restaurant in the opposite direction to myself.

In a preface which he wrote for the *Grand Véfour*, Jean Cocteau referred to the *Comédie Humaine* and described the ghosts of Rumbempré and Rastignac hovering among the tables. This was the time of the apogee of the *Rocher de Cancale*, of Very who joined forces with Véfour, and of the *Boeuf à la Mode*. Madame de Nucingen was to give the *cabinets particuliers* a touch of snobbery which some years later Sainte-Beuve carried on. He insisted upon greeting the Prince Imperial from one of the first floor drawing rooms.

When the Prince President took over from the Second Republic, he found the way pleasantly smooth. Times were most favourable to gastronomy, and there was nothing now to impede the expansion of good eating; for the first time on record, conditions were eminently encouraging: agriculture, cattle raising, fishing, transport and above all equipment were responsible. French gastronomy was about to be born in the guise in which it is now familiar to us. This was still not the end of the road. Far from it. The Imperial feast was to end in 1870 and people were soon to look back on the famine and the siege of Paris. If rats and probably human flesh were eaten then – a common phenomenon during famines – it did not retard the progress of cookery for long. Strange as it seems, potatoes were requisitioned, as was wheat. The potato had been brought into favour by Auguste Parmentier with the help of Louis XVI, who once wore a potato flower in his buttonhole.

Convinced that bread could be made from potato flour, Parmentier (1737–

111

1813) grew the precious tubers at Boulogne-sur-Seine where armed guards were posted, not to prevent thieving but to keep out crop destroyers. Bread was considered a 'balanced' food, and the public was reluctant to allow it to be made of anything other than wheat flour. We know the potato's subsequent history and the further fruitless attempts made to use flours from it and other products such as maize and tapioca for making bread.

Within less than a century, the potato achieved great popularity. All the big restaurants which sprang up after the Revolution and which were to carry on until the present day cooked potatoes and served them as specialities, each in its own style. Some of these were to remain famous, like the 'Mayor' potato. We must bear in mind the enormous number of cooks at the time who brought French cooking to its peak of glory. At the end of the last century and the beginning of this, during the immense prosperity that characterized the Third Republic, there was a huge demand for them, and by their side, for another race of cooks, now practically extinct, the plain people of bourgeois families. We owe a great deal to them. It was they who, above all others, created modern French cookery. They had plenty of time, it is true, but that did not automatically endow them with the talent and skill they so consistently displayed. Emulation was certainly a powerful goad to their imaginations. From 1870 onwards foreigners joined our ranks, and at the same time, the world magnates, the Rockefellers and the Krupps, the sovereigns of England, Russia, Spain and Germany, employed French chefs, Swiss pastry cooks, and Viennese bakers. The Société des Cuisiniers in Paris became a rich and powerful organization with ramifications all over the world. In Escoffier, the great cooks found a superb standard bearer to carry the French colours to victory in London, while, in Paris, Prosper Montagné gave the lead to a whole generation of erudite and poetic cooks who were to codify the technique of a hundred years of progress.

They were not able entirely to shed a certain traditional heavy-handedness; to this day the great basic sauces are still used and braising takes pride of place. But the impetus had been given. French cooks have now their own bible, and a good number of shorter works on individual subjects. No matter where they find themselves they must conform to a universal law. As in literature so in cookery and we may joyfully cap, 'Enfin Malherbe vint!' with 'Enfin vint

Fashionable pâtissier, Paris, 1835

Escoffier!' Detractors and the envious, often one and the same, have said that he did not write his books himself but merely signed them. It makes little difference; obviously an Achille Ozane, or among the galaxy of chefs, Perraut, Colombier, Maumene, Emile Maison, Ansaldi, Reboul and others could well have codified their collective inheritance.

At certain difficult periods in our professional lives, such as the one we are at present passing through, vast defensive and protective movements build up. The need for classification makes itself felt. Then, like the story of the Loch Ness monster, the Tournedos Rossini pops up: that slice of fried fillet of beef set on fried bread, capped with foie gras, crowned with truffles and coated with Périgueux sauce. The controversy is about the relative quantity of foie gras and truffles – that is, for those who have their feet on the ground and only look at this dish simply as providing an opportunity for disloyal competition. But others go much further. The foie gras must be absolutely fresh (Rossini would use no other); the bread must be fried in the fat of the foie gras and not in vulgar butter; the truffle must not be an ornament but a generous accompaniment; and finally the Madeira must be from the island, and substitutes sedulously avoided. I have noticed, in this new battle of Hernani, that nobody seems much concerned with the actual beef fillet. I have no personal views about it; I am like the English St Thomas who ought to have said, 'the proof of the pudding is in the eating'. There is no doubt that any criticism before a dish has been tasted is worthless. I once left the jury which was to elect the best *ouvrier de cuisine* in France because its president wanted to eliminate a competitor who had added an ingredient (onion, as it happens) to the recipe for chicken marengo. It seems more serious to me to omit an ingredient, though it can't be said to constitute a rule.

I know two most excellent restaurateurs, one of whom serves a tournedos half the size of the other's, though both stick to the recipe. What seems curious is that the price for each is about the same. The reasons are simple enough; in one case it is a question of general expense, and in the other, of the type of customer. The restaurant which serves the small tournedos has a very sophisticated decor, extremely good waiter service, a largely feminine clientele, and music. The other has floral decorations, only a small choice of dishes, waitress service, and customers interested in the rustic style of the food. As general expenses account for about half of turnover, they have to be differently allocated according to circumstances. The object of the restaurateur is above all to satisfy his customer and one should guard against any a priori criticisms. One has to admit that the restaurateur, on a different scale from the family cook, provides a cookery of intention.

After the 1914-18 war came the 'roaring twenties' when, strange as it seems, the gastronomic tendency was to cling to tradition. During the first years of the twenties, nothing seemed to have changed; the most famous restaurants were still going strong, the big hotels still kept a fine table, and the kitchen was staffed by as many workers as pre-war; and yet there was change in the air.

The first sign of this became noticeable when well known gastronomes decided in favour of the single dish. It was a first and deserved shot, but the

114

Bread and poultry market on the Quai des Augustins, Paris, c. 1670

start of a revolution. A minor journalist, cowardly and untalented, had succeeded in setting fire to the powder-barrel which sparked off the French Revolution; gastronomy in 1925 also had its Camille Desmoulins.

The 'single dish' itself did not kill the gastronomy of the Third Republic, but it so happened that the vogue for it coincided with the tolling of the bells for most of the great restaurants. The main cause of this was because no one could afford the necessary staff.

When a trade or an industry is dying, neither medicine nor the patient's will to live, can prevent it. There is no known example of a lucrative business, however difficult or dangerous, failing to be carried on. Conversely, when the struggle and the difficulties involved exceed possible profits, the rats leave the sinking ship. After 1918 it was difficult to maintain a balance; everything changed too fast. The restaurant trade lost more victims then than had been accounted for by Big Bertha.

What did the restaurant workers do then? What became of the cooks from *Foyot*, the *Café Anglais*, *Marguery*, *Paillard*, *Maire* and their peers? They set up on their own. Never before had Paris, the suburbs and the provinces known

Family supper: child presenting 'the king's cake' by Le Canot, eighteenth century

such a quantity of good little restaurants. (After the 1939–45 war it was the turn of the bistros.) The proliferation of family businesses was to flourish shortly after.

At the same time, as the market became more stable, the great restaurants rallied, to survive until after the second world war. Among them were the *Café de Paris*, *Larue*, *La Crémaillère*, *Les Ambassadeurs* and a few others. How-

116

ever, at the same time came the collapse of nearly all the restaurants in those great hotels which had been the nurseries for the best French cooks.

What have we lost and what have we gained?

The democratization of gastronomy is not a loose term, and what was lost by the restaurants was gained by family kitchens. It is the rising standard of living that has harmed the restaurant trade, but only relatively speaking, for it is not a question of its extinction, but rather of its transformation. Prices are responsible for this, but not as far as the customer is concerned. The rising spiral of costs has been such that however hard they tried, restaurateurs have been unable to charge enough to cover the increasing cost of raw materials. It is commonly agreed that a restaurant must charge double the cost of its

'Boys eating Pancakes' by Lépicié, eighteenth century

supplies if it is to make a reasonable profit, a generalization that is sometimes true and sometimes false; excessive in some cases, and derisory in others.

At a time when restaurants, even those of the highest quality, were frequented by regulars, people who ate five or six times a week at the same table, served by the same waiter, as part of their normal routine, the cry suddenly went up – alas truthfully – that restaurants were a luxury and therefore only to be visited rarely. It coincided with the closure of popular restaurants, and with tables no longer being reserved all the year round in the smart ones. The balance had altered. This was not due to the war which, like all disasters, simply shifted wealth from one to another, and changed habits faster but no more surely than do time's sickle and the hourglass.

How long does it take for a new and forward-looking business to succeed or fail? There is no rule any longer, since there is no more limit to speed; Mach 3 or 2 is normal, so why try to copy a seventeenth-century meal? We are, however, indebted to the evolution of the restaurant of today, and oddly enough, of tomorrow, for major developments in equipment, a subject to which I shall revert.

3 Wine

Wine and Gastronomy

I have already said that I do not consider myself enough of a connoisseur to write a chapter on this subject, but I cannot omit discussion of the importance of wine to gastronomy and especially its influence upon cookery.

The only thing that matters, both in oenology and cookery, is success.

In my part of the world there is a very old adage which says 'There is no great château, there are no great years, there are only great bottles'. I should like to have this proverb carved in letters of gold over the door of my personal cellar if I ever own one worthy of the name.

I know I shall shock people when I say that I buy wines to drink them, and if I sometimes drink them too soon, I seldom find them hard to replace. On the other hand, I like to live with my wines, just as it is often said that to bring children up properly one must live with them. Something of the kind must be true about wines. The wine charts which were fairly popular fifteen years ago, under the aegis of the late Raymond Baudoin, were a very silly invention indeed. How can one cover a whole wine harvest with one label denoting its quality, when one knows perfectly well that there will always be clumsy vintners who will fail with their processing, either through ignorance or through greed? Conversely, what right has one to condemn a perfectly successful wine (obtained by conscientiousness or skill) when other neighbouring growers have missed the bus?

All through my youth I heard stories of the kind. I listened to the slanders of vine growers accusing their neighbours of over-sugaring their morning coffee to such an extent that they were ordering lorry-loads of brown sugar. I also witnessed the trials and tribulations of pioneers in search of forgotten wine-making processes, and those of the apostles of natural wines. All this only convinces me that one must discover one's pleasures for oneself; nobody can do my wine-tasting for me. Do not misunderstand me; I have nothing against the dealer who advises, the taster who selects and the broker who sells. I think they are all useful and necessary. But I simply owe it to myself to confirm their verdict, not because of what I am led to expect, but insofar as it enables me to clarify my personal taste.

There can be no rules about how wine should be drunk, nor on its proper place in a meal. In the same way, there are no kitchen wines.

White wines cannot be exclusively reserved for fish courses, nor Burgundies for game, any more than it is compulsory to chill white wines or to serve red ones at room temperature.

Vin rosé and pink champagne are merely fancy wines.

Really, each and every wine should be drunk, not according to a set of rules, but to suit one's own temperament. I like large glasses and sufficient quantities to quench my thirst. If some day you have only one bottle of Haut Brion 1955 and there are four of us to drink it, keep it in your cellar until I am alone with you! I do not care for drunkards but I have a deep contempt for tiny glasses which I cannot imagine being useful in any circumstances. I have the profoundest respect for exceptionally old bottles, which interest me greatly; that is, if I have been invited to drink them. I can understand an enthusiast wishing to share his knowledge and to have one participate in his pleasure at owning a few treasures of this kind. But the special bottle should never be more than an experiment and must be part of a larger cellar. I have the feeling that no wine should be *chambré*. All of them improve by being decanted. The very great ones should be decanted on the spot where they have grown old and be served at the temperature of the cellar. Very young wines sometimes benefit by being cooled, whatever their quality and their origin. When I say cooled, I do not mean iced. Simply set the bottle for twenty minutes in a bucket of very cold water containing a few ice cubes. White wines should not be cooled for more than a few hours at most before serving, and if possible this should be done on ice. The use of the refrigerator is in fact

'Still Life' by Jean Baptiste Chardin, eighteenth century

only harmful when the wine is left there too long, but as one does not always know how long it will have to wait, I generally advise avoiding the refrigerator.

I like all wines; this is probably a great fault. But I prefer two wines to all others: Champagne and Bordeaux. In a scale of absolute values I should never try to list the other vineyards, for my preferences are arbitrary. I have a special fondness for the wines and the friendships of Sauternes because they remind me of my youth. When I am far from home and depression gets the better of my usually sanguine temperament, when I seem to brood endlessly, then only Sauternes restores me. When I say Sauternes, I mean Sauternes, not Sainte Croix du Mont or Loupiac, though these are as close to my native Langon as

'A Cook' by Jean Baptiste Chardin, eighteenth century

is Château Yquem. I remember once, when I was quite alone, laughing aloud like an idiot as I sipped a glass of Rayne-Vigneau. I seemed once more to hear the Vicomte de Roton, that distinguished Hellenist and lapidary, telling me with conviction that his wine owed its exceptional qualities to a whirlpool not unlike the maelstrom when the Flood covered the earth! True, at that time

Noah was sailing towards his first hangover, but the Vicomte had not thought of that.

This distant feeling returned to me one day in Australia. I was visiting a vineyard in New South Wales and the owner showed me his personal cellar with several bottles of Bordeaux in it. When I examined one closely and could not help smiling, the amiable vinegrower asked me why. I showed him the label which said something like 'Chaize Frères, Négociants à Meymac, près de Bordeaux'. 'Why,' he asked, 'isn't Meymac near Bordeaux?' I had to think for a moment before realizing that compared with the distance between me and France at that moment, Meymac was indeed very close to Bordeaux.

In the course of my travels around the world, I often chance to taste foreign wines. They are frequently most attractive; South African or Latin-American, Australian, California or Israeli wines. I have never tried to compare them with ours, but simply to drink them, rather than taste them, with the maximum of pleasure.

It is this pleasure which I have always sought when using the most widely differing wines in cookery. Some are not adaptable; they are never the great ones. Besides, the great ones have no defects. I cannot resist telling a story which Père Vinceau, a delegate from some vintners' association or other,

'The Oyster Eaters' by Jean Teissier, 1778

brought up at every winegrowers' meeting. 'The old Marquis de Lur Saluces, father of the present owner of Château Yquem, had planned a fishing party. It was the old Marquis, the one who was such a rabid royalist that he got himself killed by the Bordeaux express in Barsac station because he was so absorbed in reading *L'Action Française*. Well, the party set out for the estuary, starting near the Château de Beychevelle so charmingly situated overlooking the Gironde, in charge of a strictly fresh-water helmsman. After fishing for a while, it was time for refreshment. The Marquis (*noblesse oblige*) had brought a bottle of Yquem which everyone thoroughly enjoyed. Then a storm blew up, the swell made the boat roll, and the helmsman felt ill. In the purest tradition of pleasure boating, he leaned over the side and abandoned his hard-earned snack to the fishes. This done, glassy-eyed but dutiful, he resumed his post and said gratefully to the Marquis, "that Yquem, you know, it is good, even on the way back".'

I have done a lot of cooking with Sauternes, not always successfully, and I remember with affection the first editorial article written in 1935 by Paul Emile Cadilhac in *L'Illustration*. It was about a dish of sweetbreads with Château Guiraud; a very simple recipe. I remember it well, because in his article, Cadilhac had mixed up the dishes a bit. There were, I'm sure, fillets of perch with grape juice, and then sweetbreads. There was certainly a third dish which may have been an entrecôte *Maître de Chais*, which I later called Porteneuve. I do not wish here to describe the creation of dishes but simply to show the importance of wine in cookery. The fillets of perch should have been with verjuice – that was my notion. But my old friend Edmond Coste, a wine dealer at Langon and our purveyor for generations, had undertaken to popularize grape juice, supported by another old friend of mine, Dr Max Eylau, an apostle of wine and of grape diets. They got round me so well that I decided to use grape must for certain dishes. I admit to my brief shame that I added lemon juice and rind, and that plenty of shallots and cayenne pepper successfully masked the sickly sweetness. Determined to serve a meal which would be both original and very *Sauternais*, I had felt I had to include some of our wine too. I chose the finest blanched and flattened sweetbreads, and larded them with little pieces of Bayonne ham until they looked like hedge-hogs. Then I floured them lightly and fried them slowly in goose fat, uncovered, and let them finish cooking on the side of the stove for a few minutes. I drained off the fat, moistened them with Sauternes and brought it to the boil. Meanwhile, I fried one golden-brown slice of bread for each sweetbread in the goose fat which I had used for the cooking, with a little more as necessary. I put each sweetbread on to its *croûton*, when it was ready, reduced the wine until there was hardly any left, added a lump of butter to enrich the sauce, away from the heat, and put a spoonful of it on each sweetbread, serving at once. There was very little sauce so it did not soften the fried bread. A great friend of mine, Erwin Schleyen, now alas dead, who made a great success of the *Mirabelle* in London, declared this recipe to be sublime and tried repeatedly to reproduce it for himself and for his clients in London society.

I have always cooked lampreys. My father had slightly modified my grandmother's recipe; he had not quite broken free from the old methods and still liked to use basic sauces. He therefore started with a mixture containing onions, carrots, ham, herbs, garlic, etc. He used the wine we served in carafes, bought from our friend Coste. It was generally Côtes de Fronsac, if not a Bourg, my favourite. The results were amazing, and I have never eaten better lampreys although I have tasted some as good and which we prepared far more easily. They were just 'moistened' with one of the great wines, either a St Emilion or a Graves. This is my point; the amount of trouble taken by my father, the numerous ingredients he used and the reduction of the sauce made the dish just as dear. Is it not therefore better to use a great wine to enhance one's talent? A paradoxical but inescapable question.

This did not prevent me from hating a Bordeaux dealer who said that lampreys were better at St Emilion because the wine used for the sauce there was better. I never managed to make him understand that we did not produce red wines at Langon, and that St Emilion was closer to us than Algeria.

I must admit that my father's influence upon my cooking was enormous. Indeed, I cook bouillabaisse as my father used to cook lampreys, using white wine, which has involved me in many a Marseillais argument. The cook is often surprised when he discovers that the finished dish does not have the same taste as that of the wine. This does not arise with fortified wines, such as port, Madeira or Malaga which can be added neat to a sauce at the last

125

'Silverware and Fruits' by François Desportes, eighteenth century

moment and thus retain their aroma. But Sauternes, with its subtle bouquet, cannot be used in the same way for, as soon as it is reduced, it may become too sweet and will have lost its original flavour. I have tried unsuccessfully to make zabaglione or sabayon with Sauternes; the result was worth while, but could not compare with a port, much less a kirsch, sabayon.

A very amusing recipe which illustrates my point is shad-broth. I have sometimes tried to improve upon it, or more exactly to discipline it, without ever succeeding. I shall analyse the reasons why. In the first place, like fisherman's bouillabaisse, it is a recipe of such Biblical simplicity that it cannot be properly prepared except near its fishing ground.

Prepare the soup tureen with slices of bread mixed with sliced garlic. Salt,

126

'Still Life' by Meiffren Conte, eighteenth century

and put in plenty of pepper. In the shad season there is young garlic shooting, and this is best for this recipe since one should use a good deal of the green stem.

Put half a bottle of red wine per head into a stewpan. As soon as the wine begins to be covered with froth, cut off the head of one shad per person over the pan so that the blood as well as the head falls into it. Avoid boiling. Put in a little salt and a clove if possible. Leave for ten minutes at most, and then sieve it on to the bread. The gills must not be removed nor must the fish be scaled or scrubbed, and the garlic must be raw.

It is not a great dish nor can it be considered great cookery, but it cannot be modified for those who love it and to whom it represents a tradition, for

127

that is indeed what it is. Do not imagine that fishermen eat shad-broth every day. When they do, it is a reward, a feast and a symbol; some happy event, such as a lucky catch, is necessary. I cannot remember how many fish must be caught in the net at a single stroke, but it is a great many and, if I am not mistaken, must be a multiple of seven.

One must realize that to make this dish one has to mutilate a number of fish, and their value is thereby somewhat depreciated unless they are sold by the slice as often happens at the fishing ports. There is usually an old fisher-man or fishwife using ancient scales and according to the formula, 'the knife that killed Henri IV', always a very large old knife in an appalling condition.

This tradition dates from time immemorial, but was of particular interest during the Hundred Years' War. The Black Prince was staying at the time at La Réole or Saint Macaire. Langon was in opposition. Shad-broth was already being made with the red wine of La Réole which was called *Clairet*. The song about it says:

> When I drink Clairet,
> Everything goes round and round
> In the inn . . .

If the English took home with them the name Claret, which they now use to designate all red Bordeaux wines, they gave us in exchange the *Chabrot*.

'*Faire Chabrot*' is to add red wine to one's soup. Shad is the English word for *alose*, and broth their word for *potage*. Shad-broth, the soup containing red wine which I have described, gave its name by analogy to a very pleasant old custom. The word shad which sounds like *chat* probably also left its mark on the vernacular in the shape of the word *gat* or *gatte* for cat and is used to describe false shad. In pure patois, real shad is called cat too, but in the feminine: *gatte*, whereas the false brew stays masculine *gat*. This tradition of using the feminine for anything exceptionally good also gave us *la lèbre* for hare instead of *le lièvre* to emphasize quality or rarity.

If one takes shad to be a kind of sardine (to which family it belongs) one can easily understand that this is a one-way recipe and all attempts to sophisti-cate it are doomed to failure.

Since I have mentioned the Hundred Years' War and its shad-broth, I

Dinner with Madame Dubarry at Louveciennes by Moreau-le-Jeune, 1771

should like to go back a little further and retrace the path of wine in its gastronomic career.

Noah invented wine at the foot of Mount Ararat in Turkey, near Pontus which Lucullus was later to conquer. The Roman legions brought back the vine which took root quickly in Gaul, then a conquered but willing country.

129

In the *Georgics*, Virgil says it was thanks to the agricultural genius of the Gauls that vine-growing spread and prospered. There were already vines in Corsica and on the Côte d'Azur before Lucullus. The Phoceans, worried about the Carthaginians and the Tyrrhenians, had planted both vines and olives in ancient Cyrnos and the Var.

Until then the Gauls had drunk barley beer and mead. The first was beer and the second fermented honey-water. When wine made its first appearance in Gaul it was an exclusive perquisite of the rich and though fashionable, extremely expensive. From the time of the Roman occupation, vine-growing was intensified and wine became more popular. The vines almost reached the Cevennes.

Unfortunately, the year 92 was calamitous for the cereal crops and Domitian, then Emperor, had the vines torn up to make room for wheat. It was not until 282 that Probus abrogated Domitian's decrees and restored the vines to their hillsides. What were those wines like and how would they compare with those of today? We know they kept badly and in order to preserve them were mixed and cooked. Herbs of the most varied kinds were added, including aloes, and above all, resins. Water was added to make them drinkable. Wine from Marseilles was reputed to be heavy, and Pliny also complained of the thickness of Narbonne wine. Columella mentions *picatum* wine, which he loved (the ancestor of our grandfathers' *piquette*) which was harvested in the Dauphiné near Condrieux and into which the Allobroges mixed pitch.

Viticulture and the transport of wine was all the more popular with the Gauls since they were good coopers. The wooden barrels were made there and called *cupoe*, and for the Gauls there was not much of a gap twixt cup(oe) and lip. It was clear that the barrel was superior in every way to the heavy and fragile amphorae which held very little wine.

However, foreign wines were still imported from Syria and Gaza, and the many varieties of beer provided competition for our wines from the Midi, Auvergne and Champagne. There was the sparkling *brumalis-canna* containing ginger (probably the ancestor of ginger-beer) and the *alixone* mentioned in St Alvic's testament, both highly thought of. Cider, fennel, wormwood wine and perry continued to be very popular. Wine was already used in

Eighteenth-century Provençal kitchen by Antoine Raspal

cooking and to mask poison. The great d'Aussy, in *La Vie Privée des Français* says that Frédégonde used wormwood wine for administering poison. However, its culinary use was not all so dramatic; small amounts were beginning to be used in recipes. Wine cooked in the kitchen, *vinum coctum*, is still drunk in Gascony and Provence and is made with grape juice boiled down to a third of its original volume.

Scented wines became more and more popular. First, there was the Hippocras, which Guillaume Tirel dedicated to Hippocratus, and then nectar, *medon* and *claretum*. Some of these names have stayed with us and it is likely that Ausonius took the *claretum* of Moselle to La Réole. *Vina odoramentis inmixta* were those highly spiced. At Aix-la-Chapelle in 817 the Council decreed that these should be reserved for solemn feast days.

Distilling began at this time. The first distillers were probably the Phoenicians, but the Arabs, the Syrians and the Jews who were expert alchemists, may have brewed an early form of brandy.

Natural wine was the most widely used for the already common practice of drinking toasts. One drank to health, long life, happiness, the saints, and at meal times, to the souls of friends. Charlemagne found the last two practices blasphemous and anathemized them in his Capitularies. He even went so far as to inflict physical punishment on drunkards, depriving them of the right to testify in court, and simultaneously forbade Bacchic jousting which consisted of challenging one's neighbour with a wine jug.

Drinking customs and habits varied according to districts: the farther east one went, the less wine was drunk with meals and the more at other times. In the Mediterranean, wine was only drunk with food, and was even served during highbrow entertainments posing as poetry recitals or concerts.

The vine grew over almost all of France, including Brittany, Picardy and

Vivandière and hussars, 1803

Normandy. But the reputation of some vineyards was already greater than others: in the Middle Ages, first Gascony, then Burgundy, Champagne, Provence, Languedoc, Auvergne, Saintonge, the Orléanais, Poitou and Alsace. But there were vines everywhere else, including Flanders, the whole of the Ile de France and the Vexin. Philip Augustus even owned a vineyard in the grounds of the Louvre and went to a great deal of trouble to popularize the wines of Anet, Fontainebleau and Angoulême among others. This was a far from disinterested action since the King collected the dues, sometimes in kind, which to a confirmed drinker like himself was not unimportant. Saint Louis took advantage of the same privileges.

Litigants in the twelfth century had to ply the judges with clerks' wine, and parents having their children christened provided parsons' wine. Burgesses entertained by their mayor drank burgesses' wine and business deals were sealed with a *pot de vin* or *vin du marché*. Bakers owed the king an annual hogshead of wine which the monarch never found to his taste and regularly converted into chinking gold coins. Then there was messengers' wine and marriage wine, perfect examples of indirect taxation.

Today people about to be executed are entitled to a cigarette and a glass of rum, but the wretches who were sent to the gibbets of Montfaucon had two glasses of wine to drink before they were tortured; it was known as the condemned man's wine, but it was also served to the judges. In this way wine throve and became increasingly important to French eating habits. At the same time, it began to be used in the composition of dishes. Though very discreet at first, the part it played increased steadily and one can follow the evolution of a liking for spice-mixed wines or those of Mediterranean origin. One notes in particular the appearance on the market at that time of Spanish wines, and the survival of the passion for those of Cyprus. Malvoisie came from both Naples and Cyprus and when mixed with herbs such as hyssop or wormwood was called a 'herbed' wine.

Towards the beginning of the fourteenth century, *eau-de-vie* became very popular; contemporary authors writing about it were convinced that it was both a cure-all and a youth philtre. We are less convinced of this, but have nothing against the notion!

Danzig *eau-de-vie* with real gold sequins floating in it is probably a survival

133

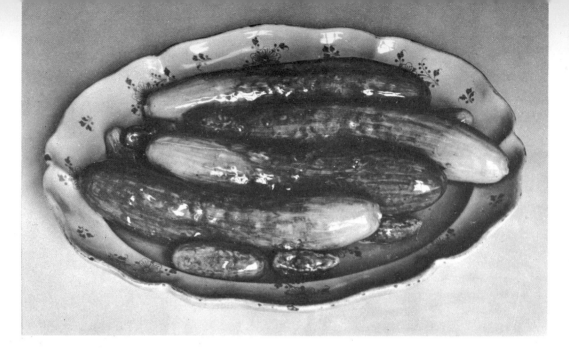

Plate of cucumbers: eighteenth-century faience from the Midi

Plate of beans: eighteenth-century faience

Cabbage: faience from Strasbourg by Joseph Hannong, c. 1758

from the most ancient of all liqueurs which contained an infusion of saffron; hence its name, drinkable gold or *aurum potabile*. Soon after their invention, spirits of every kind were used in the preparation of dishes, especially pastries, but I have to repeat that only the privileged classes had access to them.

Under Philip the Brave, *Les Comptes de la Table du Roy* devoted an important chapter to the royal cup-bearers, and their functions. It was not uncommon for one goblet to be used by several guests, and therefore impolite not to empty it before passing it to the lady beside one. She would then ask a servant to hold a dish under her chin while she drank so as not to dirty herself.

The vine grew all over France but the wines were of widely differing quality. There was a story about a Breton who told François I that three things in Brittany were better than anywhere else in France: the dogs, the wine and the men. The *Roi Chevalier* was prepared to agree about the men and the dogs, but said firmly that the Breton wines were 'the greenest and sourest of the kingdom'. He added that when his dog tried to reach a bunch

Coffee or chocolate pot: faience from St Clement, late eighteenth century

of grapes near Rennes, it was so disgusted that it 'barked with rage at the vine'.

It was François I who started the tradition of reserving Champagne for the exclusive use of the court, and during his reign the expression 'to kill the worm' was invented. At the autopsy carried out on the wife of Monsieur de la Vernade, a worm was found in her heart, after which her widowed husband would only eat bread soaked in wine. The ancient Roman custom of soaking bread in wine at breakfast had just been reborn, and people still say that to take a drop on an empty stomach is to 'kill the worm'.

It was also during this reign that they began cooling wines. Rabelais thought (as I do) that wines should always be drunk cool. Those who had no ice exposed the wine barrels to the sun under wet cloths, or in porous jugs moistened on the outside. The habit had long been current in the Near East but it seems that it was not commonly used in France until the building of the Renaissance châteaux. Camphor was also put into the cooling water to lower its temperature.

As he did for agriculture in general, Olivier de Serre helped viticulture even more than did Sully. He gave valuable advice on both vine-growing and wine-making. Thenceforward wine-makers turned more and more towards natural wine and shed the artificial additions of spices and herbs.

Under Catherine de' Medici, the rules for proper wine-serving were laid down. There were also a great many *eaux-de-vie* and liqueurs, for the art of distilling was becoming very popular.

The custom of 'giving the toast' also dates from then. It had long been customary to drink healths, to challenge someone while holding a glass, and to raise the glass to the king's glory. It became the current thing to put a crust of bread in the bottom of a goblet from which each drank one after another until the last one, to whom they bowed and who was then entitled to eat the *toustée* which was the grilled crust, or *taostée*. The word comes from *tostus*: which is to grill or roast.

Dom Pérignon is the link between ancient and modern wine-making. At the time when the wines of Champagne became white instead of red, and sparkling instead of still, present day taste was born and never looked back.

The Cistercian monks who sugared the musts of Clos Vougeot, and the Carthusians preparing their simple beverages all helped to promote ratafia, Cassis and *Parfait-Amour*. It was now liqueurs based on *eau-de-vie* that were adulterated while wine enjoyed a period of purification.

From the eighteenth century to today, wine-making has made constant progress, and wine, increasingly natural, has become a popular beverage. Happy people, they say, have no history; wine however has a long one throughout this time. I leave it to those with more detailed knowledge than myself to describe the two great crises: the first was just before the classification of 1855, and the second was the catastrophe of the phylloxera which endangered the whole vine crop between 1876 and 1885.

Having paid homage to the wines which have always improved high class cooking, let us see what happened to table wines.

Milk jugs, sugar bowl, cup and saucer: Sèvres porcelain, 1757

Sèvres bowl from the dinner service of the 1st Viscount Melbourne, c. 1760

It is generally admitted that only vine-growing countries have a developing gastronomy. To this axiom I would add a corollary 'as long as the wines themselves can go on developing'. Certain countries which produce wine, though subject to the normal laws of 'good and bad years', as for example, Portugal, have an output of uniform and almost standard character. These countries have their gastronomy, certainly, but it is a static one. We may think that America began to take a real interest in gastronomy at the moment when she began to produce wine. Although still at the research stage, one may hope that a national gastronomy will emerge from it. The great obsession of wine lovers has always been the proper marriage of wines and dishes. The German preference for beer at table and wine after the meal is admirable for those in doubt.

One can certainly succeed by choosing a wine to go with a dish but how much more by choosing the dish to go with the wine. First, the range of dishes is much wider than the range of wines, and secondly, a dish is adaptable which makes it easy to use – a quality one could not ask of a wine. This of course only applies in either case to fine wines. It is pointless to wear oneself out trying to find the perfect wine to accompany Irish stew. Of the two courses open to us, the wine must either be of good enough quality to allow for some risky dishes or it is so delicate that one cannot have too great a consideration for it. In classical cookery there are more biting acidities than those of salad vinegar. Wine-growers have a fear of vinegar which is understandable since its presence during the harvest endangers the wine. But excess of any kind is an error. I know salads containing vinegar and mustard which take kindly to a *Saint Amour*.

In my home in the Gironde, they say that '*blanc sur rouge, rien ne bouge*' but '*rouge sur blanc, tout fout le camp*'. Nowadays it is almost impossible to imagine a meal which does not begin with white wine with hors d'oeuvre, sea-food, fish or eggs, and end with red. Around Bordeaux, the meal traditionally began with red wine and the white came in with the 'white' roast and went on to conclude the meal. True, fish was seldom served at a gala meal, except for lamprey or salmon, to which I think red wine is well suited.

I am often asked when lecturing what the ideal wine to drink with foie gras is. I reply (treacherously) all wines, and probably best of all, Champagne. I try to carry on and explain that foie gras, like cheese, marries happily with every wine, etc. . . . till a voice (anonymous, more often than not) pipes up with, 'And Sauternes?' Need I say I expected the interruption? I then explain my theory which is: yes indeed, Sauternes and foie gras make a brilliant couple, to the benefit of the foie gras. Indeed, Sauternes is the most difficult wine to match to a dish, for it needs a great one. Foie gras has the merit of allowing Sauternes to be seen at its best.

The Marquis de Lur Saluces does not altogether agree with me; he likes to serve his Château Yquem with turbot and hollandaise sauce; others like it with almond or walnut pastries (almonds and walnuts go well with wines). Paul Rival I think is wiser, and convinced that Sauternes has the same place as port; he likes it after a meal with cheese savouries, at tea-time, or better still during the *cinq à sept*. When it is old, even if it is not better, it is good before a meal and rated highly as an aperitif by gourmets. It is my belief that unusual wines have unusual destinies and one cannot treat them like others without risking failure. If I have perhaps rather laboured the status that can be conceded to a Sauternes accompanying a meal, it is because I realize that it is one of the most difficult wines to do justice to.

Oil and vinegar servers: silver and glass, 1776-7

There is a whole range of white, *rosé* and red wines with a high alcoholic content which present no problems to the amateur. I advise those who are interested to experiment and take notes. If I know that I intend to serve a Dodin-Bouffant *pot-au-feu* (boiled beef) next Saturday, then today I shall try two or three of my wines on a stewed shin of beef which will give me a very good idea of what the effect will be with a *pot-au-feu*. As with the match of Sauternes and foie gras, the two can only gain by the combination. I shall note my reactions which will then remain valid till I have tried other wines.

Which should be the successive wines at a rather grand meal? The higher the fewer, so to speak. The better the wines, the fewer we can use – generally only two, a white and a red, plus Champagne.

I like to start with Champagne as an aperitif and continue with it, though not necessarily with the same *marque*, till the main course. Till then the glasses should be kept well filled with Champagne. Then there should be a fine red

Bordeaux until and including the cheese, but not with the dessert when once again Champagne should be served. This suggestion for wines relies heavily on the quality of the Champagne. When a meal includes more than two wines, I like them all to be served again with the cheese, which affords an opportunity for tasting them once more in ideal circumstances. This gives the guests a chance to compare the wines and to enjoy what they have barely tasted during the meal. A careful wine-waiter can contribute a great deal to our pleasure but should he be inattentive, we must not allow ourselves to be. A host who does not personally see to the wine service when he entertains is, whatever his other intrinsic qualities, unworthy of his guests. This responsibility is limited exclusively to the choice and service of the wines.

To balance a modern meal, and if one agrees with my principles, I think one should concentrate on the red wine and see that it is a good one, whatever one eats with it.

To exaggerate a little, I think salad is dangerous: the only solution then is to sacrifice a wine (without the chance to make an excuse if this turns out to be a mistake). Once the red wine is chosen, the white which precedes it has

Table knives made in 1884 for Baroness James de Rothschild

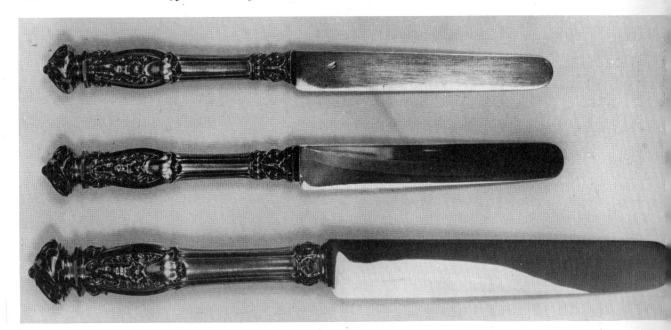

141

no other purpose than to quench the thirst of the guests and to enhance the qualities of the red. In fact, I would go so far as to advise a meal geared to a single wine, in which everything, from the flowers to the *petits-fours*, the table cloth and the glasses, should be chosen to set it off to perfection. One could discuss the system endlessly.

Silver spoons, Paris, 1770–88; silver corkscrew, Amsterdam, mid eighteenth century

I have always loved, and still love, new wines. There may be some Freudian explanation for this, but not I think in my case. I like the first fruit but I do not like it green. As children, we used to get from Sauternes sweet wine which was called rough wine elsewhere; it was grape juice, barely fermented, the sparkle of which teased the tongue and tightened the gums. With it we

143

ate chestnuts cooked in a copper cauldron with fig leaves. The fig leaf was not there by accident: it ensures proper peeling of the chestnuts and imparts an indefinable aroma which can be heightened by adding aniseed or fennel. There are few occasions as traditional and symbolic as were those autumn evenings. In the south-west of France and especially the Great Landes, they had an almost ceremonial quality: girls became engaged then, or properties changed hands. That is why I often tried to flout convention and served my friends wines of the same year which were barely ready.

What was my idea? In the first place I think that wines which are already listed have no surprises to offer (which, from another point of view, is eminently desirable). I have said before that when I am abroad and feel home-sick for the banks of the Garonne nothing disperses the gloom better than Sauternes, in which I recapture the happy hours of childhood and the tender echoes of my first loves. Between the physiology of taste and pleasant memories there is an association which is invariably cheering.

When I ally a new dish to a new wine, my object is to awaken the imagination and open the road for further experiments. A new dish, as long as its inspiration follows conventional rules, can safely be served with a traditional wine whose possibilities one can confidently foresee. To eat Dutch cheese with Château Lafite or walnuts with Château Yquem is perfectly safe but unoriginal.

Conversely, if one serves a young Haut Brion with a salad of wild chicory, Abella nuts and duck's livers . . . if the smoothness of fresh walnut oil adds an exotic note to a humdrum vinegar . . . if the chives are so discreet that one has to call for silence to identify them . . . then one has performed a piece of transcendental gastronomy.

It is within the field of research – not necessarily eccentric, but thoughtful research – that the most successful experiments are carried out. Gastronomy is an education, a long and arduous one. It is for us, the cooks, to pass on the message; but it is for us, the gastronomes, to ensure that there is no dis-integration in an art which needs to stay young and therefore constantly to renew itself.

Wine in Cookery

In a chapter devoted to cookery books, I make a point of the fact that it was a long time before the need was felt for any kind of Bacchic literature. Let me make myself clear; I mean not oenological but gastronomic literature. From very early days song and poetry were happily associated with the pleasures of the table.

It was not until the nineteenth century that wines were included on menus or their order regulated. My views on wine merchants' shibboleths designed to ensnare the naive are well known. Wine is too serious a matter to be entrusted to speculators. To recognize the merits of a wine and to sing its praises is worthy and I think entirely to the credit of the vintner. I will not bow to Draconian laws. Wine is graciousness; gastronomy is pleasure; greed is delight. To entertain is to make a guest happy, not subject him to regulations.

Let us first see how wine reached cookery. From the outset the main question was preservation. I need not recapitulate the various phases of the vine-growers' attempts to make wine every year. It is not difficult to imagine that before the advent of chemistry (before Chaptal, so to speak) if a wine was kept it was good. The wine of a bad year, which was difficult to preserve, very soon became one of the bases of popular cookery.

The wines of ancient Greece or all those of the Mediterranean basin, from Turkey or from Crete, were worked on, transformed, cooked, honeyed, pitched or infused. They were used in cookery as yellow wine is in Chinese recipes. We know that there was no contact between oriental and western civilizations during Antiquity; however, there were analogies in the use of wine in cookery.

First, one must emphasize that the yellow wine of China is only a wine in name. It is the product of fermentation in fruits of every kind, which may well have included grapes. Wine was added to food to improve it. This idea has been current for 5,000 years and we still add the final drop of Madeira or the ultimate touch of port to certain sauces. In that respect, nothing has changed. Both in Chinese and Mediterranean cookery the addition at the last moment of a little good wine is an old habit.

In bad years when wine lacks stability, it turns to vinegar: a dangerous partner which, with good reason, many suspect. Not comparable to wine, it is sometimes used in its stead. I could write a whole chapter about vinegars. For a vine-grower, vinegar spells defeat, mistakes, broken rules and an unfavourable moon. I know some who fear vinegar as they do the devil.

However, man cannot be defeated in battles of his own making; so he tries to make the best of the situation. Indeed he is naturally led to do so. Vinegar keeps better than wine. Its use in cookery stimulates the appetite. It ages well and is easy to prepare. It is the unquestioned ally of preservation. It has an aseptic action. It enjoys sunlight, rose petals, benjamin, cinnamon, tarragon and camomile. It settles down happily with gherkins, green tomatoes, walnut cordial, pimentos, mushrooms and corn on the cob; and is invaluable in marinating game. You think I have forgotten salads? Not at all. But if salad has its proper place in gastronomy only certain salads can successfully be teamed with vinegar.

The most elaborate vinegars, the most sophisticated, the most subtle, either the 'quatre voleurs',* rose, saffron or bergamot vinegars bring out unsuspected qualities in a lettuce salad. It is more forceful in some sauces such as *saupiquet*, *mironton*, *sauce diable*, *sauce Robert* or *charcutière*.

Finally there is the greatness of Béarnaise sauce which was invented at Henri IV's villa in St Germain-en-Laye, the christening of which had repercussions as great as that of sauce Américaine.

Of course only wine vinegar counts though nowadays consumer problems compel manufacturers to make artificial vinegars which we shall not discuss here, not because of contempt but because some things are best forgotten. When I say vinegar must be wine vinegar, I must correct myself, because there are cider vinegars, pear and raspberry vinegars which are splendid, and beer and milk vinegars which are amusing curiosities. But our prejudice holds good.

*A slang corruption of the *quatre mendiants*; a vinegar so-called because it contained white and black pepper etc., the colours taken from the habits worn by friars.

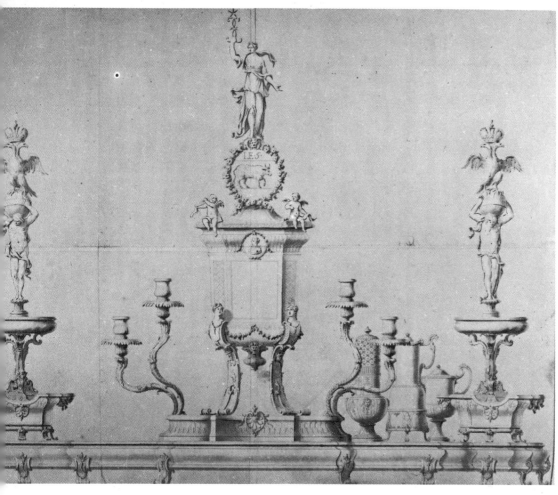

Design for a table centre for the Russian court by Nicolas Pineau, c. 1720

Can vinegar replace wine? That is the essential question which automatically comes to mind when one considers the importance assumed by the corollary to the detriment of the theorem. In absolute theory, no – in practice, yes. We all know methods of cooking fish with vinegar or lemon juice, both sworn foes of wine, which have in fact eliminated wine as a competitor, but that is not very serious.

A lobster cooked in a *court-bouillon* in ideal conditions would probably taste better if vinegar were used instead of wine. In any case, it would generally be less risky to do so. To put it another way, vinegar is easier to use, more popular, of standard strength, and therefore yielding standard results. *Nages* which are nothing more than *court-bouillons*, are more delicate, more difficult to season properly, and for that very reason less spectacular if made with wine. Moreover, one can readily appreciate the vogue for vinegar when one wants the flesh to contract quickly and there is not enough cooking time to permit the aromas of the herbs to penetrate satisfactorily. For example, vinegar is preferable to wine when the food (lobster for instance) must be highly seasoned so that within a few minutes one can produce an adequate dish. One has therefore to be heavy-handed with spices, herbs and acidity.

There is also marinading, a practice far less common since the increased use of the refrigerator. But for many centuries, keeping meat and game was the problem and to marinade it was the most practical and the safest solution. The principle consists, as we know, of keeping the meat from contact with the air. One immerses it, or even better, covers it with oil. Naturally there is some evaporation and contact with the vessel, which requires constant attention. To start with one must see that the meat is generously covered. Of course one can add many herbs and spices to marinades, but no salt for, as we shall see, it would soon permeate the meat. Instead, as soon as the marinade looks cloudy, one should change the container or simply clean it thoroughly. Then the marinade must be brought to the boil, strained through a cloth, cooled and reconstituted. To do this one adds vinegar, herbs, etc. Peppercorns, roughly crushed, are an excellent protection against bacteria. Only black pepper should be used for it is the case of the grain which contains the essential germicidal and scenting properties.

Wine has the same properties and its use in this way has gradually become more common. Meat has been soaked in concentrated vinegar for a long time past whereas it is only recently that wine has been employed. I drew attention at the beginning of this chapter to that fact that wine only entered into the composition of a dish as an ingredient. This excluded wine as the starting point. In other words, *coq-au-vin* as we make it today was unimaginable a hundred years ago. It was only at the beginning of the nineteenth century that wine in cookery acquired this importance.

'The Luncheon' by Paul Signac, c. 1887

The reasons for this change are that wine was popularized at the same time as gastronomy became democratic. Moreover, it takes a long time to alter eating habits. Recipe books have only a fairly recent history. Taillevent's recipes were not published until 100 years after his death and the second edition came out more than 200 years after the first manuscript. Cookery was probably much the same before the birth of Guillaume Tirel. So it hardly takes advanced mathematics to see that the same cooking methods existed practically unchanged for 500 years. One must also remember the facilities offered today by the retail trade. At the beginning of the nineteenth century few lower middle class people normally had wine in their homes. It was difficult to obtain in certain districts, quite apart from its high price. One can almost say that it was during the romantic period and with the advent of Nicolas that things became easier. Père Lathuile not only fricasséed chicken, he also simmered Burgundy. I have sometimes compared the potter's art with that of roasting. Both put something into the oven and take it out again. The essential difference is that the roasting-cook must know what will come out and in what condition, whereas for the ceramist, there is always some leeway; a blue may turn green, a red purple, a yellow brown and so on.

When cooking with wine one must choose the best. My father thought that wine for cooking should be young and strong. One must of course avoid the mediocre. The first time I saw my wife pour a bottle of Haut Brion 1945 into a jugged rabbit with cabbage I was shocked at what seemed to me a sacrilege. It was the best jugged rabbit I have ever eaten, and without wishing to detract from the undoubted talent of my wife, it was definitely the Haut Brion which did the trick.

The late Marquis de Lur Saluces, father of the present owner of Château Yquem, used to say that anyone could produce a good Sauternes: 'They all reach fifteen degrees, to go a tenth higher than the others is what is difficult.' In other words, it is the summit which is hardest to reach. Whatever sacrifices are needed to achieve semi-perfection, the game is worth the candle. A principle now become almost a rule consists of serving with each dish the same

'The Skate' by Jean Baptiste Chardin (1699–1779)

Domestic scene by Chodowiecki, eighteenth century

wine as was used in its cooking. In the case of the famous jugged rabbit, nothing but Haut Brion 1945 would have done. It is a defensible formula, and in that particular case not without charm.

Cooking with wine in my opinion is more suited to my father's method which allows one to drink chilled wine, a custom I find particularly pleasant, especially with highly-seasoned sauces. Successful gastronomy, I think, depends upon a fine balance: one must drink up if one is thirsty. I do not mean that one should gulp down an exceptional wine. Although a wine cannot be too good, it may be too heavy or simply too rare. I like nothing better than the great wines of unimportant years. At the beginning of this century during a period of middle class affluence, following the *belle époque*, many people

Supper in polite society, eighteenth century

bought cooking wines. These wines, nearly always from the Minervois, were in great demand for a long time, but increasing adulteration spoiled them and the custom died out completely.

The origins of cooking with wine in its present form are difficult to establish. One would suppose it to be in Burgundy or the region round Bordeaux, but other regions like the Rhône Valley, the Var, the Narbonnais or Auvergne have equal claims. In fact, it probably took place almost everywhere at the same time. Because *coq-au-vin* from Chanturge came first, it has claimed pride of place among fowls cooked in wine. Jugged hare in its present form may have originated in the Dombes or in Lower Burgundy, for there is little likelihood of its being from the Bordelais where it was preferred roasted.

Distilling: from the 'Livre de Prouffitz Champêtres', 1529 edition

Wine is today so closely linked with French cookery that the origins of both seem to blend into each other. In fact, French cookery owes much to wine; so close is the association that the one cannot do without the other. Cheese would never have become so popular in our provinces if it had not found wine as a travelling companion.

This is such a truism that since America has been producing good wines, Americans have taken a passionate interest in French cheeses. There is no enmity between wine and cheese, and little incompatibility between wines and dishes. Let that reassure us, and back up our choice: quality is the best guarantee.

Brandy and Spirits

Distilling fermented drinks only began in the Middle Ages and contributed to cookery from then on, though at first very slowly.

Spirits were then regarded mainly as medicinal; they were rare and costly and their use in cookery developed along much the same lines as that of wine. I should therefore be repeating myself if I traced its history. Spirits went through the same trials and tribulations as wine, with, however, one significant difference: setting them alight, that spectacular phenomenon.

Setting light to spirits originally had two purposes: first to seal meat quickly, best achieved by contact with an open flame; and secondly to eliminate the alcohol in order to retain only the scent. The first seems reasonable, although the results are not always conclusive. Anyway, the whole performance took place in the kitchen. One fine day, fate, which does things so well, set fire to the rum on the Christmas pudding, which gave people ideas, and in next to no time babas, omelettes and pancakes were gaily ignited. This spectacle was now promoted to the dining room, and the kitchen, feeling left out, followed suit by flaming kidneys, steak, lobster and – away with meanness – *loup* with fennel which really didn't need it. In restaurant circles there was a positive rush to fire. Russian restaurants flamed shashliks shaped like torches, and Creole restaurants produced coffee *brûlot*. If soup was not set alight, it was not for want of trying.

It is true that spirits *flambé* leave a bitter taste, so that adding them at the last moment may be a mistake. Spirits for flaming purposes have indeed always been something of a problem for good restaurants, since one cannot judge by the flavour of the raw spirit what it will taste like once burned.

I do not deny the spectacular charm of flaming, especially if this is the specific attraction of a dark and sophisticated restaurant. Actually, it is useless three times out of four, and risky half the time. All cooking should be done in the kitchen; there are very few exceptions to this rule.

'Silverware' by Charles Bouillon, 1761

Besides spirits, there are aromatics, which were neglected for a long time as were the ingredients with fixative properties of which I have spoken elsewhere. At a recent flower festival, a timid attempt was made to resuscitate them. Without any previous agreement between the cooks involved, the test was applied to fish. Among these, red mullet was chosen by most; a curious choice, for in fact *rouget* has the most pleasant smell and its aroma is so subtle I should personally hesitate to tamper with it at all. Undoubtedly, the most successful effort was red mullet with jasmine.

Quite apart from such bold experiments, there is a tradition of cookery with beer, cider and fancy *eaux-de-vie*. Beer cooks badly, cider not very well. Hence a whole technique, often very simple, aimed at protecting the dish from the disaster of over-reducing. Beer soup, Vallée d'Auge fowls, juniper thrushes, quails with *marc*, lobster with whisky, duck with peaches are all so many attempts to marry scents and dishes.

Taking the most rational attitude towards these combinations, some inspired cooks have attempted to synthesize cider and Calvados, peaches and

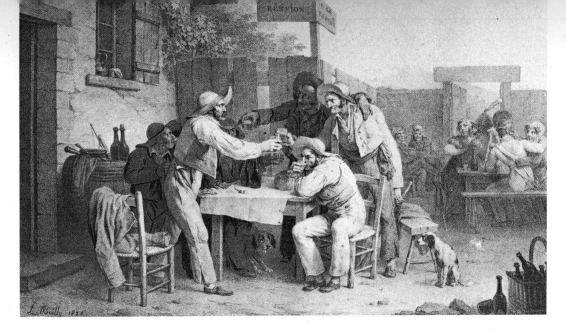

'*A Suburban Inn*' *by L. Boilly, early nineteenth century*

peach brandy, grape skins and *marc*, and so on. A symphony can be attained and the reinforcement of the *leitmotiv* compared with an *allegro* or an *andantino*. There are classics such as *Tripe à la mode de Caen* which are more amenable than others to the addition of strong spirits. Certain other combinations have to be more subtle. Soups to which alcohol is added, such as consommé with sherry, turtle soup with port, or gratinéed soups with Madeira or brandy will only accept the wines or spirits raw and added at the last minute. In any case moderation must be the rule just as the Cayenne pepper must be unobtrusive in a *crème germiny*.

In ancient cookery there was little use for alcohols or fermented drinks, and vodka, whisky, Calvados, *mirabelles*, *quetsch* or *framboise* were completely unknown. *Kirsch* was used and nut liqueur and *maraschino* (which are first cousins), and a little *Curaçao* which we no longer use, for it was dry at that time and is now only available as a sweet liqueur. Rum and *ratafia* were by far the most popular.

The recipe for roast snipe or doves according to old Gascon tradition only permits a few drops of red wine and a few of rum. I do not want to resurrect the question of the subtle alchemy of the golden number, rhythm and magic, but I must point out that while only tiny amounts should be used yet nothing can replace them. I have tried for instance to eliminate the red wine where

157

Advertisement for a sweetmakers shop and factory, Paris, c. 1840

the amount seemed to me ridiculously small. One can certainly not put in more because the sauce then becomes liquid and unusable. Using larger amounts, say of rum or yellow Armagnac, upsets the balance with disappointing results. Perfection requires harmony wherein halftones are more important than violent colours.

It is easy to make these rules but more difficult to practise them; herein lies the perfection of the great cook.

158

Wine with Cheese

Cheese is wine's best friend – this can be taken as an axiom. We all know Brillat-Savarin's aphorism: 'A dessert without cheese is like a one-eyed beauty.' Confucius said that 'A meal without rice is a one-eyed beauty.' One may ponder on one-eyed beauties in various latitudes.

Obviously cheese emerged from the need of primitive populations to preserve the foods available to them. The solidification of milk greatly favoured the popularity of cheese; shaped like a ball, or moulded, its ease of handling and transportation, and its nutritive value made it an ideal food for a large number of mountain dwellers. Indeed, it seems that cheese originated from the high pasture lands for good reasons still valid, though different, today. Cheese was clearly invented after cattle raising became established. The flocks watched over by Moses' shepherds or by those of Arcadia produced little milk; those of the Gauls little more. Asses', mares' and cows' milk were mixed with the more abundant and popular milk of ewes and goats. The same shepherds, from Abel onwards, were the first cheese-makers.

When the Romans conquered Gaul they found a real cheese industry already established there. Cantal of that period was similar to today's product and there was also a ewe-milk cheese not unlike our blue Auvergne and the *fourme* of Ambert.

A certain monk of Saint Gall recorded a story about blue cheese and Charlemagne. The monarch had stopped on a Friday at a monastery where he was offered cheese and nothing else. The Emperor, thinking it was mouldy, avoided the blue bits. When the Prior whispered that he was leaving the best part, Charlemagne tasted it and found it was so. He liked it so much that he ordered some to be sent to him regularly at Aix la Chapelle. This story is also told of Brie and the cheese from Causses.

Auvergne *fourmage* and Brie *angelots* appeared early in the kitchen. The Romans ate cheese at breakfast, and the Gauls, and especially the Franks, made real meals of it. Mountain people eat it after soup, or add it to the soup when it is meatless. Cheese was not considered 'meatless' in the Lenten sense of the word by the early Christians, nor indeed were eggs; butter was practically unknown at the beginning of the first century, and ways were soon found to circumvent laws more Jewish than Christian.

I consider that the person who chooses and buys his own bread, wine and cheese, however humble his social status, is behaving like a true gastronome.

I still remember morning tastings in the cellars of the Médoc, where in an autumn dawn I sipped Château Margaux, Beychevelle or Lafite and nibbled crumbly shavings of Dutch cheese, the subtle scent of which enhanced the magnificence of the wine.

How many of us gastronomes have promised ourselves to return to these rustic joys, and tried vainly to resurrect a lost mood! You know the story of the epicure who was asked to describe his fondest gastronomic memory?

> I was lost in the mountains in the fog. After walking all day, at dusk I saw a light and knocked on a shepherd's door. He received me courteously and offered me food; all he had was stale bread, stinking goat's cheese and the choice of a bowl of goat's milk or a gourd of *piquette* wine. None of these things had ever tempted me before, and I had despised them. But if today I could find that bread again, and that milk and cheese . . .

Brillat-Savarin says that not until food became abundant was cheese served as a dessert. Some call it 'the drunkard's biscuit'. In fact, for a long time, it remained, and still is, a complement intended to balance a meal; it is easy to apportion according to each person's appetite. Its role in gastronomy is a dual one: as an ingredient in actual cooking, and as an addition to a meal.

We know that butter did not become popular until comparatively late. It was certainly known before our era, but mainly among northern peoples. The Franks used it more than did the Gauls, and the latter more than the Romans; but its range was extremely limited. Fats were animal fats which were easy to preserve and convenient to use. The first pastries therefore combined flour, eggs, honey and lard, and very soon after, cheese. We know that brioche was originally a pastry made with Brie cheese. The Americans still have a recipe for a cheese tart which must date from the Merovingian era if not earlier. The recipe was taken over by the companions of Jacques Cartier, together with the pre-medieval traditions of the *tourtière* and pea soup.

Some American cookery, and especially some Canadian, is a survival of French gastronomy, much like the Sleeping Beauty. The same is true of Iceland, where medieval Danish is still spoken and medieval cookery still practised. In some regions of France, especially in the Lyonnais, cheese (nearly always Gruyère) figures in almost every dish, just as cream does in Normandy

'Duck' by Jean Baptiste Chardin, eighteenth century

and garlic in Provence. I myself find it difficult to use any cheese other than Gruyère in cookery. According to my father, the ideal mixture for *gratin* was 50 per cent Gruyère, 25 per cent of very dry Dutch cheese and 25 per cent of Parmesan. One could reduce the quantity of Parmesan and increase the Gruyère at will. I remember going to buy grated cheese from an old woman grocer of Langon, Madame Rivière, just after the 1914-18 war, when I was still a boy. The grocer had had her hour of glory before the war when her late lamented husband was alive. I remembered him as resembling the portrait of Tartarin on the cover of Daudet's book. She served me carefully with 'Gruyère, my dear little boy? Oh, I know your Daddy – it's Emmenthal he wants. Nothing but the best for him, ever . . .' When, much later, I learned that at that time Emmenthal was decidedly more rustic than Gruyère, and that big holes were not a guarantee of superior quality, the scales fell from my eyes and I was saddened to witness the destruction of one of the firmest tenets of Gascon gastronomy.

The fashion for rum with Dutch cheese spread throughout the southwest from Bordeaux, a region which will never become a cheese producing one. Indeed, the Pyrenees and the Valley of Ossau only just manage a respectable cheese. I think it was the heavy sea traffic between the ports of Amsterdam and Bordeaux which spoilt the market and provided a competition which the Gascons could not sustain. One must admit that the cheese known as 'death's head' is more suited than any other to accompany tasting of the white Bordeaux wines. Did the Bordelais, so vain as to put their wines into uncoloured bottles, did they never feel a pang of regret when obeying the rule of the blond, beer-drinking, *Schiedam* quaffing cheese-makers?

And finally, cheese makes possible a recapitulation at the end of the meal. A recapitulation and confrontation. That is why after drinking the wines with the dishes to which they are matched, I like to measure them all up against the single yardstick of cheese, and to compare their various qualities in relation to one or several cheeses. To paraphrase a famous aphorism, I would end this chapter by saying that England has a few good cheeses and a fair number of poor religions, whereas France is short on religion but rich in good cheeses. I can still hear Sir Winston Churchill's voice saying 'a country which has 365 cheeses cannot fail' . . .

4 Bouillabaisse

I think there is no longer any doubt that cookery is one of the humanities whose entire philosophy is in step with the progress of civilization throughout the centuries, reflecting the development of man as surely through a recipe as through the Capitularies of Charlemagne or the *Code Napoléon*. The evolution of cookery follows an ethical progression geared to an unceasing search for greater comfort.

To choose *bouillabaisse* as a theme is to select the most vibrant and passionate example (whether of loathing or love) of a dish which in itself represents a whole region and its deepest motivations and symbols.

Among Mediterranean traditions, *bouillabaisse* is as non-Marseillais as possible. Let us understand each other: I begrudge the Marseillais nothing, neither *bouillabaisse*, nor *aïoli*, but I want to be as objective as possible in retracing the former's origins and history to date. We must analyse the dish itself and assemble the pieces of the jigsaw puzzle: first the recipe itself and all the phases of its development, and then its etymology with its specifically Provençal character.

Apparently, the Phoenicians taught the method to Ulysses, Achilles and Agammemnon. Pythagoras left a recipe which was taken up by Pliny the Elder 500 years later. I am convinced that in Antiquity, the best scorpion-fish soup was made at Syracuse, and that Archimedes, a sound gastronome, knew it. By the way, two ancient gastronomes paid dearly for their status: Archimedes, who, fleeing the Roman soldiery, refused to hide in a bean field because he disliked beans, and Pliny the Elder who was barbecued on Vesuvius. Predestination?

From Pliny onwards, we have a written tradition concerning a soup which contains *rascasse*. The classical *bouillabaisse* so fiercely defended by the Marseillais must contain *rascasse*. The reason for this is curious though ill-defined. *Rascasse*, or scorpion-fish, owes its name to a poison it secretes between its skin and flesh which earned it the name of sea-scorpion. It is a less violent poison, and more difficult to inject into a victim than the venom of the stingfish, and rapidly loses its strength when exposed to air. Its main property, apart from being poisonous, is that of a fixative. In cookery, as in scent-making, the lighter and more delicate the aroma, the more difficult it is to preserve. Though modern cookery has abandoned certain fixing methods of the past, such as the use of musk or ambergris, it has unconsciously retained certain empirical processes: the inclusion of whole live *rascasses* or the red part of carrots is a survival of these methods. The fat used in the distillation of perfume (extract of rose or jasmine) is widely used in cookery and preserves certain delicate nuances in sauces and consommés which are otherwise difficult to keep. Oil has the same properties as fat.

Although *bouillabaisse* is a soup in the full sense of the word, with slices of bread and with broth, the juice must not be too liquid. It must be smooth, an effect obtained by emulsifying the ingredients. The whole thing must be very light which is one of the reasons why fish from rocks are used exclusively, whereas in *bourride*, for instance, fatty fish are acceptable. Originally *bourride* was a soup of sardines bound with *aïoli*, and one knows that sardines are fatty fish. *Bourride* and *bouillabaisse* have had parallel careers although *bourride* has excited no passions.

To start with, *bouillabaisse* was a fish soup, consisting mainly of *rascasse* with olive oil, garlic, leek, onion, and sea water. Later, in Greco-Roman times, herbs and spices were added; then after Arab supremacy, saffron; and after the discovery of America, tomatoes and potatoes. The great vogue for *bouillabaisse* is contemporary with the apogee of French cookery at the beginning of the twentieth century. Its status was slow to be established, step by step, until it became a classic with its own strict rules. These were, first of all and without question, that it should contain fish from the rocks, *rascasse*, leek, saffron, oil, tomato and fennel. Not until the end of the eighteenth century did it assume the name of *bouille abaisse* in two words, then later in three words and finally in one.

In 1785 the word was printed for the first time with the spelling 'Bouille-Baisso' in the *Dictionnaire de Provence et du Comté Venaissin* (Vol. 2, p. 109), printed by Jean Mossy at Marseilles with the king's permission. The definition given is: 'fishermen's term, sort of stew made by boiling fish in sea water. One says *bouille-baisso* because as soon as the pot boils (*bout*) it is taken off the fire (*abaissé*).

In 1818, at Toulon, there appeared an *Essai sur la Préparation, la Conservation et la Désinfection des Substances Alimentaires* by J. B. Fournier which gives, on p. 410, a recipe for *Bouille-Baisse*. From then onwards, many books give the word, beginning with Durand, who spells it *Bouil-Abaïsse* and gives several recipes for it including one using river fish. In 1839, the *Néo-Physiologie du Goût* did give several recipes with the spelling in three words: *Bouille a Baisse*. Conversely, this same *Néo-Physiologie* (later plagiarized by the publishers of Alexandre Dumas' posthumous dictionary of cookery) started a controversy which is still insoluble. A certain Abbé de Sade, who published one single work, a sentimental trifle, is said to have written that his ancestress, Laure de Noves (Petrarch's Laura) dined on *bouillabaisse* every Friday. If this had appeared in the original Amsterdam edition of 1763-7, it would have been for the first time. But it was not, and I have not been able to find either there, at Méjane, or elsewhere any trace of the letter. I once mentioned it in the course of a lecture, and many erudite Provençaux undertook to help in my search, with no more success than I had had. However, I owe them a great debt of gratitude, because that was how I learned that Prosper Mérimée, having written a letter from Cannes about *bouillabaisse*, introduced the recipe at Biarritz to the Imperial Court. André Billy very kindly helped me too. All this strengthened my conviction that the great period of *bouillabaisse* started in the middle of the nineteenth century to reach its peak about 1900.

I am the fortunate owner of the manuscript of Mistral's piece on *bouillabaisse*, and of his copy of *Les Iles d'Or* in which it was first published. One thing may seem rather odd: the spelling in the book is not that of the manuscript. Now, Mistral had given a very detailed definition of the word in his

Trésor du Felibrige as regards the spelling; in Nice as *Boui Abaisso* or *Bouille-Abaisso*, in Languedoc as *Boulhobaisso*, in the Narbonnais as *Boulh-Abais*. He must therefore have changed his mind between the time of writing and publication. We know how meticulous he was, and it is enough to read his carefully-penned, almost calligraphic manuscript to realize that his proofs must have been thoroughly checked and corrected. For the first time he writes *bouillabaisse* in one word in the French translation and in today's spelling, but continues to write it in two words in Provençal.

Professor Louis Roule, the eminent ichthyologist, in *Les Poissons et le Monde Vivant des Eaux*, gives another definition which is used every now and again. Though for Mistral there was no doubt that the pot had to be *abaissé* (or removed from the fire when it boiled), Louis Roule says that one must boil the fish. The fishermen, he says, boil sardines and mackerel. As for the *pêcheur au gangui* (the scavenging fisherman) – he just boils the remains. In Provençal, *bouillie de peis*, then *bouille-peis*, and finally *bouillebaisse*. From this, it just boils down to making a soup from the leftovers. This theory was enthusiastically supported by Brun of Marseilles, whom Charles Maurras and Léon Daudet, his friends, dared not contradict, and who swore black and blue that only noble fishes were for grilling and that *bouillabaisse* was a commercial gimmick for selling bad fish.

As far as ingredients are concerned, the variants of *bouillabaisse* are chiefly a matter of condiments. Dried orange peel, thyme, a *bouquet garni* (parsley, thyme, bay leaf) and white wine to which carrot was added are the main ones. Fashion, daughter of success, stimulates competition, and the restaurants plunged into battle. At the time, the prevalent techniques demanded basic sauces and extracts. Therefore, a classical *fumet* (fish stock) was used to moisten the *bouillabaisse*. One used very fine fish to make this stock but because of their size they were excluded from the dish itself. They are *saran* and *girelle*. The *fumet* is made with carrots, onions, shallots, the green part of leeks and a little white wine. It is allowed to cook for a few minutes, after which the fish is added and the whole stock cooked for five to eight minutes. It is then strained through a sieve and a fine cloth, and used to moisten the

Bouillabaisse

bouillabaisse. This secret was taught to me by a famous old woman, still very much alive and kicking, at Le Brusc, or by Mère Salvador, whose establishment, which is still called *La Bouillabaisse* (even on the Michelin map), I bought from her. In fact, in the same district there are two restaurants called *La Bouillabaisse*: one at St Tropez and the other, to which I allude, at La Croix Valmer. I forgot to mention that the word was originally in the masculine gender and that its present use in the feminine is a comparatively recent development.

The second secret is the marinade. The fish, as I told you, must not be cut into slices, but scaled, gutted and washed in sea water, all very swiftly. It is then marinated with olive oil, saffron and a little aniseed liqueur. *Pastis* has a fennel base rather than one of aniseed, and also contains some liquorice. This idea gave some specialists the idea of using essences and scents. Vanilla, in tiny quantities, produced that enigmatic flavour which has been responsible for the fame of so many exclusive recipes. Lemon peel, orange or grapefruit rind are in current use.

Yet another clue resides in knowing the moment at which to add the saffron. Traditionally, it is set to marinate with the fish. The secret, some say, is to divide it into equal parts, the first to be cooked with the soup and the second, diluted in a little fennel liqueur added one minute before serving. This method is closely related to that of using port and Madeira at the last moment as I mention when discussing cooked wines.

The rules for *bouillabaisse* as we know it were laid down in the sixteenth century, and its new cradle was Marseilles. Perhaps indeed, it was invented by the Catalans living there since it was they who brought saffron with them.

When I recently told my friend Emmanuel Berl my views about the influence of Phoenician cooking methods on Provençal cookery, he told me that Julius Caesar, after invading Gaul, signed a pact of non-aggression with the Jews. The Phoenicians were not Jews, though they were neighbours and had a similar culture and language. There were then 60,000 of them at Phocea (Marseilles). If one compares the French colony abandoned in Canada in 1763, then also of some 60,000 souls, with today's population of 6,000,000,

'*The Oyster Party*' *by Jean François de Troy, 1734*

one wonders about the question Peyrefitte neglected in *Les Juifs Connus et Inconnus*. How many Mariuses and Tituses can there be with the blood of Christ flowing in their veins?

After the 1914–18 war, *bouillabaisse* like the rest of French cookery, was exposed to two opposing influences. One was that of the traditionalists, defended by the great gastronomic clubs, the psychologists of taste, the *Club des Cent*, the *Académie des Gastronomes*, and several restaurateurs such as Basso and Aimé Gardane at Marseilles. The other was inclined to favour a simplification, some said a purification, but which is really no more than an attempt to make it easier. The Marseillais at once all became fishermen, since they all had a friend who had a friend who had a boat, and another friend of the friend had a fishing hut. It was understood that they should fish for their *bouillabaisse* and cook it in the hut. I know many of them of whom I am very fond, who tell each other the recipe for 'the *bouillabaisse* that . . . the *bouillabaisse* which . . . the *bouillabaisse* when . . .' and who have never in their lives peeled a clove of garlic to rub on their bread. But it doesn't matter, since poetry is alive and the Muses were among them.

After all, there are traditions, and someone, some day, had to invent 'the' *bouillabaisse*. The poet Méry claimed that an abbess had invented this *bouille* one Good Friday. An odd sort of pot-boiler, an abbess who had nothing better to do than stoke the fire. Another poetic version is that of a very poor old woman living most miserably in a cheap suburb between L'Estaque and La Madrague. One day, the children playing around her saw her weeping bitterly and asked her why. She told them that she expected a visit from her son, and was grieved to have nothing to offer him. The children put their heads together, and all their parents being fisherfolk, they either begged or stole a fish each from home which they brought to the old woman. Bewildered at the variety of small fish, none of which was large enough to make a dish, nor resembled one another, she racked her brains and finally decided to make a soup with garlic from the garden, a tomato borrowed from a neighbour, and the oil preciously stored for high days and holidays. *Bouillabaisse* sprang from

---

Napoleon entertaining the Czar of Russia, the King and Queen of Prussia, Prince Constantine, Prince Henry and the Duc de Berry at Tilsit, 1806

170

171

the Boy Scout's good deed long before such a thing was heard of. A charming and moral tale.

My own view is that *bouillabaisse* came originally from Martigues, since the best fish for the purpose is caught off Carry le Rouet. It is no accident; the seabed, rich in *algae*, gives the fish a particular flavour. In some rather exotic recipes, certain seaweeds are included for their aroma and even today sea-tomatoes or sea-nettles – that is sea-anemones – are used. Indeed there is no reason for not using them provided that all the sand is carefully washed away. There is a Carry le Rouet saying to the effect that *bouillabaisse* demands a large sting-fish and a small John Dory, a balance with which I agree. The traditions of Martigues are preserved in old salts' lore. Some of the rites are distinctly curious, such as that of *bouillabaisse au panneau*. The *panneau* is a hatch-cover, which, well-scrubbed and soaked in fresh water, does not leak. It is quite functional when used for this purpose since it is so large. Picturesque, but so are the set rules governing the ritual. When setting sail each sailor was allocated a portion of potatoes and so that each should get his share, the potatoes were cut into different shapes for each man: cubes, fingers, rounds, etc. The cabin-boy whose duty was to clean the pot was fed by the others. The *bouillabaisse* was poured into the *panneau* and the cabin-boy's share was left in the pot. Everyone sat down around the *panneau* eating the fish he found directly in front of him, but picking out his own potatoes from the broth.

Another legend from Martigues says that *rouille*, the highly seasoned pimento sauce which sets *bouillabaisse* afire in one's mouth, also originated in the Venice of Provence, which may indeed be so, as canals play an important part in the story.

A sailor, in the best tradition, poor but honest, was in love with the most beautiful girl in Martigues. He too was handsome, and had he not been so poor she would have favoured him. Along came a rich ship-owner, probably of Greek origin, who, charmed by her beauty, offered her a passage in his ship to the Saintes Maries where she could pray to her patron saint, Sarah. As she was leaving port, she saw her lover sitting sadly on the quay, busily mending nets. Wishing to humiliate him, she threw him the liver of a *rascasse* which the ship's cook was cleaning on deck, and said, 'There! that's for you!' The poor fisherman did not want anything her fingers had touched to serve for

'The Drunkards' by
L. Boilly, 1828

anything but his own meal; he crushed the liver with garlic and oil, added pimento, and from that moment on found all the girls pretty. The reason that *bouillabaisse* has a world reputation is because it is aphrodisiac. As *rouille* increases its erotic properties a hundredfold, the girl was forgotten on the spot. Once more, a fairy tale with a happy ending.

It was Martigues that Léon Daudet used as a setting for the fraternal royalist love feasts at which the famous black *bouillabaisse* was eaten. Endless conjecture is possible since he gives no recipe but there must be some logic in it. It is only a step to believe that it contained squid (*pourpre* locally and etymo-

173

Soup tureen: Marseilles faience by Joseph Robert, second half of eighteenth century

logically) with its ink left in. Since sepia has a double gastronomic quality, that of scent and binding properties, it is more than likely that experiments were tried with it.

Bouillabaisse is sometimes called golden soup. There was a golden soup in the Middle Ages which was made with bread, milk and egg yolks, but it did not survive and it can be overlooked in favour of this most popular of fish soups.

I have collected a considerable number of recipes and I have carried out as many experiments. I have frequented all the restaurants from Collioure to Ventimiglia which purport to serve the real, the only *bouillabaisse*. Some of those I have eaten were splendid but often, it is true, the better is the enemy of the good. I suppose that after so much research, desire and selection, I ought to have a definite and proven opinion. Well, I haven't; as far as *bouillabaisse* is concerned, I am still open minded. In the first place, it is no longer really a restaurant dish, except in occasional circumstances, because it is too

174

Plate: Marseilles faience from the factory of the Widow Perrin, mid eighteenth century

dear. The shortage of the necessary fish adds to the difficulty of balancing supply and demand. One can eat excellent *bouillabaisse* at my friend Bérot's at *L'Escale* at Carry le Rouet, at *Mère Terrats* at La Napoule, *Lei Mouscardins*, or the *Auberge des Maures* at St Tropez, and elsewhere, such as Madame Baudoin's *La Bonne Auberge* at Antibes or at the *Réserve* at Beaulieu. Yes, one can, but one must be able to combine one's longing for *bouillabaisse* with the mistral, the game of bowls, and the First Communion of the fisherman's niece.

Do you know this story of the Parisian who wanted to buy fish for his *bouillabaisse* and harangued a lazy fisherman? At last he said to the Tropézien who parried that although 'there might be some mistral, if the Bretons were as timid they would not often put out to sea. 'You've been to Brittany?' asked the fisherman. 'Yes, I have been to Brittany.' 'Well, if you've been there, you've seen the cemeteries.'

But this is only one Provençal sailor's story; on the whole they are neither lazier nor more heroic than any others. It is simply that they have the patois and enjoy playing the prophet.

But since I have mentioned the mistral, sworn foe of fishermen and ally of forest fires, I must also mention false *bouillabaisses*.

When Flemish fishermen could not put to sea because of fog or storm, they made *waterzoï* with chicken. Originally, *waterzoï* was the *bouillabaisse* of the Low Countries. This gave me the idea of making a chicken *bouillabaisse* basing my recipe exactly on the Flemish example. So my *rascasse* sported a red crest and there is not far to go between a chicken and a capon! Of course one should know that the Provençals call a large (preferably red) *rascasse* a capon. To my knowledge, there is no more difference between *rascasses* any more than there is between a dark or a red-headed Marseillais who may well be brothers. This recipe was warmly greeted throughout France except in Marseilles where it was strongly criticized. Certain columnists even said it was blasphemous! I knew very well that before giving my imagination a free rein my folly would have to justify itself by those good intentions with which the road to hell is paved. I also knew that there were such things as cod and even egg *bouilla-baisse*! After being attacked I therefore did some research and then found that there were ten types of *bouillabaisse* which contained no fish whatsoever: made of snails, of slugs, of eggs, of spinach, of peas, of cheese, etc. Others contained no *rascasse* but were made of conger-eel, of *favouille*, of skate, cod, sardines, etc., and then there were Parisian, Fécamp, American, African, Tunisian and Hindu *bouillabaisses*.

Finally, which I had not known at all, I found that my creation had already been invented. A chicken *bouillabaisse* was prominent in *Le Trésor de la Cuisine du Bassin Méditerranéen*. Like M. Jourdan, I was adding plagiarism to ignor-ance. But I was not accused of that. I was accused, as a Parisian (O, how little a Parisian, though!) of laying impious hands on Marseillais folklore which

'Supper' by Honoré Daumier, nineteenth century

has always been a personal property. I admit this shook me, because for reasons of accent, Mediterranean origins and personal sympathy I was not far from considering myself as one of them. I must admit that it was only the journalists who attacked me, and every time I go to Marseilles I receive the warmest welcome elsewhere. One gesture of sympathy which touched me deeply was that of a dumb man in the old port, who, unable to express his feelings, went into a café to write on a scrap of paper that he was happy to see me and to congratulate me, and had to run after me in the street to deliver

177

his '*poulet*' (a little note). Other more recent memories, always full of kindness, make me love Marseilles unreservedly.

Back to *bouillabaisse* as a recipe; for *bouillabaisses* to be faked there must be some incentive. In principle, no one imitates the banal. In all the false *bouillabaisses* we find the same ingredients which have become essential; garlic, onion, saffron, tomato, olive oil, fennel. If today in some radio or television competition people were asked what went into a *bouillabaisse*, the answer would probably be: *rascasse*, rock fishes, garlic, onion, tomato, saffron and olive oil; salt and pepper being included by implication. All the other ingredients are optional, and, indeed, questioned by the purists. However, I cannot accept a limit to the number of ingredients; the result is all that matters. I am perfectly familiar with the arguments in favour of simplicity. The great difficulty is, as Maurice Saillant says, to preserve the intrinsic taste of foods. In *bouillabaisse* therefore, it is essential to retain all the delicacy of the fish and never to debase through too much zeal a symphony of tastes which is so hard to achieve. I have spoken of aromatic herbs, of scents, of citrus rind, even of vanilla; the art of using them is entirely one of *nuances*. Fennel is a classic, and parsley is quite usual. One must also take into account the volume and weight of the ingredients and the technical facilities available. Remember too that the cooking time is very short and therefore insufficient to release the full strength of the aromatics; this is most important. Hence the technique of using a basic sauce or a *fumet* – not always justified, but generally worth while. I even wish to make an apology; during the last few years I have revised my own method, perhaps thanks to Gardanne, Bérot and Jacques Méry, but the results I obtain now, however simplified, are not better though they are more burdensome.

Thus, willy-nilly, I have followed in others' footsteps and my humanism has bowed to the same rules as theirs. I have resisted, I have tried to preserve traditions, though extraordinary as it may seem it was precisely for my attempts to remain orthodox that I have been censured; or perhaps it was because a lad familiar with the *langue d'oc* came to meddle in what was none of his business?

I think we can now draw some conclusions.

Over the centuries (in fact, over a couple of thousand years) a tradition grew up. What matter whether it came from Egypt or Greece, or already

Banquet at the Hotel de Ville held during the Paris Exhibition, 1867

existed locally? The Romans came along with their perfected techniques, and little by little all those who appreciated the exceptional qualities of fish caught off Martigues modified that tradition by adding their own personal touch of genius to it. Improvement followed improvement until the precise moment when perfection seemed to have been achieved. But in order for all this to happen, saffron growing had to be reborn, Columbus had to return from America, Sir Walter Ralegh to settle Virginia and Parmentier to launch the potato. This incredible series of adventures ended up somewhat prosaically with the recipe which begins 'Take a *rascasse* . . .'. It is understandable that a child brought up with legends dear to him, told in the accent of Provence, hearing the cicadas and delighting in sunlight and garlic should wish to preserve the pristine splendour of his dreams.

Court picnic at Fontainebleau during the Second Empire

Anyway, I am pursuing no iconoclastic purpose. I want to be objective and the subject is as serious to me as a religious matter. There are endless examples of carefully preserved myths. For the Marseillais, *bouillabaisse* is part and parcel of his patrimony on the one hand, and on the other a storehouse of confirmed values which he can use at will to support him in his superiority.

All basic ancient Mediterranean cookery survives in that of Provence. However, the particular property of this type of cookery (undeniably an exceptional one) is its suppleness and almost stark simplicity. This seems at variance with the expansive, demonstrative southern temperament of the Marseillais. There the man in the street is a wag, and not without wit. Certainly, the Parisian *titi* gets his laughs in the same way, and as in the case of his Marseillais peer, largely owing to his accent. Both use slang, but it is a colourful, logical slang which requires no translation. The joke would fall flat anyway without its accompanying wink.

For the Marseillais, *bouillabaisse* is daily bread. Show no incredulity when a Marseillais tells you he often eats it in his fishing hut. He has, of course, no fishing hut and no idea how to make *bouillabaisse*. But he will invite you to share it, and if you accept, the miracle will happen. Do not, in the meanwhile, try to find out whether he built the hut himself or how he learned to make *bouillabaisse*. The point is that around every Marseillais there is a network of relatives and friends ever ready to do this sort of good turn on which regional honour depends. For, do not be mistaken, southern hospitality is less lavish than in the north. This is due to the climate. Eight or ten months of the year the temperature is mild enough to allow everyone to manage, leaving everyone free to please himself. This freedom which one grants to others one also insists upon for oneself. Nothing is more absorbing or more paralysing than entertaining, which interferes with one's normal habits, and in matters of food more than in anything else. Indeed, one has to wait for 'St John's grass' before planning a *bouillabaisse* between friends. Contrary to what one might be led to expect, *bouillabaisse* is a fiction rather than truth. It is a symbol and it is not necessary to taste it to exalt its virtues.

At the height of its glory, this soup had to choose its destiny and opted for heroism. It is impossible to remain static: one must advance, retreat or move into legend and *bouillabaisse* chose the third. At one time I blamed sheer laziness for over-simplification – I was wrong. Giving the lie to ready-made assumptions about nonchalant southerners, facts prove that there is virtually no pause in their struggle for existence. But in the Midi, the lazy are to be found out of doors where they can most easily be counted.

When I am in Mexico or South Africa and I ask friends what they would like me to cook for them, they nearly always ask for *bouillabaisse*. As I am deeply respectful of Provençal folklore, I only agree to do this if suitable ingredients are to hand. More often than not, I cook a *thorre*, a *zarzuella* or a *cotriade* which I christen, according to the inspiration of the moment, with the name of some friend or gastronome whom I wish to honour. It would never occur to me to confuse fish soup and *bouillabaisse*. When I made *bouillabaisse* on television, I was at the *Mont Rose* of La Madrague. The fishermen came to the foot of the terrace on which this took place, and in order not to betray the spirit of Marseilles, I allowed the locals to choose both the fish and the recipes. The running commentary was in pure Marseillais. And even that was not enough. Even the soul of a maternal great-grandfather of Catalan origins and of Marseillais adoption was powerless to protect me!

'Enjoy being criticized' adjured Montaigne. If you really do, go to Marseilles, speak of *bouillabaisse*, and you will surely find some ignoramus to explain to you that as France is basically Marseilles, so *bouillabaisse* is the final word in French cookery. Whatever you do, don't laugh! You will hear this truth echoed in Toulouse about *cassoulet*, in Bordeaux about lampreys, in Périgord about truffles, in Alsace about foie gras, in the Lyonnais about *quenelles*, and all are quite right. They have good reason to love their little county, their folklore, and their recipes, for their chauvinism is merely a form of patriotism. They revere their forbears who share their own generous intentions. If the Marseillais are a little more unfair than the others, it is because love is blind, and who can blame them for being in love with such a beauty?

Bouille-Baisse

For 8–10 persons, choose 6 lb. fish, such as whiting, sole, carp, sting-ray, etc., and 24 or 30 mussels, 6 onions cut into quarters, 2 sieved tomatoes, 2 dry bay leaves, 2 slices of lemon, dried orange peel, 4 cloves tied together, salt, pepper, a little saffron, a good pinch of finely-chopped parsley and a pint of white wine. Put the lot into a saucepan, having first thoroughly washed, scaled and sliced the fish. Add a pint of fine oil and water to cover. Boil fast for 40 minutes. Slice bread, 2 or 3 slices per head; remove the fish and the cloves from the pan, place them aside on a dish and pour the rest over the bread which is then served as broth, or everything together.

(*La Cuisinière de la Campagne et de la Ville*, 1862)

Provençal Bouille-à-Baisse

Put into a casserole slices of onion, of carrot, a piece of celery, lettuce, chervil, parsley, bay leaf, cloves, garlic clove, salt and pepper, and water to cover, and boil.

Cut off the heads of the fish to be used for the *bouille-à-baisse*, put them in the pot and allow to boil. Then take the pot off the fire and strain the broth through a hair-sieve or a cloth. That is the fish broth for a start.

Put a little olive oil and chopped onion in a big pot and set on the fire; then, at the bottom of the pot, put fish such as sea-perch, whiting, *moraine, rascasse,* lobster and several others, sliced and seasoned with parsley and garlic finely chopped, a slice of lemon and a little tomato purée, salt, pepper and powdered saffron; moisten the fish with good olive oil and a glass of white wine, add the prepared fish broth, covering the contents of the pot, and boil fast.

When the liquid is reduced by half, pour into a hollow dish over rather thick bread slices; put the pieces of fish in another dish, and serve all together. One can, if necessary, omit the fish broth which is a refinement, and simply moisten with water.

(*La Petite Cuisine* by Baron Prisse, 1875)

Bouillabaisse

Prepare a *mirepoix* consisting of carrots, onions, leeks, parsley, thyme, garlic and bay leaf; cut into large cubes and fry the whole gently in 4 oz. good olive oil; season with salt, peppercorns and grated nutmeg; moisten with a bottle of very dry white wine and 4 pints of water. Cook for 2 hours and strain through a fine sieve. Having obtained the requisite fish, red gurnet, red mullet, *barbet*, congers, sting fish and whiting, gut and wash the fish, cut it into slices; put the prepared broth back on the fire and when it boils throw in the fish, except the whiting which goes in later as it cooks faster; let the fish cook for 20 minutes, and during the cooking add a little powdered saffron, and a pinch of cayenne pepper; grill slices of bread, put them in a tureen, arrange the fish in a pile in a hollow dish. Pour the broth over the bread and serve at the same time.

(*Nouveau Traité de Cuisine Pratique et Elémentaire* by Dubusc, 1884)

Bouillabaisse of Martigues

Put into a cast-iron pot called *pignatte*, John Dory, *galinettes, capelan* (a kind of whiting), *baudroie* (also known as sea-devil or sea-frog) which have all been swiftly gutted and washed. They are salted and peppered, crushed garlic scents them, parsley and tomatoes finely chopped add their aromas, and a goodly dose of olive oil moistens the mixture of fishes which half an hour's marinating prepares for their high mission. To this, saffron adds its own personal perfume.

Now cover the whole with water, boil fast for a quarter of an hour and the *bouillabaisse* is ready. The broth, gilded by the saffron, is then poured over slices of bread laid in a china bowl, and upon the *cousado* (a round slab of oak hollowed out to serve as a dish) the fish are placed in layers to provide pot-luck.

During this time you have prepared the *rouille*: here is the formula. In a marble mortar pound one clove of garlic and a red pepper; a lump of soaked bread dough is added and the paste scented with garlic and highly seasoned with pimento diluted by the addition of one spoonful of the *bouillabaisse* broth and one of the finest olive oil.

No need then for the traditional 'Madame is served'; the fishermen are already seated at the table eagerly forking up the fish piled up in the *cousado* and dipping into the china bowl for the saffron-soup-soaked slices of bread.

That is real *bouillabaisse*, the fisherman's *bouillabaisse*, and the most complicated recipes, wrong because of their complication, will never compare with the simple methods of the Martigues fisherfolk.

(*L'Art Culinaire* by C. Meynier, 15 July 1897)

Fishless Bouillabaisse – Aigo Saou D'uous

Slice a leek and an onion and put them together in a saucepan with a few spoonfuls of oil. Fry for a moment, then add a chopped tomato or a spoonful of tomato purée, 3 or 4 chopped crushed cloves of garlic, a piece of fennel, a *bouquet garni*, a piece of orange rind, a quart of water, a pinch of saffron and a pound of potatoes sliced a quarter of an inch thick.

Season highly and boil swiftly. (Choose yellow potatoes which do not break during cooking.) As soon as they yield to the finger, break 5 or 6 eggs into the boiling liquid, remove the pot from the fire and allow the eggs to poach slowly.

Pour the broth over half-inch thick bread slices arranged in the dish. Put the potatoes on another dish having carefully removed the *bouquet garni*; put the eggs on top of them, sprinkle the whole with chopped parsley, and most important, serve very hot.

(*L'Art Culinaire* by Mistralat, 15 July 1897)

The Gourmet's Bouillabaisse

For 12 persons you need 7 lb. of fish of different kinds. These are the names of those famous for the purpose in Provençal cookery: *rascasse*, John Dory, *muraena*, lobster, *boudreuil*, red mullet, or thick red gurnet, *chapon*, very thick sole (and very white), and large whiting. Cut the fish into slices of equal size and trim them. In a deep frying pan containing a fifth of a pint of fine virgin olive oil, fry gently and without letting them colour, $4\frac{1}{2}$ oz. onion with 3 chopped leek-whites. Add 3 fine peeled and crushed tomatoes, with their seeds removed, 3 crushed garlic cloves, a pinch of savoury, a bay leaf and a sprig of thyme. On top of these lay the tough-fleshed fish and keep the tender ones to add later. Wet the whole with a light fish *fumet*, add salt, and peppercorns and ground pepper, then season with a generous pinch of saffron. Boil rapidly for 15–20 minutes.

Then arrange in a pyramid in a round dish the various fish, and a lobster or crayfish, shelled. The broth, served separately, is poured over 12 slices of bread which have been dried in the oven.

(*L'Heptameron des Gourmets*, MCMXIX)

Bouillabaisse

Bouillabaisse is a Provençal soup made of sea fish and shellfish which is served with the ingredients used in the cooking. There are many *bouillabaisses* which differ from each other mainly in their constituents.

To be tasty, all must combine a great variety of different fish, each with its own particular taste and scent which marry to produce a harmonious combination of smells and tastes. Consequently, you cannot make a good *bouillabaisse* in small quantities: for a really delicious one, you need at least 5 or 6 lb. of fish. Similarly the quality of the *bouillabaisse* depends on the freshness and quality of the ingredients, which is why it is best by the seaside.

French *bouillabaisses* can be divided into three categories: that of the Mediterranean seaboard which is the mother of all the others, that of the Atlantic coast, and finally the inland *bouillabaisse* of which the prototype is the Parisian.

The ingredients currently used for *bouillabaisse* in the Mediterranean area are: *Fish*: conger eel (*Conger vulgaris,* sp. *muraenidae*), baudroie (*lupius piscatorius* and *lophius budegassa,* sp. *lophidae*), black conger or black *muraena, daurade* (sp. *sparidae*), *gallina* (*trigla lyra,* sp. *triglidae*), *girelle* (*julis vulgaris,* sp. *labridae*), *grondin* (*trigla pini,* sp. *triglidae*), *loup* (sea-perch), whiting, grey mullet, *muraena* (*muraena Helena,* sp. *muraenidae*), *rascasses* (essential), *scorpoena scrofa et scorpoena porcus,* sp. *triglidae*), *rougets* (red mullet), *sar* (*sragus rondeletii,* sp. *sparidae*), John Dory (*zee forgeron, zeus faber,* sp. *scomberidae*), turbot and sting-fish (*trachinus braco,* sp. *trachinidae*); as shellfish: *cigales de mer* (sea-cicadas) (*scyllares,* sp. *palinuridae*), crabs, lobster, and crayfish.

Some of these are particularly excellent along the Algerian coast which is why one often eats splendid *bouillabaisse* there.

Here is a practical method of making a Mediterranean *bouillabaisse* prepared with ingredients selected from the list above.

For 10 people take 12 lb. assorted fish and shellfish (e.g. a slice of *baudroie*, a slice of conger eel, a small *daurade*, a *gallina*, a *loup*, a *muraena*, a *rascasse*, 3 red mullets, 1 John Dory, 10 sea-cicadas and a crayfish).

1 lb. sliced onion

4 oz. olive oil
3½ oz. fish livers such as *boudroie*, whiting, *rascasse*, etc.
1 oz. chopped shallots
1 oz. sweet peppers
½ oz. parsley
½ oz. fennel
pinch crushed garlic
pinch powdered saffron
7 pints fish stock
2 fine peeled, seeded and sliced tomatoes
2 bay leaves
2 cloves
1 piece orange peel
few sprigs thyme
salt and pepper

Clean the fish, removing guts and gills, then cut them and the shellfish into slices. Place separately in two dishes, on one the softer meats such as *loup*, whiting, red mullet, John Dory, etc., on the other the tougher pieces such as *baudroie*, conger eel, *rascasse*, stingfish, crab, lobster and crayfish, etc.

Pour a little oil into a pan and gently fry the onions, shallots, garlic, tomatoes, peppers, parsley, fennel, thyme and bay leaf; add the rest of the oil, the cloves, the orange peel, the fish broth, the tougher fishes, salt, pepper and boil fast. After 5 minutes add the tender fish and cook for a further 5 minutes. Then remove the pot from the fire, take out the fish and shellfish, drain them and remove any other ingredients adhering to them, and keep warm.

Sieve the broth, add the saffron, reduce the liquid to 4 pints, taste, adjust the seasoning which should be strong, and bind with the crushed livers. (This last operation is often omitted.)

In a hollow dish put half-inch thick slices of bread and pour the fish broth over them. Set the fish slices and shellfish slices in another dish, sprinkle with blanched parsley, well chopped, and serve all together.

An alternative is the *bouillabaisse* known as 'the fishermen's' in which the aromatic herbs are not cooked and which usually does not contain saffron.

Atlantic *bouillabaisse* is prepared with ingredients chosen from the following:

Fish: sea eels, brill, black conger, *daurade*, red gurnet, *lieu* (a yellow whiting, *gadus polliachus*, sp. *gadidae*), mackerel, red mullet, John Dory, *vieille de roche* or *labre* (*labrus bergylta*, sp. *labridae*), and stingfish.

Shellfish and molluscs: sea-spider (*maja suinado*, sp. *majides*), lobster, crayfish, mussels, sea-urchins, clams (common name of several eatable molluscs: *bucardes, venus, donax, tapes,* etc.), sea-grasshoppers (common name of several crustaceans: *cytherae, gamarae,* prawns, *salicoques, parsiphees, crangon,* etc.) or *chevrettes* and *tourteau* (*cancer pagurus*, sp. *cancridae*).

The preparation is the same as for Mediterranean *bouillabaisse* except that the mussels, clams and sea-urchins are made to open separately over a brisk fire and the juice strained and added to the broth, but they must only be added at the moment of serving so they do not harden. Only the coral of the sea-urchin is used and this is also added to the soup at the last moment without being cooked.

In Paris, the easiest ingredients to find are:
Fish: black conger, *daurade,* red gurnet, dab (*platessa limanda*, sp. *pleuronectidae*), whiting, mackerel, plaice (*pleuronectidae platessa*, sp. *pleuronectidae*), sole, turbot.
Shellfish and molluscs: crabs, prawns, lobster, crayfish, mussels, sea-urchins and clams.

The preparation is very similar. However, in Paris, Sauternes is often added, sweet peppers replaced by pepper, and the consommé thickened with butter. The fish is not usually sprinkled with parsley.

Another variant is the *bouillabaisse* of river fish and shrimps which is pleasant but cannot compare with those described above.

Finally, certain similar preparations of a single species of fish which is often accompanied by vegetables are also known by the name of *bouillabaisse,* such as cod *bouillabaisse* with potatoes. In fact these dishes have nothing but the name in common with *bouillabaisse.*
(*Gastronomie Pratique* by Ali Bab, 1928)

Scorpion Fish: Sauce for boiled scorpion fish

Pepper, caraway, parsley, caryot dates, honey, vinegar, *garum,* mustard, oil and cooked wine (*defrutum*).

Scorpene (scorpio). Xenocrates says that scorpion fish have tough meat and contain evil humours 'and therefore they need seasoning; one must however admit that they assist excretion'. 'Against any poison, either drunk or injected by a sting or a bite,' says Pliny (XXXII, 17), 'there is no better remedy than sting-fish broth and that of sea-scorpion.' In another chapter Pliny says (XXXII, 31), 'The *court bouillon* of all fish is laxative and diuretic too, especially with wine. The best is made with scorpion fish, *girelle* and all the *saxatilae* providing they do not smell bad and are not fatty; they must be cooked with *aneth*, *ache*, coriander, leek, oil and salt.'

It was in fact an early variety of *bouillabaisse*.

(*Les Dix Livres de Cuisine d'Apicius* translated from the Latin by Bertrand Guégan, 1933)·

Bouillabaisse

Most dictionaries give the following definition for *bouillabaisse*: 'A Provençal dish consisting of fish cooked in water or white wine, flavoured with garlic, parsley, saffron, pepper, bay leaf, etc.' In that 'etc.' the editors no doubt include the other essential elements of the preparation such as, for example, the oil and the tomato without which there would be no *bouillabaisse*.

As we have said, the varieties of *bouillabaisse* are legion and prepared right along the Mediterranean coast. In certain regions, especially at Perpignan, *bouillabaisse* is made with potatoes as an accompaniment, and often without saffron which makes this rather like *soupe de la chaudrée* or *cotriade*. At Sète there is a fish soup with garlic which is not unlike Flemish *waterzoï*. And finally, in several different places, they make *bourrides* which are, in the final analysis, kinds of *bouillabaisse* or rather *cotriades* similar to those of the Breton fishermen.

Ingredients: Provençal *bouillabaisse*, or rather Marseillais *bouillabaisse*, for that is how it is most often referred to, must be prepared with the following fish: *rascasse*, *chapon*, John Dory, conger eel, *baudroie*, red mullet, *rouquier*, whiting, *loup*; lobster, crab and other sea shellfish. All these fish, both those with tender and with tough meat and the shellfish must be cut into pieces of the same size. To all of these ingredients which are essentially Mediterranean, one should not add mussels or other shellfish as is commonly done in many Parisian restaurants. To make a *bouillabaisse* for 8–10 people one needs about 7 lb. net of these fish.

Method: In a large pot with high sides put chopped onion, 3 large tomatoes pressed and chopped, 1 oz. crushed garlic, a branch of fennel, and 3 of crushed parsley, a sprig of thyme, a bay leaf and a piece of dried orange peel. On these vegetables and herbs lay first the shellfish and on top of them the firmer-fleshed fishes. Pour on half a pint of olive oil, pepper, salt and saffron, and water to cover generously.

Boil very fast, covered, for 7–8 minutes. Then add the tender-meated fish, such as whiting and red mullet, and finish cooking over a high flame. The total cooking period for a *bouillabaisse* is no more than 14–15 minutes.

Arrange the pieces of fish and of shellfish on a large hollow dish and sieve the broth into another large deep dish containing slices of bread. Sprinkle the soup and the fish with roughly chopped parsley and serve all together.

Some authors suggest preparing *bouillabaisse* with two-thirds of onion and a third of chopped leeks.

One can, instead of using water, moisten the *bouillabaisse* with a fish stock prepared beforehand with the heads and parings of the larger fish used in the *bouillabaisse*.

The bread in the *bouillabaisse* must be neither toasted nor fried. At Marseilles a special bread is used for this purpose which is called *marette*.

An essential point for obtaining good *bouillabaisse* is to cook it as fast as possible, boiling hard. This gives a well-bound broth. To bind the broth properly in this way, certain authorities say that one should add at the last moment a spoonful or two of butter. This addition of butter to a Provençal dish seems to us quite un-suitable, and we believe that without the addition of butter the *bouillabaisse* broth should have the right consistency. Indeed, certain Parisian restaurants which specialize in *bouillabaisse* are in the habit of serving broth which is too thick. (*Larousse Gastronomique*, 1938)

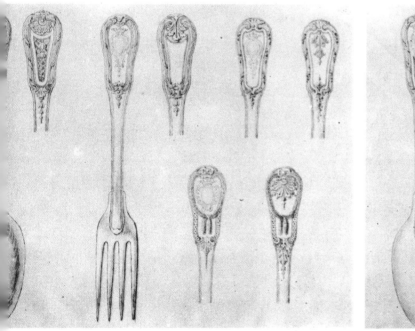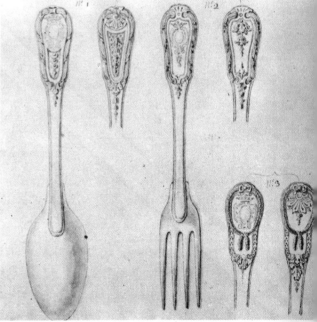

Designs for spoons and forks: attributed N. M. Langeois and L. F. Langeois, eighteenth century

'Kitchen' by Velasquez, seventeenth century

190

5   In the Kitchen

Equipment

Prehistoric man tamed fire and knew how to roast meat. As hunter, male and head of the family he was watched as he prepared the fire, the meat and the branch to be used as a spit. And when the flames leapt up, wife and children backed away gazing at the man with admiration and at the fire with terror.

Fire, once domesticated, became the prisoner of the hearth where, known and revered, it no longer inspired much fear. The eldest son was allowed to tend the fire and turn the spit in place of the father and the whole family trusted them. Later the stove was invented. Black, in a cast-iron armour, it was entrusted to the mother, and though her eyes watered a bit when lighting it, she appreciated its advantages and the extra comforts it gave such as coals for the copper warming pan and the oven itself, so convenient for roasting.

Then, one fine day, this armoury of cast- and sheet-iron, complete with metal hinges and copper ornaments, was replaced by a shiny elegant piece of furniture, delectable in stainless steel and enamel, easy to clean, and – O miracle! – to light simply by striking a match to the pilot flame for gas, or pressing a button for electricity! No more tears and no more dirty hands. The eldest daughter was promoted to the rank of priestess at this modern hearth.

Gadget was added to gadget, infra-red rays to thermostats, mechanical spits to electric ventilators. And then Papa, after so many years of frustration, installed a barbecue in the garden. Mother and children rediscovered those long-forgotten fears, and hiding in the bushes admired the man who, his waist draped in an apron and armed with a trident like Neptune or Vulcan, solemnly scorched for their pleasure what could so easily have been cooked in the latest model of electronic oven in their kitchen.

A cycle completed, a circle closed. Papa has resumed his pioneer's role just in time for the table barbecue to take its place on the family table and be tended by the youngest son aged seven – the age of reason!

Equipment is at the root of all gastronomic developments, has been so since the stone age and probably always will be. Cooking equipment such as saucepans, stewpans or frying pans have altered little throughout the ages in relation to the changes in sources of heat used. Little in shape, that is, but immensely in terms of materials. There are people who say the best stews are those cooked in earthenware vessels. This is only half true; what *is* true is that the frailness of the material made the user take the greatest possible care and the most elementary precaution was to cook on the lowest possible flame. So naturally the method was extolled by all who sang the praises of slow cooking. Do not worry if the dish tastes better when reheated; it may be because it was not completely cooked the first time.

The employee who regularly ate at a restaurant and the bourgeois who ordered his meals from the caterers, did so largely because of the enormous work involved in lighting and tending a kitchen stove, the cost of wood and transport, the need to watch the fire constantly, the inconveniences of cleaning and scouring, and the disposal of the ashes, all of which could be avoided by eating out. The stove which needs no more than a match to a pilot or a push on a knob has completely altered the general standard of living.

And what do you think will happen next? The workman and the white-collar man do not even have the time to go home to their automatic ovens because of commuting problems and the continuous working day. So they have to feed in the canteen just as their grandfathers did on bouillon Duval or *Chez Magny*. So the wheel has turned full cycle once more, but even so there has been considerable progress.

There is no doubt that the modern cooker and the refrigerator are great steps forward, not only in terms of comfort but from a gastronomic point of view. Cold storage is essential, yet often badly used; heat is better understood generally because, for thousands of years, everything had to be cooked with fire. Today, although perfection has not yet been achieved, the position is satisfactory. So is the standard of small equipment.

In searching for a form of pottery which would stand up to the speed of space travel 'pyroflam', a material practically indestructible by thermic shock, was discovered. You can remove a 'pyroflam' dish from a bed of crushed ice and put it straight into a flame of 450°C. and it does not react at all, just like platinum. It has far outreached oven-glass, itself a step forward.

Glass, china, pottery and enamelled cast-iron make a splendid range of cooks' utensils. Professionals continue to use tinned copper, an excellent metal, but other materials are slowly being used even by them. Oven-to-table ware, so useful, is now both practical and pretty.

It is obvious that research at present being undertaken for a material which will prevent food from sticking will revolutionize cooking. Silicone-based plastics have provided a partial solution but there is no doubt they still have some disadvantages, mainly their frailness and the special care they require, both of which make them difficult to use correctly for the beginner. Experiments have also been made with edible fats which have the same results but no drawbacks.

Cold storage, in the form of either the classical refrigerator or the deep freeze, has considerably altered eating habits. The use of very low temperatures in family kitchens will remain one-way for some time yet, for deep freezing can only be used on an industrial scale and the housewife can only use it for some stock-piling. This is a complex technical problem which cannot be dealt with here but in the long run it should have beneficial effects on gastronomy when it has been rationalized.

However, freezing techniques may be profoundly modified by Accelerated Freeze Drying which consists of very rapid dehydration at a very low temperature. As this technique becomes more common it will alter storing methods greatly. Freeze-dried foods can be kept in a vacuum or a sealed wrapping at ordinary room temperature without any loss of flavour or nutritional value. Imagine what possibilities this opens up.

We can at any rate be certain that gastronomic progress will continue to be influenced by equipment as it has been since the beginning.

Chefs

The layman may confuse the chef with the cook, but in fact a professor is not necessarily a great scholar and an orchestra conductor may be an indifferent instrumentalist.

A *chef de cuisine* can without harm be both a good cook and a good organizer. The cook, because for so many years considered a servant, has chosen the name of chef, a generic term. One is a chef as soon as one has ceased to be an apprentice. There is a sort of amiable mockery in the relations between cooks and their subordinates, especially the apprentices, and it is common to hear a qualified cook address an apprentice as 'mon chef'.

Among cooks, the title is respected. In the most professional quarters a chef is not judged by the height of his bonnet but by his real qualities, for which he is known. As a career, however short, it has its official requirements; it is necessary to show to whom one was apprenticed, the quality of the establishments in which one has worked and the length of stay in each. The apprentice's master plays a vital part, for his quality will affect the whole professional life of his pupil.

One therefore understands how guilds and freemasonry have had a lasting effect on the organization of our trade. I am not sure how freemasonry influences us, though I have been in touch with masons all my life. Cooks were freemasons just as were master printers, suggesting that both crafts felt the need to group together in a mystical ritual.

The Scottish fraternity's lodges numbered a great many cooks. After all, the cook, however, good or bad, is an artist whose single vocation is to make others' lives happier. He works only for the pleasure of his fellows, twice a day, for ever. His works are among the most uncertain, his techniques among the most flexible. He must constantly adapt himself, modify, interpret and in turn create; that he should be attracted to freemasonry seems obvious to me.

One must also consider methods of recruiting. Too often children are

Silver sugar bowl and coffee pot by Vever, 1889

apprenticed against their will. When a child works badly at school but eats heartily, his parents send him into the kitchen where he is sure to be well fed. I have always regretted this state of affairs and I make a point of ascertaining an apprentice's ambitions before imposing on him a trade which he might later pursue without enthusiasm.

However, be that as it may, recruiting for our profession starts at a very early stage. A primary or elementary certificate is all that seems to be needed. So-called hotel schools do not train cooks. Their pupils only do an absurdly small amount of cookery – thirty-six hours a year. These are secondary schools which train hotel keepers and hotel executives. The food schools and certain technical schools offer cookery tuition of the same standard as classical apprenticeship. In both cases students are awarded a certificate of professional aptitude (known as the C.A.P.) at the end of their studies, and as the name indicates, shows them only to be ready to start learning their trade.

At Siem-Reap I met a young Cambodian serenely convinced that his job as manager of the local grand hotel was fully justified by his C.A.P., obtained in Strasbourg. I think the natives were so impressed by this diploma acquired in so remote a place that his reputation was untarnished.

The cook has to be self-taught, sometimes by choice but more often through necessity. Few cooks can go to evening classes since they have to work when others have stopped.

Since intelligence has nothing to do with knowledge and even less with culture, the proportion of intelligent cooks is the same as that of intelligent doctors or lawyers. For them no problem exists, or rather, it is solved for them by a series of formulae applicable to all circumstances. But cooks have to decide whether or not to cross the *pons asinorum*. Those who do will become chefs, the others will remain artisans; both equally necessary.

There would be much wider scope for cooks if general culture were of a higher level and more easily attained; a limitation which restricts the possibilities open to him. Let us examine these possibilities.

In general, apprenticeship takes place between the ages of sixteen and nineteen. The boy then does eighteen months in some reputable establishment recommended by his master. Then comes national service. If there is good stuff in him, by which I mean if he gives satisfaction both by his work and his team spirit, his chef or his *patron* will look after him. He may volunteer for the Navy which takes on ships' cooks and where the work is particularly interesting. The ministries for all the armed forces also take on men with his qualifications. Therefore, nine times out of ten, the cook will do his national service in his own trade; most useful for him.

Then he returns to civilian life. He can return to his former employer if he wants to. There are some losses though; some cooks give up their trade after being demobbed. A high proportion of those who carry on, however, branch out in new directions – new both of them and for us – they turn to industrial catering. The reasons for this are clear; until they do their national service, the only daily rhythm they know is ours, and as we seem content with it, they are too. But national service, often abroad, shows them new horizons and timetables; even in the army, they have normal working hours. They see a chance to enjoy family life, leisure and friendships not necessarily confined to colleagues. Their income remains much the same; if the canteen worker earns less, he can still do overtime and in one or two weekends a month, pick up the same pay as a cook in a great restaurant. On the other hand, he has regular full-time work throughout a day lasting from 7 a.m. to 5 p.m. The cook in the restaurant does not work longer hours, but he has an afternoon break which most of the time he does not want and cannot use. When I was a young cook in Paris, I used it to visit the museums, and though I know some who still do the same, it is not for everyone. Many have not the time to go home because they live too far from work, so there is the risk that they will take to cards in some bistro and start drinking.

Alcoholism is the great danger. It is perfectly normal for a cook to be thirsty, but it is only a step to quenching that thirst. The legend of cooks drinking the Madeira or brandy intended for the sauces is discredited nowadays; it also infuriates the workers and leaders of our profession. Alcoholism in the kitchen, indeed, is waning rapidly. Personally I have laid down what seems to me a rational rule. Beer, lemonade and mineral waters are freely available, as is wine with meals. No one takes undue advantage. I think rationing creates a double problem; frustration for those who do not get enough, and selfishness on the part of those who have plenty but do not wish to part with their due. When I was young, between twenty-five and thirty, I used to make a refreshing drink for my colleagues with the juice strained from the stewed fruit, white wine, ice and water. There was always a full jug of this punch in the refrigerator with a ladle and a glass, and everyone could help himself. This was greatly approved of, from the *patron* and the chef down to the youngest apprentice.

There appears to have been a time when the *patrons* behaved badly towards their cooks. They salted the wines and liqueurs intended for the sauces before issuing them – brandy, Madeira, red and white wines and so on. My father said that in one kitchen where he had worked the chef himself insisted on pouring the white wine into the dishes for poaching fish. The fish-cook glazed the dishes with shallot and seasoning and melted butter, and the chef poured in the wine which did not mix with the butter and then it was child's play to recover it with the use of a funnel. There is also the legend of the pastry-cook who claimed he could make perfect puff pastry only by using white wine instead of water. Fables which may have been true but are not so any longer.

So, the cook returns to normal life after his national service; where will he go?

First of all, the more competent he is and the more he feels cooking to be his vocation, the more he will feel the need to learn. For he knows nothing yet. He must take the hard way and set out to acquire the knowledge he will need. There is a great corpus and his choice will be determined by one main aspect of it.

Technique comes first. Among many techniques some, such as hollandaise, béarnaise, soufflé potatoes, sauce *nantua*, bases such as consommé, jelly, curry, *coq-au-vin*, etc. are almost elementary. The result depends largely on the quality of the ingredients available, but it is only too easy to ruin a cooked dish. All these primary preparations must be carried out by a sort of reflex action which must be effortless. Then, and this is his ambition, he may tackle the difficult work; the delicate cooking, vegetables or fragile mushrooms, fish to be cooked for only a very short time, which allows him no possibility of salvaging the dish if he makes a mistake. If he takes to this kind of work, and it appeals to him, he must then make up his mind whether to be a cook or a chef.

To be a cook may well mean to run a restaurant for there are few chefs who find this sort of administration interesting. The two require different viewpoints.

A chef reaches high rank slowly by climbing the ladder and meriting each rise. The gifted cook and, of course, there is nothing to prevent the chef from being one too, often prefers to set up in business for himself. He is rightly self-confident and has often taken this decision in his days as an apprentice. I do not think it is the best solution for a talented practitioner, but no one ever stopped a man from nourishing the illusion that working for himself means freedom.

What becomes of these two men with identical training whose paths separate?

The chef has been through the mill. He has been an apprentice, then a *commis de cuisine*, then a soldier or sailor. As a cook, he would have been *premier commis*, *chef de partie*, *chef saucier*, *second* and finally *gros bonnet* (big bonnet, the accepted name of a *chef de cuisine*). Real kitchen *brigades* are now few and far between but there still are some. In Paris, one of the largest is at the *Plaza Athénée* with forty cooks. In Tokyo at the *Tokyo Kaikan* there are several hundred white bonnets for several thousand daily customers.

198

Chefs in the Restaurant Lasserre, Paris

The average French *brigade* consists of six to eight members. A chef, a *second* (generally a *saucier*), a *rôtisseur*, a *gardemanger*, and one or several assistants ranging from apprentice to kitchen boy.

Here is approximately the ideal *brigade*: a chef; a *second*; a *saucier*; an *entremettier*; a *grillardin*; a *rôtisseur*; a *poissonnier*; a *communard* and a *pâtissier*.

Each of these cooks has one or several *commis*. During the first year apprentices are responsible for basic preparations, and from the second year are allocated to a different section each month.

How is the work split up?

To the layman, only two titles may seem intriguing – the *entremettier* and the *communard*; the others' names convey their specialities.

The *communard* cooks for the staff. Clearly, in an establishment with a large *brigade*, there are a lot of employees. As soon as there are more than fifty to be fed twice a day, it is worth while for everyone to have a specialist on the job. This is not an easy task and it is often entrusted to an older cook who has some authority over the rest of the staff.

The *entremettier* is in charge of the vegetables. There was a time when this section also included a chief soup-maker. In general, it is this section that has the largest number of *commis*. The work is very important and there is a great deal of it, for the *entremettier* is responsible not only for the eggs, soufflés (salt or sweet) and pancakes (also salt or sweet), but all the vegetables except potatoes which are looked after by the *grillardin*, who seldom has a *commis*, but is usually given an apprentice.

The reasons for this exception are obvious to a professional, since the *grillardin* has almost no *mise en place*. Indeed, he only has to see to the potatoes: soufflé, straw, waffled, Pont Neuf, or chips according to the day's menu. Thanks to machines, peeling and cutting are now very simple and the actual cooking greatly facilitated by thermostatically controlled electric friers.

I must elaborate on the *mise en place*. Every morning the menu is posted up. If it is a fixed menu or one for a banquet, the number of guests will be known and will show each cook what he has to do for the day.

When it is *à la carte* the *mise en place* will differ greatly and include a large number of preparations which at the right moment have to be used for the dish ordered. Certain sauces automatically constitute part of a classical *mise en place*: mornay, hollandaise, béarnaise, veal extract, *maître d'hotel* butter, lemon juice, watercress, and so on. There are many more complicated preparations but I will not weary you with too much detail.

When the chef is running a very big *brigade* he allocates the tasks when he puts up his menu. Banquets are shown in a given colour, as are sittings. Blue can be used to indicate lunches and red for dinners, etc., and there must be the strictest adherence to the timetable.

Such a chef must be able accurately to gauge the possibilities of his workers in relation to the equipment at their disposal. A rush for a given stove, grill or pot must not be allowed to occur as it retards productivity. There are two

Nineteenth-century kitchen interior: Restaurant Lasserre, Paris

types of productivity, one from the raw materials themselves, and the other from the amount of work per head.

While in small or medium-sized businesses the output per worker is unimportant, it is a major consideration in big business. To share out the work in the most efficient way presents enormous difficulties which are only partly eased by the use of refrigeration. The chef has to plan ahead and have certain foods prepared in advance and then deep-frozen, sometimes for several days, sometimes for only a few hours, to spread the load. A chef with such responsibilities must know his trade perfectly and must also be an expert with figures. It is not he who works out the figures; the calculating machines produce the percentages. Nevertheless he must decode their message and be able to spot the weak points.

I know of one hotel which adopted the old method – one I have favoured for years: a central kitchen with distribution at the 'points of sale'. Let us consider a big hotel with five restaurants on different floors, each of a different type and standing. To these must be added the reception rooms, room service on eight floors, banquets and so forth. If one only kept an account of what left the central kitchen, one would not know where the food was being consumed. For the information to be of use and for the system to be run efficiently, each 'point of sale' must order its own food from the central kitchen. Of course, we are talking of prepared, ready-cooked food. Thus five litres of consommé, twelve *brochettes* of prawns, twelve portions of curried chicken, twenty-four apple pies might be sold and one can see the breakdown clearly between the kitchen and the selling point. A few minutes devoted to examining these figures will show up any mistakes.

It is far more difficult to check output per man-hour as this can only be gauged by observation. One must therefore know the trade inside out to be able to judge not which item but which worker yields poor returns. To the layman, using full-time employees may seem a lunatic investment, but I shall give you an example of how it works. The pastry-cook has finished the work shown on his card for the day, but he still has a couple of hours to go. In the old days, he would potter around the place, tidying up, fixing the flowers,

Street market in the rue Mouffetard, Paris

and doing odd jobs in the restaurant. Now he makes 100 kilos of croissant dough which will go, already shaped, into the deep freeze and which can be drawn upon as required over a couple of weeks. This flexibility produces better results and complete efficiency and also allows for shedding some of the load at busy times.

To govern has always meant to foresee, in cookery as in politics. The *chef de cuisine* is an important man in his profession. He must be fully trained in technique and practice from the start, and he must be capable of doing the work in any of his sections before he can organize others to run them under him. He must know his equipment and use it properly. Moreover, because he must always be in the van of progress, he must keep abreast of every new development, and at the same time, gauge the value of expensive new tools which must not only pay for themselves but also show good returns.

Banquet at the Hotel du Louvre held during the Paris Exhibition, 1867

Some people are surprised at the high position of a chef in a big establishment. They should realize that the interests he controls are of the same kind as those of an engineer in any branch of industry. The least one can do is to place on an equal footing two executives of equal worth. The chef is at a disadvantage because of staggered working hours, holidays which do not coincide with those of anybody else, the disruption of family life, and needs different from those of other people. In addition, he has constantly to remember the perishable nature of his wares and take into account wastage or losses (not necessarily due to pilfering). Finally, he has to occupy himself with recruitment. In a big international establishment the *chef de cuisine* is paid about $2,000 a month, which is normal and should not surprise anyone – least of all those incapable of doing his work, either well or badly.

An international *chef de cuisine* will, between now and the twenty-first century, have to speak three languages, know all about freezing techniques, A.F.D. and electronics; all this in addition to the professional knowledge of the trade required of his predecessors.

The first chefs who had some notion of costings were born with this century. Even a cook as remarkable as Escoffier was quite incapable of tackling figures; administrative work was not his strong point. Liberal taxation and ludicrously low wages allowed certain establishments to muddle along and just get by, but a lot of water has flowed under the bridges since those early days.

The chefs of tomorrow will have to be taught by very different methods but luckily, intelligence has always come to the rescue of technical problems. In every generation, there is some self-taught genius who ends up as a millionaire having started out as a bottle-washer. There have been Cornuche, André and Cazes. There will be many more and I have complete faith in the genius of the French and the cooks of the whole world.

Service

This is obviously not the place for a detailed study of serving at table so I shall content myself with sketching only the main outlines of development.

As soon as people began to sit or recline to eat together, it was necessary for them to be waited on. So this became a task to be filled by an individual, whether slave, courtier or a member of the family or group. For an elaborate meal no less than for a family dinner some sort of ritual had to be invented, and very gradually a whole complex of customs, rules and regulations grew up around the simple business of serving food.

Throughout the western world we can say that certain customs are generally accepted by everybody: one starts with soup, eats fish before the meat, then cheese and dessert, ending up with fruit. It is not an absolute rule, of course, but is practically universal. It was not always so.

Originally, the sequence in which food was served was chaotic, but order was later imposed simply according to fashion, for there seemed to be no reason for its classification. (To simplify matters, I shall not here compare Chinese and Western cookery.)

Experience conferred upon custom the force of law, and this was codified by two aphorisms of Brillat-Savarin: the 11th edict – the order of foods is from the most substantial to the lightest; the 12th edict – the order of drinks is from the mildest to the most powerful. The modern tendency is to disagree with the view of the nineteenth century – a tendency which I think is right. The order of foods is virtually reversed, and the wines could also be served the other way round without doing any harm, as I shall show later.

First, let us consider courses which have varied in number at different periods, rising to a maximum under Louis XIV and Louis XV when there were eight courses of eight dishes each.

I have already talked about the evolution of the *entremets*. In a ceremonial meal two out of the eight courses consisted of *entremets* and two of desserts.

There would be a soup course consisting of several soups, a fish course of several fishes, an entrée course, a roast course and a game course. Rather surprisingly, the composition of the courses could be optional, the *entremets* mainly consisted of vegetables, and the entrées (poultry or classical) could appear in the same course as the fish, shellfish, roasts and game.

Though one cannot therefore talk of strict rules, the enormous number of dishes, $8 \times 8 = 64$, remains surprising. Of course, sixty-four dishes were not eaten at the table of the Great Condé in 1671, as we shall see from the order of service.

The King's food had to be tasted before he could be served; even the swiftest tasting by two or at most three courtiers of sixty-four dishes would have taken well over an hour. So in fact they only actually tasted the ten or twelve dishes which the King intended to eat. The last course of fruit and confectionery might consist of eight dishes. Even today thirteen desserts are served at midnight on Christmas Eve in Provence. But if one eats a dried fig, a date, a prune, a piece of nougat, an apricot *tapé*, two liqueur cherries, a piece of chocolate and an almond, though not an enormous dessert, it contains eight different elements.

Louis XIV ate little of the eighth course but always asked for hard-boiled eggs after every meal and often ate several. The royal meal was served much like a meal today in a good restaurant rather than one at home. The King was served by his courtiers who cut up each piece of meat on his plate for him. This form of service is much like that which we call *à l'anglaise* where a full plate is handed to each guest and removed when empty.

More often than not the King ate alone in his bedroom. He was offered a series of dishes from which he made his choice, after which they were tasted, and the royal plate loaded. The courtiers tended to gobble up the leftovers so that severe rules had to be laid down to protect the rights of those traditionally entitled to them.

A normal meal with the company assembled round the table was rather different. Only certain dishes from certain courses were handed round, among which were the soups, the roasts and their sauces and the *entremets*. The other courses were on the table and might include tongue *à l'écarlate*; stuffed small shellfish such as shrimps, large fish, game stews, pies, and so on. Everyone helped himself, the dishes were hardly moved at all and the meal proceeded without any particular order. Each guest had a trencher in front of him often on a plate and the most disparate foods were piled indiscriminately on to this large slice of bread, also known as *soupe*. The correct thing was to let the trenchers soaked in the various juices be removed to feed the poor.

Out of sixty-four dishes, at most twenty were handed round and from these one had to help oneself more often than not. The great noblemen had their own carving grooms whose duty was to fill their lords' plates. This was not always easy, and as manners were rough and ready, the craftiest got the most food. Similar competition takes place at buffet lunches and cocktail parties today; but it all works out in the long run.

It was only with modern gastronomy that an ordered service became usual. Before the First Empire the only way to be properly served at table was to have one's own servants. In inns and monasteries there were certainly servants and lay brothers, but they only put dishes and jugs on to the table.

Service as we know it had to be invented by restaurants for obvious reasons; there had to be waiters or waitresses to fill the plates and change them when empty, and similarly with pouring out drinks, as I have already pointed out. Waiting at table became even easier when it was possible to put all the serving dishes within reach of all the guests.

There was a choice of dish within each course for some considerable time: two soups, two fish dishes, sometimes even two pâtés were offered in turn. There were also several vegetables (no longer called *entremets*) from which one could choose one or more. For a long time too, there were various desserts, of which more or less everyone partook. But by degrees, only one soup, one fish, one poultry or game entrée, one entrée, one sauce and one roast were served, with several vegetables, a salad, cheeses (again and increasingly, a choice of cheeses), desserts and fruits. That was before the 1914–18 war. The period immediately following the war was to influence our entire present gastronomy. This is important as I have already pointed out (see page 114).

Creation

Prolonged and intensive study of cookery, cooks, foods and utensils might make me suppose that everything has already been said on the subject. However, the principal themes of novels are love and death, and though it would seem that nothing more can be added to what has been said on those subjects, a goodly number of new novels appear every year. My friend Emmanuel Berl to whom I was complaining about the difficulty of writing replied that one should not try unless one had something to say and that the rest, meaning style, would come of its own accord even though it was not necessary. I am not so sure. Have something to say? Had all the people who wrote cookery books something to say? The cookery book is like its subject matter; for consumption. One uses a cookery book as one uses a wooden spoon. If one considers the fate of books in general, one is astonished at the number which have disappeared. Cookery books, especially, are roughly handled, get easily soiled and stained, their spines cracked by being held open at a given page, sometimes a page is actually torn out and the book therefore banished.

To satisfy the market, specialists who are rarely themselves cooks are employed. But they do not have enough knowledge on subjects outside their own and so borrow from others. Today there are plenty of cookery bibles containing all the correct references one wants, but just think how many are compiled from works themselves a tissue of borrowings. Have you never wanted to slough off your skin, to change house, to change wardrobe, town or country, make a clean sweep of philosophy and religion, and settle into a new world – not necessarily a desert island? I sometimes long to write a book which would omit all the 'principles' we were taught about methods available to everyone and which are circumscribed by our habits and surroundings. I should find a publisher easily enough, though probably not any readers, but he and I would differ because he would want me to talk about béchamel sauce, mayonnaise and a *ragoût* of mutton and potatoes. The spell would be broken. But of course, he would be right. A book which recorded purely personal experiments could only interest someone already in a position to carry out those same experiments, starting with the same possibilities. I tried to read Einstein's theory explained to the layman and realized that my knowledge of mathematics which stops short at logarithms forbade my going farther than page 20 or 25. The layman for whom that work was destined was far superior to me. When Maurice Hertzog explained to me that the last peak of *la Verte* was easy to climb, it did not make it any easier for me to get to the foot of the rock-face as I could certainly never overcome the obstacles between it and the hotel.

A cook learns his trade in different ways. I myself began very young with my father and in the trade as it were. I saw and lived through the struggle between the cooking of my father and the women who went before him and worked beside him. My apprenticeship was of very short duration and I therefore specialized too soon, finding great difficulty later in becoming an all-rounder. One simply must begin at A, learning to peel potatoes and asparagus, to break an egg properly, to separate yolk and white (known in the trade as 'clarifying'), and to familiarize oneself with the many operations which become second nature.

Apprenticeship lasts three years and do not imagine that this is a moment too long. Our work is governed by the seasons and sometimes we have too little time to learn enough about a given food; shad, lamprey, ortolans, field mushrooms, so many things which we can enjoy for only a few brief days each year. At the end of the three years, the cook is called a '*petit ouvrier*' or a 'little *commis*' (which of course, has nothing to do with his size), then *commis*, first *commis*, and finally *ouvrier*. From then on he is a *chef*. A chef can work alone or helped by an apprentice or a *commis*, or he can join a *brigade* in which case he will either be a *chef de partie* or a *gros bonnet*. The *chef de partie* is the specialist in charge of a kitchen section, i.e. larder, roasts, sauces, etc. . . . The *gros bonnet* is in charge of the whole team and responsible for the entire kitchen and in some cases, buying and costing.

These are *ouvriers* in the widest sense of the word, manual workers who have acquired from different sources an education which is theoretically identical. In practice, it is not so. Regionalism affects their training. However, they have

210

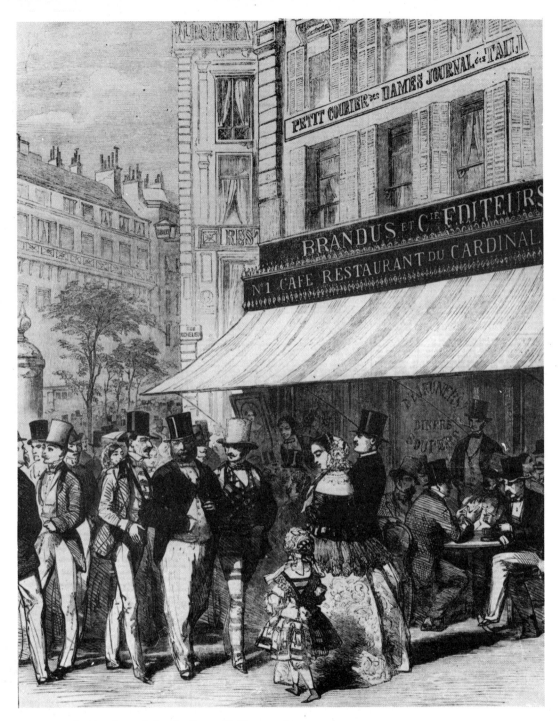

Scene in the Boulevard des Italiens, Paris, c. 1860

211

now reached a level where it is easy to adapt themselves, especially if their training has been thorough. To keep up this standard, an examination has been instituted, known as the C.A.P. Some chefs go to great trouble to train their young men to an even higher level than that required for this examination and courses in theory are also compulsory for apprentices. All this is excellent.

The cook has therefore become a master of his trade. He has had a chance either to compete for one of the prizes, such as the Prosper Montagné, or others, which are the Goncourts, Renaudots and Interalliés of gastronomy, or for the annual title of the 'best *ouvrier* in France'. Even at this stage, training is seldom bolstered by theory. The cook is a repository of the great traditions. He will only start to create when he is stimulated by a particularly successful performance or by the need to show off. This often occurs when he becomes a *patron*; then he becomes his own master and can give free rein to his imagination as he uses his talents for himself. He creates according to his temperament, his environment and his tastes. He will be influenced, first of all, by his wife (and her influence can be decisive), his staff, his suppliers, the area in which he works with its regional products, his local customers and especially the really important ones who will have a great responsibility for his creativeness. Cookery is the result of intentions, which situates creativeness in both a time and a space relationship. The painter transposes an emotion on to canvas at the very moment when he is inspired. It is not impossible for a cook to create in similar circumstances. It is more difficult, of course, but there is no doubt that the habit of serving meals at fixed times has disciplined a whole mental and physical process which takes place pretty consistently between midday and 8 p.m. One does not create every day, nor twice a day, but one has to reproduce twice a day a creation which itself may therefore be influenced by this fact alone. Hence the use of successful as an adjective in terms of cooking. One does or does not succeed with a *tournedos au poivre* or a mustard sauce. This has always worried me, and yet it is an incontrovertible fact. What has led to success or failure; the phase of the moon, the tenderness of the meat, a phone call (to which you may say there was no need to reply), a cut finger, two drops of scalding water on one's foot, bad temper, a poor appetite? Yesterday's masterpiece in which the touch of magic was manifest turns out badly today. A cook's main preoccupation from his earliest days consists of trying to eliminate the unexpected. This does not mean a lowering of standards; on the contrary. Certain great restaurateurs, by specializing, eliminate any risk by severely restricting their selection of raw materials. This method only works when they see their customers about once a year, as they usually do.

How does culinary creation take place? Often by seeking for the unexpected, or what the workman thinks is unexpected. He may think up something unexpected because he wishes to break the rules, although they were created for very good reasons. Aubergines should be fried, meat is not stuffed with fish, red meats are not served with white sauces, and so on but he will attempt a *tournedos au gratin*, a *salmis* of salmon, or aubergines *flambées*. But there is always an audience ready for the unusual, especially when an enthusiastic creator has set the scene well; though this is rare, it is the starting point of a whole process.

The seeker finds his search spell-binding and it strengthens his love for his profession even when faced with obstacles. On the whole, most culinary inventions have been the result of chance, of which the most famous examples are the soufflé potato, mayonnaise, chicken *nantua* and chicken *marengo*. There are many versions of the origin of this last recipe. The first says it occurred on 14 June 1800 on the day of the famous battle. The Bank of France financed the campaign. The French troops, commanded by Generals Lannes and Victor, were joined by an anxious Bonaparte who, in mufti and surreptitiously, came to rally his friends. In the night of 13-14, the Austrian troop movements worried the Little Corporal. He tried to localize the danger, and decided to attack at dawn in order to reduce the enemy's numerical advantage. The longest battle in history (save perhaps that of Joshua before the walls of Jericho) was about to take place. Its outcome was so confused that the Austrians believed themselves victorious and sent a messenger to Vienna to tell the Emperor, who was so angry when the news proved false that he had the messenger executed. One would not have thought the atmosphere of the battle to be particularly conducive to gastronomic research. At the usual time for a meal, the army cook wanted to serve the French Emperor who was far too busy and refused. But the pangs of hunger finally got the better of him

State banquet in the Tuileries, 1869

and he asked what there was to eat. The cook said, 'Olives and anchovies, fried eggs with tomato, and chicken stew.' 'Put it all on the same plate,' Bonaparte is alleged to have said, 'I haven't time.' And so chicken marengo was born. It is a charming and very plausible legend which has always delighted Bonapartists.

In any case, though the battle was fought at Marengo, the Piedmontese, who were the pawn in the game, took no part in it. Indeed, the Bank of France had insisted that exceptional care be taken not to offend them, but to win them over, and declared pillage punishable by death.

The second version of the legend takes this into account. To make it more credible it accredits to Napoleon a famous cook, Dunand. Advocates of this view claim that there were in fact two Dunands, and play upon a father-son duality. In fact, the Dunand who was later cook at the Imperial court was then in the service of the Prince de Condé. He later accompanied him into exile and only returned to France and the service of the Emperor in 1804. How could it have been Dunand whom the Emperor asked for his meal?

Nevertheless, according to this version, Dunand had nothing but garlic, olive oil and anchovies, and sent his orderlies out to find what delicacies they could. In the Piedmontese countryside they found what one would still find there today: chicken, eggs, tomatoes, and, in the stream meandering across the plain, crayfish. There was culinary creation in all its splendour. Dunand gently fried the chicken in olive oil with garlic, added the crushed tomato, cooked the crayfish and fried the eggs. When everything was ready, he arranged pieces of chicken on a dish, then the sauce made with the tomatoes, the fried eggs on their *croûtons*, crowned with fillets of anchovy. He surrounded the whole with the crayfish and a few olives, and there was the 'very simple dish' he constructed under fire from the Austrians. But two ingredients which are today part of the recipe were lacking: Bayonne ham and mushrooms. Apparently, Dunand always had olive oil, olives, anchovies and garlic; thus, wherever he might be, he could always prepare a meal for his master. Napoleon stuck to the eating habits he had acquired as Bonaparte.

But to continue with the recipe and the missing Bayonne ham and mushrooms so dear to purist 'white bonnets'. This is where a third version of the story comes in, and it is to my mind the most attractive. We know that the battle was very long, since it began in the middle of the night with troop movements and continued until dusk on the following day. We also know that there was doubt about the outcome as late as the middle of the afternoon when the messenger was sent to Vienna. Bonaparte, alive to the danger, ordered Desaix to carry out a particularly dangerous sortie, and although aware of the strategic risk, Desaix went through with it. He was badly wounded, and died in the arms of Bonaparte in the early hours of 15 June. Bonaparte had sacrificed his best lieutenant, his companion of the Egyptian expedition, and his friend, but he had won.

The years went by. The cynical Talleyrand was in London where Louis-Philippe had appointed him ambassador. Faithful to his own traditions, he kept open house and served France well, regardless of who ruled her. During a particularly successful dinner party, he offered his guests chicken marengo. Everyone went into ecstasies over the elegance of the dish and its exceptional qualities but one guest (perhaps with Machiavellian intentions?) asked, 'Why Marengo?' Talleyrand told him why. 'The battle of Marengo was won by sacrificing Desaix at the last moment. A meal is always a battle; as it happens I won the battle of poulet Marengo by sacrificing a tomato at the last moment.' It is certainly a curious history for a recipe – to have been born in England thirty-three years after a battle whose name it took, to commemorate a victory and its hero. After all this, it behoves me to give you *my* recipe for the dish.

> For 4 people: a 3 lb. chicken, salt, pepper, $\frac{1}{3}$ pint olive oil, 1 clove of garlic, 20 mushroom caps, 1 lemon, 4 large ripe tomatoes, 8 freshwater crayfish, 1 nut butter, 1 spoonful brandy, 4 rounds of bread, 4 eggs, 20 stoned olives (12 green and 8 black), 8 fillets of anchovy, $\frac{1}{4}$ glass dry white wine, 4 *bouquets garnis* (very small: parsley stalks and leaves, a sprig of thyme, $\frac{1}{4}$ bay leaf), cayenne pepper, 4 small slices Bayonne ham.

It is necessary to make this dish up at the last moment in some haste so it is important that all the constituents be prepared beforehand so that the operation is easy once begun. The chicken is cut up. There is the classical method which I no longer recommend; rather cut it into 12 pieces, carcass included, taking care to keep all the pieces the same size. Salt and pepper them, add a little of the olive oil and let them marinade in the kitchen (not in the refrigerator) while you prepare the other ingredients. Peel the garlic, leaving the skin on one clove out of two. Peel the mushrooms, wash them and put them in lemon juice. Peel very ripe tomatoes by dipping them for a few seconds into a large pot of boiling water, and then put them into very cold water. Take off the stalk and the skin. Cut the tomatoes in half vertically, remove pips and water, let them soak on a grid, sieve or cloth, and after draining them, chop them roughly and put on a small plate or bowl.

'Castrate' the crayfish by pulling out the central wing sheath from the tail. For this, you hold the shellfish tightly, so that it can neither bite nor move, in the left hand, while seizing the central wing sheath between the finger and thumb of the right hand, being careful to take it at the root. By a twisting movement of the right hand, break it gently. Then pull very gently so as to remove the digestive tube which comes out easily. This is an essential operation, intended to avoid bitterness. Then have ready a small saucepan in which you have put a nut of

216

butter and a dessertspoonful of oil; heat, put in the crayfish, salt, pepper, allow to colour (to 'cardinalize'), add the brandy, set it alight and cover at once. Keep it tepid without doing any more. Cut the bread about an inch thick to fit the fried eggs.

Stone the olives and blanch them. Put them in a saucepan containing two or three times their volume of cold water and bring to the boil. They do not need to reach boiling point and indeed, must not be boiled. Drain off the hot water and replace by cold. Drain. Put the anchovy fillets on a small dish well separated from each other so that you can pick them up easily at the last moment. Put the wine in a vessel. The *bouquets garnis* must be small, for given the short cooking time, a large one four times the size would be useless. You need to have at your hand salt and ground black pepper for the chicken and cayenne for the tomatoes. One must produce this dish fast because each ingredient must be very hot. There is no need to be a virtuoso if one keeps a Pyrex dish of the right size very hot in a low oven.

Put 3 generous spoonfuls of olive oil into a thick casserole, preferably of enamelled cast-iron with a tight-fitting lid, and allow to get very hot but not to smoke. Put in the pieces of chicken and brown them all over; turn the pieces over without piercing them by using a wooden spoon or spatula. When they are nicely browned add the garlic and push it under the pieces of chicken with the 4 *bouquets garnis*. Add a pinch of salt, bearing in mind that the pieces of chicken have already been salted. Cover and keep just warm. The cooking will last 20 minutes from the time when all the chicken is in the pot. While it is cooking, all the rest is prepared. The crayfish, olives and anchovy fillets are ready, so start with the *croûtons*; take a small frying pan, which you will use later, and fry the slices of bread in oil until they are golden. Put them one by one in a warmed dish so they do not get in the way of later operations. Put the ham, heated in the same pan for 2 seconds, on either side of each *croûton*.

Add some more oil to the pan, heat it gently, break in the eggs, tilting the pan slightly by leaning on the handle, and with a spatula or wooden spoon keep the egg from spreading. One can flip them over but personally, I prefer to let a little yolk show, and make the white look fluffy. It is very pretty. As soon as an egg is cooked put it on the ham which itself is on a *croûton*. Salt the white of the egg very lightly. Remember the ham is salty and the whole dish fairly highly seasoned.

The chicken will now be cooked. Remove the lid and take out the pieces of chicken. Arrange them on the dish at once. Also remove the garlic and the *bouquets garnis*. Put the pan on a very high flame and when it is hot enough, put in the mushrooms to colour, add the crushed tomato, salt and cayenne. Stir with a wooden spoon scraping the bottom of the pot well. This operation must not take more than 5 minutes. Then add the white wine without ceasing to stir, and boil fast. Add the olives and pour the sauce over the whole dish. Put 2 anchovy fillets on each egg and a crayfish either side of each *croûton* and serve. I do not remove the garlic cloves when I make this for myself but I eat only the cloves which have not been peeled.

This recipe seems to fit into the Talleyrand tradition; one knows how difficult it is to do work of such elaboration in trying circumstances.

However, if Dunand could not have been at Marengo, it was equally impossible that chicken, egg, olives, *croûton* etc., could have been served on Napoleon's 'campaign dish' which was tiny.

There is also a *pied noir* tradition. In Algeria there is a small area no larger than Marengo in the Piedmont. There they have olive oil, garlic, tomatoes; and perhaps a chef of genius or inspired cook; confess, it would be a shame.... Thus the story of chicken marengo has brought home to us the process of discovering and christening a new dish.

Naming a dish is probably less important than creating the recipe, but it gives one more ideas. It was in this way that the Marquis d'Uxelles and the Marquis de Bechameil immortalized themselves. Thank goodness the recipes dedicated to both, although they have survived time and the insults of mis-spelling, are no longer more than the pale ghosts of what they were. Today a *duxelles* is a purée of mushrooms and béchamel is a milk sauce.

Modern recipes are often very simplified. It is not the professionals who have let the side down, but the housewives who would make the noblemens' hair stand on end by their shamelessly over-familiar attitude to their favourite recipes.

A béchamel (one also says *béchamelle*) in the seventeenth century was a very complicated sauce which contained a number of vegetables and wines as well as old hens and old partridges, and after being strained several times was finished with reduced cream and cooked in the oven. Not so very long ago, a béchamel was cooked in the oven with ham, chopped onions coloured in

Alexandre Dumas' dining table: a modern reconstruction

butter and a *bouquet garni*. It was turned out and strained through a hair sieve, double cream was added and the sauce was stirred and reduced again.

Today, in most cases, one boils milk with salt and nutmeg (sometimes a sprig of thyme is added and a bay leaf) and a pinch of cayenne pepper. You make a *roux* of 2 oz. flour per pint of milk, and about 3 oz. butter. The *roux* is not allowed to colour and is cooled. The milk is poured over the *roux* through a fine sieve, the whole is well beaten, and brought to the boil. Add 1 gill thick fresh cream and allow to boil for a few seconds. Butter is then put on the surface and the whole is ready.

True, in most great French kitchens this preparation is vulgarly known as glue, and is only a primary one on which more elaborate sauces are based. It is also true that yesterday's béchamel served the same purpose. If *sauce allemande* has simply vanished from our stoves as from our vocabulary, it may be because of its name and not because of the recipe which is now called *velouté*, rather in the same way as béchamel is called glue.

To name a dish after a gastronome or a personality is a compliment or a gesture of thanks. The artist's modesty and sometimes that of the recipient, do not reveal the deeper reasons for such naming. In some cases, the name given to a dish refers to the gastronomic preferences of the person it is named after. We know that Rossini himself invented the *tournedos* which bears his name, but we don't know the origin of the word *tournedos*. We also know that he married his cook. We know that Comte Pilet-Will liked cocks' crests and kidneys, and that the *financière* garnish which resulted from this liking is served in a *vol-au-vent* whose etymological origins are unknown. Melba liked gooseberry jam, peaches and vanilla ice-cream; Escoffier's genius was to win his own battle of Marengo by adding at the last moment chopped, toasted and caramelized almonds.

Erato and Polyhymnia are frequent visitors to our stoves and our kitchens where they provide inspiration for our cooks; and if they sometimes overdo it, the intention which has always been the basis of inspired cookery must justify the deed, even if the results are not always those hoped for.

'The Poultry Vendor' by Jean Baptiste Chardin, eighteenth century

Dish of apples: faience from the Midi, mid eighteenth century

Dish of asparagus: Moustiers faience, eighteenth century

6 Aphrodisiac Cookery

In the aphrodisiac meal as we now conceive it the number of dishes should be extremely limited. If possible, one should make do with a single dish and in no circumstances should one eat one's fill. In fact, even if all goes very well, it is preferable to restore one's forces after two or three hours of an engagement. These two or three hours would not be sufficient for the digestion of a heavy meal.

In very favourable conditions, the effects of an aphrodisiac meal are almost instantaneous. Grimod de la Reynière used to say that there were only two essentials for an apartment, the kitchen and the bedroom. The Romans simplified this aphorism by combining both essentials in the triclinium. They were wise in their generation for it would be presumptuous to say at what moment the solace of one room would outweigh that of the other. The same intelligent perception led to the development (in certain restaurants) of the private dining room or *cabinet particulier* which was equipped to serve more than a single purpose. These had the added advantage of obviating any risk for those who made use of them.

In the distant past, gout used to be called the queen of diseases. At the end of the second world war, in France, the medical faculty used to complain of its almost total disappearance, and therefore of the difficulties which professors were undergoing in finding cases from which to illustrate to their pupils the clinical symptoms of this illness. Since then, the creature has taken a new lease of life. It is, alas, an unhappy fact that an aphrodisiac diet is the most heavily loaded with *urate* and that one is therefore forced to choose between rather tepid sentiments on one hand or an occasional treatment of colchicum on the other. We tend to overlook the symbolism in certain traditional acts, simply because we take them as automatic. This applies to the banquet of celebration and so, by extension, to any meal.

Clearly it is still possible to find in the ordered routine of a meal a real and unmixed pleasure. Nonetheless it is possible to suppose that a certain interest in the meal has been displaced and diluted. The deeper awareness of ritual has been forgotten and the pleasure is by that much lessened. To come back to the banquet, this ceremony has undergone alterations which have changed its character. By tradition, it used to follow a leisurely rhythm, itself dependent on a knowledge of well-defined ritual. The performance of this ritual has not been entirely lost and one finds echoes of it in certain harmonious (and ancestral) gestures the tradition of which is preserved in certain parts of our countryside, particularly in the Basque country, Provence, the Massif Central, Savoy, Brittany, Lorraine, Alsace and to some extent Flanders, Artois and the vineyard areas. In much of France, in fact, traces subsist, with wide variations probably stemming from different origins. One could imagine that by a deliberate act of will, dictated by a precise set of rules, one might attempt to perform a perfectly ordinary, symbolically empty, act in such a way that it could take on a deeper significance by which the act could be transformed and magnified. Deprived of this will, and this ritual, the banquet has replaced ceremony with vulgarity and is now stripped of the intelligence which informed its true meaning.

It is likely that, in citing these symbols, I am opening a door through which it might be as well to pass. Without entering into delicate and sometimes rather uncertain details, I should just like to mention one or two symbolic customs, such as marking loaves with the sign of the cross before baking; the saying of Grace; salad mixed by the hands of the lady of the house; the carving of meat by the head of the household; the preparation of flour by the grandmother; the thirteen puddings at Christmas-time; the three tablecloths; the prayer offered as the Christmas cake is made, and a multitude of other gestures which seem harmless and even mildly ridiculous because they lose their power at the moment when the performers lose their faith. On the other hand, certain rites are to be found intact in very primitive religions and (even more vigorously) among the non-religious. This is true of Jews, Shintoists and Buddhists on the one hand, of the Japanese and Kanakas on the other. It is clear that one cannot analyse each ritual gesture but one must grant nevertheless that they constitute a form of religion or belief and take the place of a more logical philosophy. I think that a certain proportion of religious ritual has always concerned itself with food and drink and that the banquet was an example of one of its more solemn forms.

If we turn to the practical framework of erotic cookery, while we are aware of a considerable body of literature on the subject, there is at the same time a disappointing similarity between the methods proposed. For the most part they are discredited. They were addressed to another era, and having been constantly repeated, they are of little interest to us. Today we have a food hygiene and a form of life which cannot properly be compared with those of even a few generations ago. To judge by certain manuals everything could be considered aphrodisiac: spices, fish, mushrooms, shellfish, almonds, liqueurs. In fact, our constitution is more demanding, more individual. One man's aphrodisiac can be another man's disappointment. It is probably true to say that the cook does dispose of the best and most effective means to this end. My theories, as a cook, cannot go beyond my own terms of reference. Nevertheless, before returning to the heart of the matter we should cast an eye over the conditions in which this type of meal is likely to be most successful.

The first postulate is that the two protagonists are agreed on the trial; the second, that only one has it in mind. If they are both agreed, then we have mainly to consider the man since he is generally the instigator of the idea. It is therefore more or less of an egoistic meal. The man's gastronomic concern will hardly go beyond mellowing his companion so that, assisted by a glass or two of champagne, she will not adopt any pose of false modesty! I think one might quote Grimod de la Reynière and bear his formula in mind:

> In cooking, as in love, a little help can be invaluable and if a man were always thrown back on his own resources he could not do justice to what under so many guises is offered to his senses. Stimulants, therefore, are not only useful but desirable. There are many occasions where a lover or a trencherman would be far below his best form if art did not come to the aid of nature.

If the fire of love burn bright enough, then the cook need only help the man to make full use of his talents. In the present day, when the expectation of life is so much longer, the problem is very different from what it was a hundred years ago. Provided he is not half-hearted, his intelligence can come to the aid of the seducer. Erotic cookery, for this reason, is essentially honeymoon cookery, and honeymoons may well be repeated frequently and over a long period. With few exceptions, however, it can be of no service to a long-standing love attempting, like the phoenix, to rise from its own ashes. Potiphar's wife failed for this very reason. Imagination playing the great role it does, it is most important that it be stimulated in the man. The woman in love, therefore, should only use erotic cookery to the extent that her lover desires it, and in minor ways. She will also need to be distinctly gifted if she attempts to direct the proceedings which in general (and for no very good reason) are entrusted to the male sex. The formulas and recipes to be found later on are therefore subject to adaptation in one way or another. It seems (and indeed is) logical that erotic cookery be designed for bachelors. In the same way that personal appearance and dress require particular attention before a lovers' meeting, so also should the preliminary meal be carefully planned.

Our habits of mind and our attitudes of courtesy forbid for this reason the use of garlic which is well known as an aphrodisiac, and one much appreciated by Henri IV, the *Vert Galant*. On the other hand, we are willing enough, in France, to sprinkle our hair or our manly bosom with lavender or *cuir de Russie*, depending on whether our conquest-to-be is dark or fair. We generally make the mistake of wishing to excel at the first instant, an attitude which can well prejudice everything to follow, always assuming that we wish anything to follow. If we do, why force the pace? Granted that appearances must not be overlooked, and that the cuisine of love will come to our aid by effacing our lassitude or our fatigue. Here it should be mentioned in passing that the greatest faith can be placed in the simplest recipes, but that these are by no means always the least costly! The deliberate addition of aphrodisiac concentrates to food, drink or tobacco go beyond my brief. This method only

'A Delectable Supper' by Moreau-le-Jeune, 1781

influences women and it is therefore of minor interest. It is not my intention to venture beyond the study of aphrodisiac dishes and ways of preparing them. This, of course, verges on alchemy, so that the actual method of cooking is of capital importance. We know, for instance, that in order to produce their full effect, Mexican mushrooms must be eaten raw. Those experiments with them which I have been privileged to attend were disappointing because, being prepared by a woman, the aim was dissipated in a dish which at the same time modified the flavour and the desired effect. In fact, my curiosity would have been much more titillated had I been aware of the experiment.

Mushrooms are aphrodisiac. Raw morels (which are poisonous, but not fatal) can yield remarkable results. I would not recommend their use in the raw state but, very lightly cooked and in combination with eggs, they are capable of producing solid results. The cultivated mushroom (commonly known as the *champignon de Paris*) is only any good for this purpose when eaten raw, and extremely fresh. Since freshness is all, the new process of Accelerated Freeze Drying will do great service in the future. The *cèpe* (an edible boletus) is also excellent, but cooked slowly in olive oil, as is the general practice, it loses its powers. It should be cut into thin strips and cooked quickly. Only those with firm flesh should be selected. As an accompaniment to this sort of dish one should not underestimate the value of fresh herbs. The most aphrodisiac mushroom is, of course, the truffle, which is best eaten raw and very fresh. Once truffles are cooked, and particularly in heavy wines or spirits, they will only retain part of their powers, and in this case, they should be considered in terms of a steady, long-term, diet; not as an immediate stimulant.

Another mushroom notable for its stimulant ability is the *Amanita*. It is perhaps time to record some recipes as illustrations to the foregoing remarks. All recipes are for two portions.

Croûte aux morilles

Take 2 small puff-pastry cases. In an enamelled ironware casserole dish reduce by two-thirds 8 dessertspoons of double cream to which have been added a teaspoonful of paprika and 2 pinches of Cayenne pepper.

At the same time, melt in an enamelled or earthenware pan a dessertspoonful of oil and the equivalent of butter. Heat without allowing to brown. Add the morels after washing them and drying them thoroughly. Increase the heat for not more than 3 minutes and then turn out the morels into the casserole containing the cream. Stir for a few seconds. Pour the mixture into the pastry cases. Sprinkle with a mixture of chopped yolks of 2 eggs (which have been boiled for 9 minutes) and an equal quantity of *fines herbes* consisting in this case of two-thirds chervil, one-sixth parsley, one-sixth tarragon. Serve at once.

Note: Metal is not suitable for this type of preparation, hence the need for an enamelled surface. The exceptions are gold and silver, which are admirable! For this reason the Regent and Louis XV used them in their kitchens. Today Pyrex or enamelled metal are perfectly satisfactory.

La Salade de champignons de Paris

The best mushrooms are those of a slightly golden colour and of medium size. They should be peeled and the stems should be left on. Wipe them, but only a very little, and in no circumstances wash them. Cut them into even dice, squeeze lemon juice freely over them and leave them to marinate for half an hour. During this time crush 4 leaves of basil in a mortar. If no fresh basil is available, use the equivalent in dried form. Add the same quantity of marjoram and add a little oil and nutmeg in order to blend more easily. Today the operation can be carried out even more simply in a blender. When the mixture is smooth add enough oil to ensure 2 tablespoonfuls of it. Pass the mixture through a fine sieve. Dry the mushrooms. Sprinkle lightly with salt and briskly with freshly ground black pepper. Mix well. Taste and, if necessary, add a little of the remaining lemon juice.

Note: The dish should be served in a glass or porcelain bowl for the sake of an elegant presentation, always a factor of importance. Furthermore, in serving an aphrodisiac meal there should be no helping at table. The portions should be allocated before serving and it is most important that service should not be slow. Timing is everything.

Cèpes

Select either 2 large mushrooms (edible boletus in this case) weighing between 6 and 7 oz. each) or enough small ones to give the same weight. Wipe them, *do not wash them*, cut them into strips.

In an earthenware or enamelled ironware pan warm 2 tablespoonfuls of oil, 3 oz. of butter and 12 cloves of garlic cleaned but not peeled. Warm gently with the lid on for 10 or 12 minutes without allowing the butter to brown. Then take the lid off, turn the heat full on and add the strips of mushroom. At the last moment add a little salt and a lot of freshly ground black pepper. When the mushrooms turn golden brown withdraw the pan from the fire in order to withdraw the garlic cloves.

Depending on one's companion one can then either throw the cloves away or squeeze them out of their peel and add them to the mushrooms. Break 2 duck eggs into the pan and stir them into the mixture with a wooden spoon, making sure that they do not cook too long since the eggs should add a smooth look to the dish.

Note: Black pepper and white are the same, but the latter has been freed of its black case. This case is more perfumed but less hot than its contents. The case, however, possesses essential qualities which must not be lost, though the white pepper which acts as a dilating agent is therefore favourable to the matter in hand.

Truffles

It is evident that the best way in which to employ truffles is to scrape them, wash them, soak them in Cognac and eat them raw with a little salt.

Rosy salt is especially suitable and this is made by mixing a soup spoon of fine salt with a tablespoonful of paprika and a coffeespoonful of Cayenne. Blend the mixture well. Initiates pinch this mixture (like snuff) between the thumb and index finger of the left hand and sprinkle as much as they require on the truffle (or on a peewit's egg).

All combinations of truffle with lobsters, eggs, fish, champagne or game are said to be aphrodisiac. For those who might hesitate to eat raw truffles as described above, and particularly for the gentle sex, a salad offers a more elegant method of presentation.

In a porcelain salad bowl mix oil, freshly ground black pepper, salt and a little wine vinegar. Add the hearts of 2 fine lettuces, well washed and dried between 2 cloths. Add 7 oz. of truffles sliced fine, mix and serve. Neither herbs, nor other ingredients, such as mustard or paprika, should be added.

Eggs: Eggs are a good restorative. In the circumstances which we are discussing rapid digestion is a prime consideration. The dialogue of love, even if it were not limited in time by the pace of modern life, should not be delayed too long. *Carpe diem* has never been more applicable.

The egg was considered by the Chinese to be the ideal form of food because it contained both the positive and the negative, the Yin and the Yen, the sun (yolk) and the moon (white). Cooking, however, dissipates considerably the not very aphrodisiac properties of the hen's egg. The most satisfactory egg from our point of view is that of the plover, followed by that of the peewit, the wild duck and the duck. These in turn are followed by the roes of fish, which are dealt with later.

Eggs should therefore be eaten raw. They may be swallowed whole, and if they are not too fresh – say forty-eight hours old – they are perfectly digestible. Truly new-laid eggs can adversely affect a delicate liver. The drink known as flip which consists of raw egg-yolks, sugar, some fortified wine such as port or madeira, a little additional spirit or liqueur and some added spice such as nutmeg – are typical love potions and act effectively as restoratives.

To make the best use of eggs, therefore, for aphrodisiac purposes, they should be cooked as little as possible. On the evidence available, scrambled eggs with truffles are the most satisfactory, for plain scrambled eggs and even scrambled eggs with caviar are disappointing. In any case one must not forget to ensure that the quality of the dish is also pleasant to one's palate.

I do not believe that one can replace an aphrodisiac meal by some pharmaceutical product directed to the same purpose. At a pinch, the two might possibly complement one another, but in my view the pharmacopoeia should not be devoted to these purposes.

To prepare the best scrambled eggs, be careful not to cook them too long.

For 2 people, take 7 eggs. Once cooked, in my opinion, two-thirds should be served to the man, one-third to his companion. The butter should just be melted before adding the raw sliced truffles and the eggs, which should be beaten only just enough to blend yolks and whites and which should be anything but whipped to a froth. Pour the mixture into a thick casserole dish over a moderate fire. As soon as the eggs begin to solidify, withdraw the dish from the flame because they will continue to cook from the mere heat of the casserole and they must above all be kept creamy. Season very carefully with a pinch of salt and the equivalent of Cayenne on each egg. Serve without bread and eat with a spoon.

Another excellent method is to put eggs – in their shells – into cold water and then bring the water to boiling point. The eggs should then be withdrawn from the water and broken into a warm bowl, the whites scooped out with a teaspoon and salt and pepper added, along with a truffle cut into thin strips. This dish should be eaten at once.

Plovers' eggs, ducks' eggs, peewits' eggs can all be treated in the same way or with the addition of the rosy salt described above.

Roe: All roes are not necessarily active but they are all rich in phosphates and these are much prized by the amorously inclined. They are particularly interesting from the man's standpoint. The old saw, that women enjoy the wine of Burgundy most particularly when their husbands have drunk of it, can be applied here. In a lovers' luncheon, the lion's share of caviar should go to the man despite the woman's inclination towards this delicate dish.

Caviar has the advantage of being both fresh and raw. The inhabitants of Iceland in their search for a restorative (and boredom sets in without difficulty in Iceland) have found a substitute caviar, as far as chemical properties are concerned. They allow large hunks of sharks' meat to rot in barrels which they leave open to the four winds. The climate not being favourable to corruption, they have to wait for a certain time (two or three years) before cutting the results into little half-inch cubes. These they spear with cocktail sticks, to the delight and improvement of the island's males.

To revert to our roe, however, shad, herring and cods' roe, smoked and raw, are among the most estimable for our purposes. All roe is good, save that of the roach, which is mildly poisonous, as is the roe of certain tropical fish though only during particular phases of the moon.

Allium: The onion, which has sometimes been used as a symbol of virility, and garlic are both aphrodisiac. There are today however two grave disadvantages opposed to their use in the dialogue of love. First, that not everybody can digest them readily, second their smell. Henri IV was worried by neither of them. He used to crack garlic in his teeth and his breath could fell an ox at twenty paces. Nevertheless, one cannot afford to neglect garlic and the solution is to take courses of it. When the new season's garlic appears one should bake it in the ashes and eat one's fill. One can also make good use of it during a bachelor weekend or a weekend's hunting. Garlic absorbed in this way is a delicious and nourishing food holding real promise for the future. From the standpoint of aphrodisiac cookery, it may appear that I am contradicting myself at times, but in fact, it is a question simply of preparing the ground for better harvests to follow.

Garlic on tour

Take an iron or enamelled iron casserole, invite your guests, and for each guest provide the following:

a large cup or bowl
from 3–5 cloves of garlic
an egg
a spoonful of wine vinegar
a spoonful of goosefat or lard
salt and pepper

Put some bouillon into a saucepan and heat it. Melt the fat in a casserole and throw in the garlic, peeled, crushed and chopped up. Let it brown a little and as soon as it begins to stick to the wooden spoon with which you are stirring it, add the water and the seasoning.

Let it simmer for a few minutes. Drop the egg whites into the boiling bouillon so that they are well mixed with it. In a bowl mix the yolks with the vinegar and stir into this liaison a little of the hot bouillon. Withdraw the casserole to the edge of the flame and blend the liaison into the contents. Pour over thin slices of bread and serve.

This garlic soup, known as *touring* in the south-west, as *aigo bouillado* in Provence, will seem very simple to you. Let us therefore try one or two different procedures.

First formula

Start in the way described above and wait until your bouillon has cooked for a few minutes, then set it aside. In a separate double-boiler cook the egg whites. Turn them out on to a platter and let them cool off before cutting them into little pieces. Mix the yolks with a purée of avocado pears (1 avocado to 6 people). Pass the blend through a fine sieve and make the liaison with the soup, taking the usual precaution of not letting it boil. Serve garnished with the little pieces of egg white.

Second formula

Proceed with the bouillon as described above and poach in it a handful of vermicelli per person. Beat the egg whites so that they become liquid, but no more. Place a little metal filter, of the kind used for coffee, over the boiling bouillon and pour the egg whites into it. This will cause them to sieve through into the bouillon in hair-fine threads. Make the liaison with the yolks but use coconut milk instead of vinegar.

You can compose from these variations any number of others which will be both original and good.

Avocado pears: I have written elsewhere and at some length on the subject of avocados. It is undeniable that we are dealing with a fruit whose stimulating and restorative virtues are in practice only one of several considerations. The qualities are, moreover, only in evidence at the moment of perfect ripeness. It is true to say that nature's alchemy plays a decisive part here, as with other forms of food, and that good timing is vital. Even just before or just after maturity the qualities of fruit can be modified. Without claiming that a moment here or there will throw everything away, attention must still be paid in order to achieve satisfying results. All recipes dealing with raw avocados are worth while, but avocados cooked are like overripe fruit and little can be expected from them in the aphrodisiac field. One can, however, add peeled avocados to garlic soup and, without waiting for them to cook, serve up soup and all. It is enough, in this case, just to heat them through. Perhaps the best erotic combination with this fruit is a mixed salad with shell-fish and walnuts.

Ducks' eggs with avocados

Ducks' eggs, so agreeably white and translucent, have a flavour all their own. Cook them for 12 minutes in lightly salted, gently simmering water. Drop them instantly into very cold water and shell them. Cut half the flesh of an avocado into little dice, crush the other half and mix with a pinch of curry powder, 3 pinches of celery salt and a dessertspoonful of coconut milk. Cut the whites of the eggs lengthwise down the middle so that you can extract gently the yolks which you then sieve with the crushed half of the avocado. Blend the mixture well, decorate the whites of egg with the diced avocado, place them into small crisp lettuce leaves. Decorate with flowers of avocado purée by means of an icing bag and serve at once.

Avocado beignets (*fritters*)

Cut the flesh of 1 or 2 avocados, depending on their size, into long strips about ½ in. square, taken from the widest part of the fruit. Place them in a deep plate,

234

add a little salt and pepper and moisten them with white Vermouth. Leave them to soak for an hour. Prepare a batter for the beignets with $3\frac{1}{2}$ oz. flour, a spoonful of oil, salt, nutmeg and 2 whole eggs. Thin the batter with a little tepid beer. Gently dip the pieces of avocado into the batter, not forgetting to pierce them with the tines of a fork, and deep fry them in oil at $135\,°C$. Dry the beignets in a cloth as soon as they are golden and serve piping hot.

Nettles: Why are nettles no longer eaten? Personally I first made their acquaintance in the company of a band of gypsies who also gave me hedgehog and muskrat to eat.

Young nettles, not necessarily white ones, picked in a clean place (they often grow at the roadside and are covered with dust), rinsed lightly in water with a very little vinegar and cooked in butter without more ado make an absolutely excellent dish.

It seems that the Japanese use them for erotic purposes, but through massage rather than digestion. It seems probable that nettles cooked in this way are much more potent than spinach. I should stress the point that this particularly simple form of cooking, limited as it is to the shortest possible time, is the most satisfactory.

Capers: Capers, such as we know them, bottled in vinegar and often years old, are of no assistance. The fresh flower of the caper (they are to be found almost everywhere in the south of France) is, on the contrary, very effective. The Bible records that when the caper could no longer help King David, the Shunammite woman was summoned. Capers are easy to use since one need only add them to a salad. If you preserve the berries in vinegar, you can count on them retaining some of their properties at least for a few weeks. It pays, however, not to take them too often or over too long a period.

Cloves, myrtle, nasturtiums: Myrtles used to be sacred to Venus. Cloves are unquestionably aphrodisiac. Unluckily, they need to be taken in considerable quantity and our stomachs are ill-adapted to doing so. If we ever have dashing ideas after a visit to the dentist we probably attribute them to love, quite wrongly. They are more likely to be the result of the oil of cloves used by our practitioner.

235

As for nasturtiums, they have consistently been confused with cloves and capers (French *câpre*, caper, and *capucine*, nasturtium). They are nevertheless agreeable when added to a salad, this being the only way to eat them.

Pepper: Pepper, which in my native Gascony, is known as 'parson's oats' is not the most popular of aphrodisiacs. Like other stimulants it dilates the arteries and speeds up the rhythm of the heart. The effects, although ephemeral, are none the less real. Is it necessary to explain how to use it? A curious fact is that Cayenne pimento, wrongly called pepper, is almost as effective as the real thing. Cayenne is at its most effective when the pimento is still green, probably because in that state one can consume more of it.

Nux vomica: All books on aphrodisiac cookery treat nux vomica as a panacea. They all list more or less similar prescriptions: caffein; nux vomica; syrup of bitter orange-peel; Banyuls wine.

The essence of this elixir obviously lies in the combination of caffein with nux vomica. The syrup lends an aperitif flavour and the wine forms the base for the whole.

This type of concoction is perfectly suitable for use during a lovers' meeting. A liqueur glass taken before a meal should prove an agreeable reinforcement. Taken after a meal it should serve its purpose in mid-afternoon.

Sexual organs of animals: It would seem natural to seek at the source those elements which perhaps we lack. For this reason, these appendages (politely known as external kidneys) assume considerable importance in our eyes.

The little titbits which include *animelles* have always been much appreciated by lovers, and rightly so, I must admit. Therapy by gland extract has to some extent given way to hormone therapy, the value of which was for some time debated but which has in the end been accepted as effective. One may retain certain misgivings about cooked *animelles* but one can hardly deny that they are beneficial. Certain laboratories have developed extracts from bulls' testicles whose effectiveness is unquestionable. *Garniture financière* was created

'Woman eating Oysters' by James Ensor, 1882

with the undisguised intention of reinvigorating the financier John Law; not without success. I remember asking a doctor if an infusion of lime was favourable to sleep, and that he answered that it would be if one swallowed a treeful. The part which homoeopathy plays in this matter resolves itself into the question of what effect the volume consumed has on effectiveness of results. Public opinion is unquestionably in favour of bulls rather than cocks, though the two cases are closely allied. The cock is noted for its fertility though with the apparent fault that consummation is reached as rapidly as that of the sparrow or rabbit. Transposed into our terms, however, only the initial stimulus before action is of interest since we possess the techniques through which to profit by it. In any case, important though rhythm and endurance may be, the modern pharmacopoeia has provided us with simple and effective medicaments. Everything depends on one's condition at the start and this is certainly improved by this particular diet. The easiest to find on the market are rams' and if they are not too aromatic, they are both delicious to eat and easy to digest.

Cascalopes d'animelles au soleil

> Skin them (1 per person) and cut them into *cascalopes*; that is to say, in small sections, about $\frac{1}{2}$ in. thick. Add salt, pepper and a very generous allowance of paprika. Dip them in flour and fry them in a mixture of oil and butter. When they are golden on both sides, place them in an oven-proof dish and keep them warm. Throw into a hot frying-pan a *polonaise* (1 hard-boiled egg sieved or sliced fine and mixed with *fines herbes*). Sprinkle the *polonaise* over the *cascalopes* and heat in the oven for from 5-10 minutes. Do not overcook.

Turtles and swallows' nests: Turtles are more sought after for their aphrodisiac properties than for their gastronomic merit. Obviously turtles (particularly seagoing turtles) are a quality food, but their imaginary properties weigh more in people's minds than their real quality. In Polynesia their flesh is taboo, and reserved for tribal chieftains. This is a protective measure. The chieftains are jealous of their privileges, particularly if these enable them to excel. This delicate point would not have escaped Boccaccio's attention.

'The Luncheon Party' by Nicholas Lancret, eighteenth century

Restif de la Bretonne fed his heroines on what he was pleased to call *bavaroires*, the abundance of which makes one wonder . . . '*en flots luisants jusques au bord* . . .'. He made out that nothing could put them into better form either for their first sparring partners or for those who followed after.

One eats mainly the cartilaginous part of the turtle. This is to be found directly beneath the shell and constitutes the creature's carapace. It is in this gelatinous substance that the valuable elements are to be found. Through an association of ideas and indeed, in actual fact, any substance similar in texture should yield a similar result. Fish heads in particular have always been in demand for the same purpose and mock-turtle was invented using a base of calf's head. Be it said here in passing that herbs can serve the same purpose. Everyone will choose his own blend but the basis will still consist of those plants which are reputed aphrodisiac: basil, thyme, bay leaf, marjoram, savoury.

Sturgeons' heads have a well-earned reputation but it is less well known that eel-pouts' heads will serve equally well. Unluckily, for some time past, these have been sold beheaded.

Sturgeons' heads

> The actual preparation and cooking is much simpler than making turtle soup and is more akin to the traditional fish soup. In a really big casserole or cauldron melt oil and butter and add onion, a little garlic, celery finely chopped, a sprig of thyme, 1 bay leaf, 1 part of dry white wine to 3 of water, the fishes' heads, salt and pepper. The heads should be no more than barely covered by the liquid. Bring to the boil and simmer very gently for rather longer than usual – say, three-quarters of an hour. Next dissect the head, removing all the bones. Pass the balance through a sieve or *moulinette*, so that everything else is well pulverized. Next pass the results through a fine sieve. According to your fancy add vermicelli, rice, bread, chopped hard-boiled eggs, peeled shrimps, *fines herbes*, or any combination of these, and serve. The heads of turbot and John Dory are particularly recommended.

The structure of swallows' nests contain many elements in common with turtle cartilages and the gelatinous parts of fish heads. Always very rich in easily assimilable phosphorus, fish heads offer a kind of concentrate of aphrodisiac properties. The same applies to sharks' fins.

240

Soups made with swallows' nests are based on clear chicken or beef broth. Personally I like to prepare them by cooking them in an unseasoned broth and with no lid on the pan in order to secure concentration. I have also added the nests to traditional fish soup and to the soup of fish heads described above. Everyone knows that sand martins build their nests in cliffs and that these can only be collected at a certain risk. Even so, it is not so much the difficulty experienced by the bold climbers which makes them expensive. The price is caused by insatiable demand.

Eyes: Calves' eyes, like those of many animals, are sought after for aphrodisiac purposes. They are, however, out of fashion and it is only rarely that I have cooked even calves' or pigs' eyes. Their revolting aspect can easily be disguised and presented perfectly acceptably. One only needs to stuff the eyes or to serve them under a layer of *polonaise* (see above). In general, one serves them in flat earthenware dishes (like snails) and one can then cover them with a mixture of herbs and grated cheese and cook them briskly under a grill. The recipes (only a few) given in eighteenth-century cookbooks are sufficiently detailed to be perfectly practical today. The eyes of big fish such as John Dory, haddock, etc., can be prepared in the same way. In the Orient it is customary to fry them in batter.

Celery: Surely the most popular of all? Celery *remoulade*, celery in salad, or just celery by itself with salt, all these can adorn the most modest table. Perhaps for that very reason it is not as highly thought of as it deserves to be. Before devising the recipe for *croquemcoquelle* I had been much involved in research on our subject generally. It was not to be wondered at that I was tempted to try it out. There were soups to be made with celery stock, there was celery *au gratin* with a sauce *soubise*, there were salads of celery hearts and walnuts . . . any number of delicious recipes. It might even come to mind that this type of cuisine is dietetic. There is, after all, the jockey's diet as well as the lover's, although as it happens aphrodisiac dishes have the additional advantage of being palatable.

In this chapter, however, I have left on one side all sexual stimulants which are not specifically culinary. This is true, for instance, of cantharides and of ambergris, which have been known to appear disguised by the simplest of pea soups and the least exhilarating of vegetable bouillons.

Croquemcoquelle (*for two*)

    2 pig's ears previously cooked in consommé
    3 oz. fresh celery heart
    3 oz. fresh fennel
    2 soupspoons olive oil
    1½ oz. butter
    salt, pepper and paprika
    a big frying-pan (a *coquelle* with a lid)

Melt the oil and butter in the frying-pan and heat briskly. Add the pig's ears and the chopped celery and fennel and give them a rapid turn in the pan for not more than 2 minutes. Season. Turn everything out into the *croquelle* and bring it to table.

Nuts: To conclude the meal I should suggest walnuts, almonds or nuts of some sort. In parenthesis, marzipan, which is the basic concentrate for all confections in almond paste, was considered during the Italian Renaissance to be highly effective. Marie de' Medici made great use of it and her recipe has come down to us virtually unchanged. I think that when dealing with nuts one must take care to avoid dangerous combinations. A *feuilleté* pastry, if at all heavy or undercooked, will completely undo the advantages latent in the use of almonds. This is a truth which applies generally to aphrodisiac cookery. It must be light. I have already explained that we are dealing with the problem of restoring our forces or of preparing for exertions (of the most splendid order!) and to that end we must be careful of our timing. Any undue effort of digestion can only harm the results we hope for.

A marzipan tart

Set forth three-quarters of a pound of flour and mix with it in a cool place enough white of egg to reduce it to a soft paste, as it were for a *feuilletage*.

When your paste is ready, let it lie a little while that it may become easier to handle, then you must lay it on your board and draw it as thin as you can.

Directly you have rolled out your paste you must grease with lard the bottom of a patty pan and into it you will lay one end of the paste so as to make a fold which in turn you grease with lard. Then fold your paste again and grease it,

242

Title-page from the 'Singulier Traicte', Lyon, sixteenth century

a third time and grease it, but the fourth and last fold you shall not grease with lard. When the fourth fold is made you shall set upon it as much as is fitting of the following preparation which shall be at your hand as you prepare your tart.

In a cauldron set a *chopine*★ of cream, very fresh and sweet and not whipped. Add to it 4 yolks of egg, a little pinch of salt and 2 pinches of flour. Stir all these together and place them on your stove for about half an hour until all becomes thick, when it is ready.

★About a pint.

When your mixture is cooked you shall pour it into a bowl and when it is tepid add a quarter of a pound of pistachios peeled like almonds in hot water, then well beaten with a pestle and mortar as if for preparing macaroons; add at the same time 6 oz. powdered sugar, a pinch of cinnamon, a slice of candied lemon peel chopped small, 20 or so pine kernels and a good sprinkling of Corinth raisins. You may also add at this time a little ambergris and musk dissolved in half a spoonful of rose water or orange water and a piece of beef marrow half the size of an egg. Blend them all and cover the tart.

When the tart is sufficiently covered with this mixture, fold the remaining pastry four more times, greasing each time, to make the crust. Then go round the tart, pressing down the pastry at the edges with the thumb so as to make all fast and well-knit. You may also decorate the edges of the tart. You must indent the top two layers of paste with a knife taking care that it does not touch the two lower layers of the crust, lest the mixture escape. Brush the top of the tart with yolk of egg, and place in a gentle oven.

It needs about an hour to bake this piece which when ready is about six inches deep. When it is withdrawn from the oven, powder it with sugar and sprinkle on a few drops of rose water or orange water, then replace in the mouth of the oven to glaze it. This takes a quarter of an hour: and when it is ready, serve it forth at table.

In conclusion I should say that erotic cookery is not only destined to a perfect consummation, but that at the same time, it must taste perfect. A happy frame of mind is essential to certain aspects of life and there is no one so happy as the skilful gastronome!

7 Restaurants, Cookery Books, and Recipes of the Past

Restaurants

The restaurant as we know it is as old as the Palais Royal. One can indeed find earlier traces, but these are so vague that we can disregard them. To begin with, one must realize that before the reign of Louis XV, one could eat and sleep in the inns which provided lodging for man and beast, but this was nothing like what we know today. It would be rather like talking about Procope's coffee-and-ice-cream shop which drifted quite naturally towards the café, the ice-cream parlour and our familiar modern notion of a restaurant.

I do not say therefore that the first restaurant was one of those in the Palais Royal, but that a new industry developed at that time. One swallow does not make a summer, even if, as the story goes, it is painted by Carle Vernet. Apparently, one of the ceiling mirrors of the *Café de Foy* was damaged and Carle Vernet, then a child, painted a swallow over the disfigured patch – a swallow which has been preserved to this day. Let us, therefore, walk round the Palais Royal as it used to be.

Galerie de Montpensier: Nos. 7, 8, 9, 10, 11 and 12. The *Café Glacier Corazza* was on the ground floor. Created in 1787, it soon became the headquarters of the Jacobins; Chabot and Collot d'Herbois made it the ante-room of their club. Barras tells us that the 'crafty little Corsican would speechify at the *Café Corazza* and manage to forget the bill for the refreshments necessitated by the heat of conversation'. The author of those lines, Talma, Merlin de Thionville and, as we have just seen, Bonaparte, were regulars there and it later became a restaurant run by Douix, who had been Charles X's majordomo. In 1834, André Montemont revived the old *Société du Caveau* which was there until 1875.

The first floors of Nos. 9, 11 and 12 were high-class gaming rooms. No. 9 which, with No. 113, were the most famous, was the setting for a number of unlucky gamblers' suicides. Above was a ballroom, known as the 'bottom-pincher' which stayed open until 6 a.m. The *Corazza* existed until 1914.

No. 18. The *Café du Lycée des Arts* occupied the first floor during the First Republic. Chamfort apparently lived in the building before his appointment by the Roland Ministry as Keeper of the nearby Bibliothèque Nationale. When threatened with arrest during the Terror, Chamfort cut his throat on 13 April 1794.

No. 28. *Café du Phénix* in 1852.

No. 36. *Café des Mille Colonnes* (thirty columns were reflected in its mirrors). The founder's wife, Madame Romain, nicknamed *La Belle Limonadière* was indeed the most beautiful woman in Paris and crowds of her adorers were responsible for the finest hours of the establishment. Among these was Sir Walter Scott. Later, the lady, no doubt to expiate sins she probably never committed, became a nun. After the Hundred Days, the *Mille Colonnes* became a royalist rendezvous, then a gaming house, and finally, in 1850, the *Café Guillaumat*.

No. 50. *Café Hollandais* until 1850.

Nos. 57, 58, 59 and 60. The *Café de Foy* which opened in or about 1725 at what is now 46 Rue Richelieu was owned by an officer who gave it his name. His son-in-law, Jousserand, succeeded him and his son removed the café to the arcades of the Palais Royal in 1784, when the buildings put up by Philippe d'Orléans separated the Rue de Richelieu from the gardens.

The *Café de Foy* which then occupied seven arcades for which 500,000 *livres* were paid, could serve drinks, ices and lemonade in the gardens without, however, being allowed to set up tables there. Everything was served on chairs. When the rule was less strictly enforced, the café became the meeting-place of ladies of quality, then of the Jacobins and the Muscadins who took it over in turns, being careful each time to purify it by burning juniper. Under

Inside a café in the Galerie du Palais Royal, early nineteenth century

the Empire, it became a rendezvous for actors, theatre managers, literary men and politicians. It is noteworthy that Camille Desmoulins came out of the *Café de Foy* on 13 July 1789 to harangue the people of Paris a few steps away in the gardens. Put up for sale in 1836, the *Café de Foy* found no takers.

Nos. 66, 67. *Café de l'Europe* under the Directory, and *Café du Périgord* under the Restoration.

Galerie de Beaujolais: Nos. 79 to 82. Initially known as the *Café de Chartres,*

247

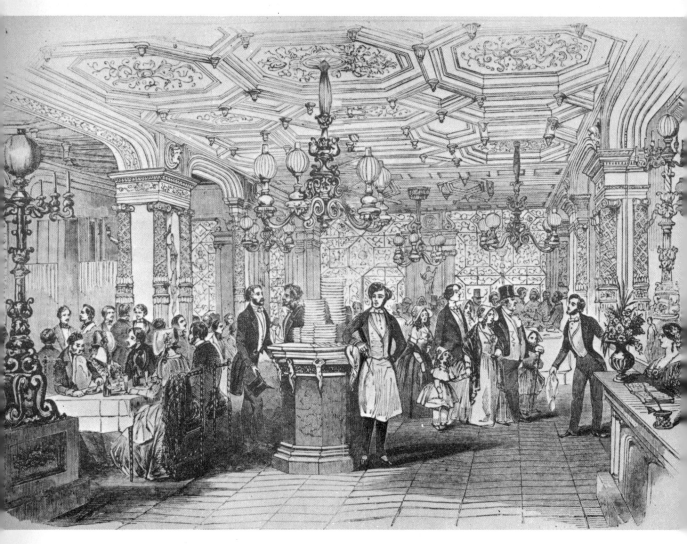

Parisian café, 1846

and a royalist headquarters, this establishment owned by the elder Véfour was known as the *Grand Véfour* and dated from 1740. It was frequented by Murat, the explorer Humboldt (whose menu was invariably vermicelli, breast of mutton and beans), Rostopchine (Governor of Moscow at the time of the Russian Campaign of tragic memory, and who was believed to have himself set fire to Moscow when the French arrived), the Duc de Berry, Lamartine, Thiers, Sainte-Beuve (who gave Victor Hugo dinner there on the

Café Turc, Paris, 1829

first night of *Hernani*), MacMahon, Pelissier, Lamoricière, Canrobert, the Duc d'Orléans, the Prince de Joinville, and the Duc d'Aumale.

On the first floor, from 1 October 1790, the actress La Montansier had her flat which connected directly with her theatre. There on one occasion she entertained together la Dugazon and Barras, Hébert and the Duc de Lauzun, Robespierre and Mademoiselle Maillard, Danton, Marat and the Duc d'Orléans. Camille Desmoulins, Joseph Chénier, Tallien, Fabré d'Eglantine,

Café Frascati, Paris, 1807

Barbaroux, Couthon and Bonaparte were also among her regular guests. She died there in 1820 at the age of ninety. Barras had lived on the second floor; a corkscrew staircase connected his flat and hers.

Nos. 83 to 86. The *Restaurant Véry* opposite the *Terrace des Feuillants* of the Tuileries Gardens. Under Duroc's protection, Véry set up in the Palais Royal in 1808 and was the first great restaurant with set prices. It was in this establishment that a waiter brought a chamber-pot to a Prussian officer who asked for coffee 'served in a cup no Frenchman had drunk from'. The *Restaurant Véry* was taken over in 1859 and became part of the *Grand Véfour*.

Little '*père*' Fragonard lived in the house and died there aged seventy-four on 22 August 1806 while eating an ice.

No. 88. The *Restaurant des Trois Frères Provençaux* which moved there in 1766 from the Rue Helvetius (today Rue Sainte Anne). The founders were Barthelémy, known as Trouin, Maneille and Simon, who were neither brothers nor Provençaux, but Marseillais who had married three sisters. Maneille managed the restaurant, and the other two stayed on as the Prince Conti's cooks until his exile. Bonaparte used to dine there which is perhaps why Blucher made it his favourite restaurant. The Provençaux sold out in 1836 to the Bellenger brothers who failed and left it to Collot. The actors of the Comédie Française celebrated Molière's birthday there every year on 15 January. Collot sold out to Duré who was succeeded by Dugléré, then by

Les Trois Frères Provençaux, Paris, 1842

Café des Aveugles, Paris, 1800

Hurel who killed himself on the premises when he went bankrupt, and finally
Goyard towards 1867. The restaurant only lasted ten years more.

Nos. 89 to 92. The old *Café du Caveau* (or *du Perron*) where the owner, the
cordial-maker Cusenier, was allowed to set up the little cannon of the Palais
Royal until it was returned to its old site in 1799. This café was the rendezvous
of the *Piccinistes* and the *Glückistes*. Since 1774 Glück had reigned over the
Opéra; Queen Marie-Antoinette whose singing teacher he had been, supported him against the Italian Piccini. The court and the town were divided
into two musical factions, and it was at the *Café du Caveau* that their partisans
waged verbal battle.

In 1797 a subscription was taken up to present a medal to Montgolfier. Cambacérès arranged for the proprietor to be allowed to erect in the gardens of the Palais, in front of the café arcades, instead of marquees, a half-moon shaped pavilion, a sort of little temple with columns which was baptised *La Rotonde*. Built by Babert, rebuilt by Chabrol, the little temple finally vanished in 1885. Boieldieu and Mehul, Talma and André Chénier, David and La Montansier, Hébert, were all faithful regulars at the *Caveau*.

Below, with an entrance on to the Rue de Beaujolais, was the *Caveau du Sauvage* where libertine customers watched shows that would make a sailor blush. The part of the Savage, they said, was played by Robespierre's former coachman.

Nos. 100 and 102. The old *Café Lemblin*, founded in 1805 and beloved of the imperialists and the half-pay men during the Restoration. It was frequented by the philosopher Ballanche, the composer Boieldieu, Brillat-Savarin, General Cambronne, Colonel Dulac, General Fournier and others. The Lemblin closed in 1870.

No. 103. In the basement and running under the *Café Lemblin* was the *Café des Aveugles*, launched during the Revolution and at first frequented by the *sans-culottes*. It was probably this café which bore the inscription: 'Here we are proud to call ourselves "citizen", we call each other *tu*, and we smoke.' Divided into twenty little decorated cellars, it was frequented by very mixed company and included the obliging of both sexes. The orchestra of four players was blind; they had been trained at the *Quinze-Vingte* and played the violin, the clarinet, the flute and the bass. One woman simply blew into the French horn. The blindness of the musicians was an advantage as they could not witness the goings-on on these premises forbidden to 'under-eighties', a peculiar mixture of the curious, prostitutes, pimps and provincials. The *Café des Aveugles* closed its doors in 1867.

No. 104. The former shop of Corcelet before its transfer to the Avenue de l'Opéra, and then the *Restaurant Philippe* in 1910.

Galerie de Valois: Nos. 106 to 112. *Restaurant du Petit Véfour* over which were gaming rooms where the favourite games were *biribi, trente et quarante* and roulette. In 1867 it was run by Guibert who refused to do wedding-parties.

No. 113. In the basement, the *Café Février* which opened there in 1784 and

Parisian café, 1886

where the guardsman Paris killed a member of the Convention called Le
Pelletier de St Fargeau the day before Louis XVI's execution. The *Café Borel*
replaced it. Borel, the owner, used to astonish his customers by his talents as
a ventriloquist. The rooms above were the most famous gaming rooms of all
the Palais Royal, with eight rooms for *trente et quarante* and six roulette tables

The Palais Royal, Paris

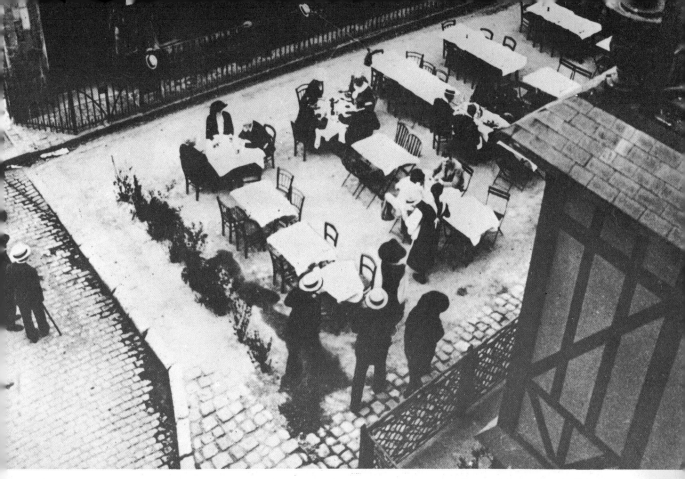

Restaurant du Coucou, Montmartre, early twentieth century

open from 2 p.m. until dawn. One night Blucher lost a fortune there at roulette – a fitting punishment for rushing to Wellington's aid at Waterloo.

> This den has three doors:
> Hope, Madness and Death.
> Go in through the first,
> Come out through the others.

No. 121. The *Café Méchanique* opened there in 1785. No waiters were seen; but food ordered by placing a message in the hollowed leg of the table was served by a lift which rose in the middle of it. This café enjoyed great success,

Sèvres dinner service, c. 1760

Smoking room or Wintergarden, Hotel du Palais, late nineteenth century

and those who could not afford to come in would stand for hours outside gazing through the windows at the food going up and down. However, this ingenious device did not prevent the bankruptcy of the owner during the Revolution.

No. 156. The site of the *Café de Valois* which, like the *Mille Colonnes* and the *Grand Véfour*, had the custom of the Household Guards and the former *émigrés*. It closed in 1841.

Above it was the *Restaurant de Beauvilliers*; the owner was a former major-domo of the Comte de Provence and opened there in 1782. For fifteen years it was the most famous of Paris restaurants. Towards the end of his life, Beauvilliers published a book on the art of cooking in *L'Art du Cuisinier (1814)*.

The question of restaurant prices has prompted many comparative studies and attempts at reasonable assessment. In fact, if we take the bill of fare at a Palais Royal restaurant, any one of them, between the end of the eighteenth

Menu of the Café de l'Europe, Paris, eighteenth century

HYVER, S.ᵉᵘʳ de VEFOUR J.ᵉ, Restaurateur, CAFÉ DE L'EUROPE,

Palais-Royal, Galerie de Valois, N.ᵒˢ 108 et 109.

CARTE DES DÉJEUNERS, DINERS ET SOUPERS.
Salons et Cabinets pour les Sociétés.

POTAGES.	Fr.	Sous.
Un Potage seul.		10
A la purée aux croûtons.		12
Au riz.		10
A la Julienne.		10
Aux choux.		10
Au macaroni.		12
Consommé.	1	
Vermicelle.		10
Riz à la turque.		10
Potage au lait d'amande.	1	

HORS-D'OEUVRE.	Fr.	Sous.
Artichaut à la poivrade.		12
Beurre frais.		4
Radis et Raves.		6
Melon, la tranche.	1	8
Deux oeufs frais.		
Huîtres vertes, la douzaine.		
Huîtres fraîches, la douzaine.		18
Citron.		6
Olives de Lucques.		6
Cornichons.		
Salade d'anchois.	1	
Canapé à l'anglaise.		
Thon mariné.		
Saucisson de Troyes.		18
Saucisson de Lyon.		16
Jambon.		18
Hure de sanglier de Troyes.		18
Andouillette de Troyes, glacée.		
Andouillette farcie aux truffes.	1	
Un boudin noir.		12
Deux saucisses.		
Saucisse farcie aux truffes.		16
Deux saucisses aux choux.		16
Petit salé aux choux.		
Choucroûte garnie.		
Pied de cochon à la Sainte-Menehould.		10
Pied de cochon sauce aux cornichons.		10
Pied de cochon farci aux truffes.		
Sardines fraîches.		10
Sardines confites à l'huile.		
Hareng frais à la sauce.		
Hareng saur.		

BOEUF.	Fr.	Sous.
Boeuf choucroûte.		
Boeuf au naturel.		8
Boeuf aux choux.		10
Boeuf à la sauce aux cornichons.		12
Boeuf à la sauce tomate.		12
Bifteck à l'anglaise.		12
Bifteck aux pommes de terre.		18
Bifteck au cresson.		18
Bifteck aux cornichons.		18
Bifteck aux pois.	1	
Bifteck au beurre d'anchois.	1	
Filet sauté dans sa glace.	1	
Filet sauté aux truffes.	1	
Filet sauté au vin de Madère.	1	
Filet aux cornichons.	1	
Filet sauce piquante.	1	
Filet à la sauce tomate.		16
Filet à la gelée.	1	
Filet de chevreuil piqué.	1	
Filet sauté aux champignons.	1	
Filet sauté aux olives.	1	
Palais de boeuf à l'italienne.		18
Roulof.		
Vinaigrette.	1	

MOUTON.	Fr.	Sous.
Deux côtelettes au naturel.	1	6
Deux côtelettes panées.	1	10
Deux côtelettes à la maître-d'hôtel.		
Deux côtelettes à la minute.		
Deux côtelettes garnies de légumes.		
Une côtelette aux champignons.		
Deux côtelettes à la chicorée.		
Deux côtelettes aux haricots.		
Deux côtelettes aux épinards.		
Deux côtelettes sauce aux cornichons.		
Deux côtelettes sauce tomate.		
Une côtelette aux pois.		
Deux côtelettes à la financière.	1	
Deux idem d'agneau aux pointes d'asperg.	2	

Suite du Mouton.	Fr.	Sous.
Poitrine aux pois.		
Côtelettes d'agneau sautées.		
Poitrine de mouton aux haricots.		12
Idem sauce tomate.		12
Idem à la Sainte-Menehould.		12
Pieds de mouton à la poulette.		
Pieds de mouton à la vinaigrette.		
Deux rognons à la brochette.		
Rognons au vin de Champagne.		
Rognons au vin de Champagne et aux truf.		18
Filet mignon à la maître-d'hôtel.		
Blanquette d'agneau.		

VOLAILLE.	Fr.	Sous.
Caisse de foie de volaille.		
Atreaux de foie.	2	
Chapon au gros sel, le quart.	2	
Chapon au riz, le quart.	2	
Poulet au riz, le quart.		10
Poulet au gros sel, le quart.		16
Poulet aux champignons, le quart.		
Poulet aux truffes, le quart.		
Poulet à l'estragon, le quart.		
Poulet à la Marengo, le quart.		
Poulet aux olives, le quart.		
Fricassée de poulet.		
Fricassée de poulet à la financière.		
Blanquette de volaille.		
Croquettes de volaille.		
Friture de volaille.		
Marinade de volaille.		
Suprême de volaille.		
Filet de poulet à l'anglaise.		
Coquille de volaille.		
Galantine de volaille.	10	
Mayonnaise de volaille.		
Salade de volaille.		
Cuisse de poulet en papillote.		
Poulet à la tartare, le quart.		
Salmi de perdreau, aux truffes.		
Perdrix aux choux ou à la purée.		
Ragoût de financiere.		
Coquille de financier.		
Pigeon à la crapaudine.		
Pigeon aux petits pois.		
Aileron de dindon au jus, aux navets.		
Mauviettes au gratin.		
Capilotade de volaille.		
Pâté de foie d'oie.		
Karic à l'indienne.	2	10
Demi-Perdrix aux choux.		
Salmi de caille, aux truffes.	2	
Salmi de bécasse.		
Caille aux pois et aux laitues.		
Demi-saloi de perdreau, aux truffes.		

VEAU.	Fr.	Sous.
Côtelette en gelée.		
Oreille en marinade.		
Oreille en vinaigrette.		
Oreille aux champignons.		
Oreille frite.		
Côtelette au naturel.		18
Côtelette panée à maître-d'hôtel.		18
Côtelette en papillote.		
Côtelette au jambon.		
Côtelette sauce tomate ou à l'italienne.		
Côtelette aux petits pois.		
Côtelette de veau aux financiers.		
Fricandeau, sauce tomate.		
Fricandeau au jus.		
Fricandeau aux pois.		
Fricandeau aux haricots.		
Fricandeau à la chicorée.		
Fricandeau aux épinards.		18
Blanquette de veau aux champignons.		18
Tête de veau en vinaigrette.		
Tête de veau à l'estragon.		
Tête de veau à la sauce tomate.		
Tête de veau en tortue.		
Langue sauce piquante.		
Langue en papillote.		
Langue aux épinards.		
Cervelle frite ou à la poulette.		
Cervelle au beurre noir.		
Idem en financière.		
Coquille de cervelle.		

Suite du Veau.	Fr.	Sous.
Veau à la rémolade ou à la gelée.	1	
Ris de veau à l'oseille ou au jus.	1	
Coquille de ris de veau.		
Ris de veau aux pois.	2	
Ris de veau financière.	2	

PATISSERIES.	Fr.	Sous.
Deux petits pâtés au naturel.		8
Deux petits pâtés au jus.		18
Vol-au-vent à la financière.	1	10
Vol-au-vent de volaille.	1	10
Vol-au-vent de cervelle.	1	10
Vol-au-vent de morue.	1	10
Vol-au-vent d'anguille.	1	10
Vol-au-vent de turbot ou de saumon.	1	

POISSONS.	Fr.	Sous.
Truite.	1	10
Saumon sauce aux câpres ou à l'huile.		10
Turbot sauce aux câpres ou à la hollandaise.		10
Morue à la maître-d'hôtel.		10
Morue à la Béchamelle.		10
Morue à la provençale.		
Morue à la hollandaise.		
Raie sauce aux câpres ou au beurre noir.		
Anguille à la tartare.		
Anguille à la broche.		10
Sole frite, à l'anglaise ou au gratin.		
Filet de sole à l'anglaise.		
Filet de sole au gratin.		
Filet de sole à l'italienne.		
Merlan frit, au gratin.		
Filet de merlan au gratin.		
Eperlans frits.		
Goujons frits.		
Maquereau à la maître-d'hôtel.	2	
Idem, la moitié.		
Moules à la poulette.		
Ecrevisses.		
Homard. La moitié.	1	
Filet de sole mayonnaise.		10
Carpe frite. La moitié.		
Brochet.		

ROTS.	Fr.	Sous.
Filet de boeuf piqué.		
Poulet gras.		
Poulet gras, la moitié.	2	10
Poulet gras, le quart.		
Perdreau gris, rouge.		
Pigeon.		
Bécasse.	2	10
Bécassine.		
Grive.		
Plovier doré.		
Mauviettes.		
Caille.	2	10
Veau rôti.		
Perdreau gris truffé, rouge.		
Demi-perdreau rôti.		

ENTREMETS.	Fr.	Sous.
Concombres au jus.		
Navets au jus.		16
Coquille aux champignons.		16
Coquilles aux huîtres.		14
Macaroni.		
Truffes au vin de Champagne.		
Truffes à l'italienne.		
Coquille aux truffes.		
Petits pois au sucre ou au naturel.		
Petits pois au lard.		
Fèves.		
Asperges à la sauce ou à l'huile.		
Asperges aux petits pois.		
Artichaut à la sauce ou à l'huile.		18
Artichaut à la barigoule.		
Artichaut frit.		
Choufleurs à la sauce ou à l'huile.		
Epinards à la crème et au jus.		
Laitue au jus.		
Chicorée à la crème ou au jus.		
Oseille au jus.		
Haricots blancs à la maître-d'hôtel.		
Haricots verts à la maître-d'hôtel.		
Salsifis frits ou à la sauce.		
Cordons à la moelle, au jus.		
Croûte aux champignons.	1	
Omelette aux fines herbes.		
Omelette au jambon.		

Suite des Entremets.	Fr.	Sous.
Omelette aux rognons.	1	10
Omelette aux truffes.		
Omelette au fromage.		
Omelette aux pointes d'asperges.		
Macédoine de légumes.		
Chou de Bruxelles.		
Carottes à la flamande.		
Aubergine à la provençale.		
Oeufs brouillés aux pointes d'asperges.		
Oeufs brouillés au jus.		
Oeufs brouillés aux truffes.		
Oeufs sur le plat.		
Oeufs brouillés au naturel.		
Oeufs brouillés au fromage.		
Oeufs pochés au jus.		18
Oeufs frits.		18
Oeufs sauce tomate.		18
Oeufs à l'oseille.		
Pommes de terre frites.		
Pommes de terre à la maître-d'hôtel.		
Pommes de terre à l'huile.		
Pommes de terre à la lyonnaise.		
Salade de concombres.		
Salade.		
Ploud pudding.	1	

ENTREMETS AU SUCRE.

	Fr.	Sous.
Petit pot de crème.		6
Omelette au sucre.	1	
Omelette aux pommes.	1	10
Omelette aux confitures.		10
Omelette soufflée.		16
Idem soufflée au riz.		16
Idem soufflée aux pommes de terre.		16
Croquette de riz.	1	
Charlotte de pommes aux confitures.		
Beignets de pommes.		
Beignets de pêches.	1	
Beignets d'abricots.		
Beignets soufflés.		10
Meringue à la crème.		10
Meringue aux confitures.	1	10

DESSERT.

	Fr.	Sous.
Tourte aux pommes.		10
Cerneaux.		
Raisin de Fontainebleau.		
Poires-Médoins.		
Marrons.		
Noix.		
Pomme.		
Poire.		
Marmelade glacée au sucre.		
Pommes à la portugaise.		
Compote de poires, de cerises.		
Compote d'oranges, d'abricots.		
Pruneaux cuits au sucre.		
Cerises.		18
Fraises au sucre.		18
Groseilles au sucre.		
Groseilles de Bar.		
Gelée de groseilles.		
Gelée de pommes de Rouen.		
Gelée de coings.		
Marmelade d'abricots.		
Confitures de cerises.		
Biscuit.		6
Biscuit de Reims.		8
Macarons.		
Prunes.		
Abricots.		
Pêche au sucre.		
Figues.		
Amandes nouvelles.		
Orange au sucre.		
Salade d'oranges.		
Chinois.		
Gelée au rhum.		
Gelée au marasquin.		
Gelée d'oranges.		
Gelée au Madère.		
Gelée au kirschenwasser.		

FROMAGES.

	Fr.	Sous.
Fromage à la crème.	1	
Fromage de Gruyère ou de Hollande.		
Fromage de Brie.		
Fromage de Roquefort.		
Fromage de Neufchâtel. La moitié.		
Fromage de Chester (anglais).		
Fromage du Mont-d'Or, près Lyon.		

On trouve à toute heure POTAGE
ET RESTAURANT.

IMPRIMERIE DE GUIRAUDET, rue des Fontaines, n.ᵒ 8, à Paris.

VINS ROUGES.	fr.	s.
Mâcon.		
Bourgogne vieux.		
Coulanges.		
Beaune ordinaire.		
Beaune, première qualité.		
Thorins.		
Pomard.		
Volnay.		
Chambertin.		
Bordeaux Saint-Émilion.		
Bordeaux Château-Margaux.		
Bordeaux-Laffitte.		
Porto.		
Tavel.		
Beaunois.		
Clos-Vougeot.		
Hermitage.		
Médoc.		

VINS BLANCS.	fr.	s.
Pouilly.		10
Chablis.		
Bourgogne.		
Meursault.		
Grave.		
Sauternes.		
Hermitage.		
Champagne.		
Champagne rosé.		
Saint-Peray.		
Côte-Rôtie.		
Tisane de Champagne.		
Champagne (Aï).		
Champagne mousseux.		
Bergerac.		
Volnay mousseux.		
Vin mousseux de Glacé.		

VINS DE LIQUEUR. (La bouteille.)	fr.	s.
Vin de Madère, sec.	7	
Malaga.	6	
Alicante.	6	
Rota.	6	
Muscat de Lunel.		
Muscat de Frontignan.	6	
Xérès.		

CAFÉ ET LIMONADE.	fr.	s.
Une tasse de café à la crème.		14
Demi-tasse d'eau.		12
Une tasse de chocolat.		15
Bavaroise au chocolat.		
Bavaroise au lait et à l'eau.		
Orgeat et Limonade.		
Un verre d'eau.		
Un thé à la crème.		
Un thé complet.		

PUNCH. (Le bol.)
	fr.	s.
Au rhum.		
Au vin de Champagne.		
A l'eau-de-vie.		
Au vin.		

LIQUEURS FINES. (Le verre.)	fr.	s.
Extrait d'absynthe.		
Crème d'absynthe.		
Eau-de-vie de Cognac.		
Eau-de-vie d'Andaye.		
Eau-de-vie de Dantzick.		
Marasquin de Zara.		
Rossoli de Turin.		
Anisette de Bordeaux.		
Anisette de Hollande.		
Curaçao de Hollande.		
Rhum vieux.		
Noyau de Phalsbourg.		
Kirschenwasser.		
Huile de Kirschenwasser.		
Crème de fleur d'orange.		
Crème de framboises.		
Crème de Menthe.		
Crème de Roi.		

Suite des Liqueurs fines. (Le verre.)	fr.	s.
Pékin, liqueur du Japon.		8
Scubac de Lorraine.		
Parfait-Amour.		
Huile de girofle.		
Huile de rose.		
Huile de Vénus.		
Huile de vanille.		
Huile de cannelle.		
Eau de la Côte.		
Genièvre de Hollande.		
Ratafia de Grenoble.		
Élixir de Garus.		

FRUITS À L'EAU-DE-VIE.
	fr.	s.
Cerises.		
Une prune.		
Un abricot.		
Une pêche.		

HAMEL frères, Restaurateurs, Succrs. de Boissier et VEFOUR,

CAFÉ DE CHARTRES, Palais-Royal, Galerie du Perron, N°. 82.

CARTE DES DÉJEUNERS, DINERS ET SOUPERS.

SALONS ET CABINETS POUR LES SOCIÉTÉS.

POTAGES.

Un potage seul.
A la purée aux croûtons.
Au riz.
A la Julienne.
Aux choux.
Au macaroni.
Consommé.
Vermicelle.
Riz à la turque
Potage au lait d'amandes.

HORS-D'ŒUVRE.

Artichaut à la poivrade.
Beurre frais.
Radis et Raves.
Melon, la tranche.
Deux œufs frais.
Huîtres vertes, la douzaine.
Huîtres fraîches, la douzaine.
Huîtres d'Ostende, la douzaine.
Huîtres marinées
Citron.
Olives de Lucques.
Cornichons.
Salade d'anchois.
Canapé à l'anglaise.
Thon mariné.
Saucisson de Troyes.
Saucisson de Lyon.
Jambon de Bayonne.
Hure de sanglier de Troyes.
Andouillette de Troyes, glacée.
Andouillette farcie aux truffes.
Un boudin noir.
Deux saucisses.
Saucisse farcie aux truffes.
Deux saucisses aux choux
Petit salé aux choux.
Choux-croûte garnie.
Pied de cochon à la Sainte-Menehould.
Pied de cochon, sauce aux cornichons.
Pied de cochon farci aux truffes.
Sardines fraîches.
Sardines confites à l'huile.
Hareng frais à la sauce
Hareng saure.

BŒUF.

Bœuf au naturel.
Bœuf aux choux.
Bœuf à la sauce aux cornichons.
Bœuf à la sauce tomate.
Bifteck à l'anglaise.
Bifteck aux pommes de terre.
Bifteck au cresson.
Bifteck aux cornichons.
Bifteck aux pois.
Bifteck au beurre d'anchois.
Filet sauté dans sa glace.
Filet sauté aux truffes.
Filet sauté au vin de Madère.
Filet aux cornichons.
Filet sauce piquante.
Filet à la sauce tomate.
Filet à la gelée.
Filet de chevreuil piqué.
Filet sauté aux champignons
Rosbif. aux pommes de terre.
Vinaigrette.
Palais à la poulette ou au gratin

MOUTON.

Deux côtelettes au naturel.
Deux côtelettes panées.
Deux côtelettes à la maître-d'hôtel.
Deux côtelettes à la minute.
Deux côtelettes garnies de légumes.
Une côtelette aux champignons.
Deux côtelettes à la chicorée.
Deux côtelettes aux haricots.
Deux côtelettes aux épinards.
Deux côtelettes, sauce aux cornichons.
Deux côtelettes sauce tomate.
Une côtelette aux pois.
Deux côtelettes à la financière.
Deux côtelettes à la provençale.
Deux *idem* d'agneau aux pointes d'asperges.
Côtelettes d'agneau sautées

Suite du Mouton.

Poitrine de mouton aux haricots.
Idem sauce tomate.
Idem à la Sainte-Menehould.
Pieds de mouton à la poulette.
Pieds de mouton à la vinaigrette.
Deux rognons à la brochette.
Rognons au vin de Champagne.
Rognons au vin de Champagne et aux truffes.
Filet mignon à la maître-d'hôtel.
Poitrine d'agneau aux légumes.

VOLAILLE.

Chapon au gros sel, le quart.
Chapon au riz, le quart.
Poulet au riz, le quart.
Poulet au gros sel, le quart.
Poulet aux champignons, le quart.
Poulet aux truffes, le quart.
Poulet à l'estragon, le quart.
Poulet à la Marengo, le quart.
Fricassée de poulet. aux truffes.
Fricassée de poulet à la financière.
Blanquette de volaille. aux truffes.
Croquettes de volaille.
Fritot de volaille.
Marinade de volaille.
Suprême de volaille. aux truffes.
Filet de poulet à l'anglaise.
Capilotade de volaille.
Poulet à la tartare, le quart.
Cuisse de poulet en papillote.
Mayonnaise de volaille.
Salade de volaille.
Karis à l'indienne.
Galantine de volaille.
Aileron de dindon. fr. s. aux navets.
Coquille de volaille. aux truffes.
Coquille de financière.
Ragoût de financière.
Pigeon en compote.
Pigeon à la crapaudine.
Pigeon aux petits pois. La moitié.
Canard.
Perdrix aux choux ou purée. la moitié.
Salmi de perdreaux. aux truffes.
Demi-Perdreau en salmi. aux truffes.
Salmi de bécasse. aux truffes.
Becassine en salmi, aux truffes.
Sarcelle en salmi aux truffes.
Mauviettes au gratin.
Caisse de mauviettes.
Caille en caisse.
Pâté de foie d'oie.
Galantine de lièvre et perdreau.

VEAU.

Oreille en marinade.
Oreille en vinaigrette.
Oreille aux champignons.
Oreille farcie frite.
Côtelette au naturel.
Côtelette panée à la maître d'hôtel.
Côtelette en papillote.
Côtelette au jambon.
Côtelette sauce tomate ou à l'italienne.
Côtelette à la provençale.
Côtelette aux petits pois.
Côtelette de veau financière.
Fricandeau au jus.
Fricandeau aux pois.
Fricandeau aux haricots.
Fricandeau à la chicorée ou aux épinards.
Blanquette de veau aux champignons.
Blanquette d'agneau.
Tête de veau en vinaigrette.
Tête de veau à l'estragon.
Tête de veau à la sauce tomate.
Tête de veau en tortue.
Langue sauce piquante.
Langue en papillote.
Langue aux épinards.
Cervelle frite ou à la poulette.
Cervelle au beurre noir.
Idem en financière.
Coquille de cervelle.
Veau à la rémolade ou à la gelée.
Ris de veau à l'oseille ou au jus.
Coquille de ris de veau.
Ris de veau aux pois.
Ris de veau financière.
Ris de veau en caisse.
Poitrine à l'oseille.

PATISSERIES.

Deux petits pâtés au naturel.
Deux petits pâtés au jus.
Deux petits pâtés à la Béchamelle.
Vol-au-vent à la financière.
Vol-au-vent de volaille.
Vol-au-vent de cervelle.
Vol-au-vent de morue.
Vol-au-vent d'anguille.
Vol-au-vent de turbot ou de saumon.

POISSONS.

Truite.
Crevettes.
Saumon aux câpres, ou à l'huile, ou au gratin.
Turbot au gratin.
Turbot sauce aux câpres ou à la hollandaise.
Morue à la maître-d'hôtel.
Morue à la Béchamelle.
Morue à la provençale.
Morue à la hollandaise.
Raie sauce aux câpres ou au beurre noir.
Anguille à la tartare ou à la poulette.
Carlet frit. au gratin.
Sole frite. au gratin.
Sole en matelotte normande.
Filets de sole à l'anglaise.
Filets de sole à l'italienne ou au gratin.
Filets de sole mayonnaise.
Filets de merlan au gratin.
Merlan frit. au gratin.
Limande frite. au gratin.
Eperlans frits.
Goujons frits.
Maquereau à la maître-d'hôtel.
Idem, la moitié.
Moules à la poulette.
Carpe frite. La moitié.
Écrevisses.
Alose à l'oseille ou à la sauce.
Homard. La moitié.
Salade de homard.

ROTS.

Faisan.
Ortolan.
Poulet gras. La moitié.
Poulet gras, le quart.
Poulet truffé.
Perdreau gris truffé.
Bécasse. Bécassine.
Bécau.
Grive.
Pluvier doré.
Mauviettes.
Caille.
Canard sauvage.
Rouge de rivière.
Sarcelle.
Pigeon.
Filet de bœuf piqué.
Veau.
Agneau.

ENTREMETS.

Coquille aux champignons.
Coquille aux truffes.
Coquille aux pointes d'asperges.
Coquille aux huîtres.
Macaroni.
Truffes au vin de Champagne.
Truffes à l'italienne.
Petits pois au sucre ou au naturel.
Petits pois au lard.
Fèves.
Asperges à la sauce ou à l'huile.
Asperges aux petits pois.
Artichaut à la sauce ou à l'huile.
Artichaut à la Barigoule.
Artichaut frit.
Choufleurs à la sauce ou à l'huile au gratin.
Épinards à la crème ou au jus.
Laitues au jus.
Chicorée à la crème ou au jus.
Oseille au jus.
Haricots blancs à la maître-d'hôtel.
Haricots verts à la maître-d'hôtel.
Salsifis frits ou à la sauce.
Cardons à la moelle. au jus.
Céleri au jus.
Croûte aux champignons.
Omelette aux fines herbes.
Omelette au jambon.
Omelette aux rognons.
Omelette aux truffes.

Suite des Entremets.

Omelette au fromage.
Omelette aux pointes d'asperges.
Choux de Bruxelles.
Macédoine de légumes.
Tomates au gratin.
Artichaut d'Espagne au gratin ou à la sauce.
Aubergine.
Lentilles à la maître-d'hôtel.
Concombres à la crème ou au jus.
Œufs brouillés aux pointes d'asperges.
Œufs brouillés au naturel ou au jus.
Œufs brouillés aux truffes.
Œufs sur le plat.
Œufs brouillés au fromage.
Œufs pochés au jus.
Trois œufs frits.
Trois œufs sauce tomate.
Deux œufs à l'oseille.
Pommes de terre frites.
Pommes de terre à la maître-d'hôtel.
Pommes de terre à l'huile.
Pommes de terre à la lyonnaise.
Salade de concombre.
Salade.

ENTREMETS AU SUCRE.

Petit pot de crème, au chocolat.
Omelette au sucre.
Omelette aux pommes.
Omelette aux confitures.
Omelette soufflée.
Idem soufflée au riz.
Idem soufflée aux pommes de terre.
Croquettes de riz.
Charlotte de pommes aux confitures.
Beignets soufflés à la crème.
Beignets de pommes.
Beignets de pêches.
Beignets d'abricots.
Méringue à la crème.
Méringue aux confitures.
Plumb puding.

DESSERT.

Cerneaux.
Raisin de Fontainebleau.
Quatre-Mendians.
Marrons.
Noix.
Pomme.
Poire.
Marmelade glacée au sucre.
Pommes à la portugaise.
Compote de poires. de cerises.
Compote d'oranges. d'abricots.
Compote de pêches. de pommes.
Pruneaux cuits au sucre.
Framboises au sucre.
Cerises. Groseilles au sucre.
Fraises au sucre.
Groseilles de Bar.
Gelée de groseilles.
Gelée de pommes de Rouen.
Gelée de coings ou quartier.
Marmelade d'abricots.
Confitures de cerises.
Biscuit de Rheims.
Macarons.
Prunes.
Abricots.
Pêche au sucre.
Figues.
Amandes nouvelles.
Orange au sucre.
Salade d'oranges.
Gelée d'oranges.
Gelée aux framboises.
Gelée au rhum.
Gelée au marasquin.
Gelée au Madère.
Gelée au kirschenwaser.
Chinois.

FROMAGES.

Fromage à la crème.
Fromage de Gruyère ou de Hollande.
Fromage de Brie.
Fromage de Roquefort.
Fromage de Neufchâtel. La moitié.
Fromage de Chester anglais.
Fromage du Mont-d'Or, près Lyon.

On trouve à toute heure Potage et Restaurant.

VINS ROUGES.

	fr.	s.
Mâcon	1	10
Bourgogne, vieux	1	10
Coulanges	1	10
Beaune ordinaire	2	
Beaune, première qualité	2	10
Thorins	2	10
Pommard	3	10
Volnay	3	10
Chambertin	5	
Bordeaux ordinaire	2	
Bordeaux Saint-Émilion	3	10
Bordeaux Château-Margaux	4	
Bordeaux-Lafitte	6	
Saint-Julien	3	10
Médoc	3	10
Bordeaux-Mouton	6	
Porto	5	
Tavel	3	
Romanée	6	
Clos-Vougeot	8	
Hermitage	6	
Nuits	4	
Corton-d'Aloxe	5	

VINS BLANCS.

	fr.	s.
Chablis	2	
Pouilly	1	16
Meursault	3	
Grave	4	
Sauterne	5	10
Hermitage	6	
Champagne	6	
Champagne rosé	6	
Sait-Perray	6	
Tisane de Champagne	4	
Champagne d'Aï	7	
Demi-bouteille de Champagne	3	
Volnay mousseux, 6 f. 1/2 bout.	3	
Mont-Rachet	4	
Côte-Rôtie	6	
Porter	1	10

On fait des demi-bouteilles de toutes sortes de vins, excepté dans les cabinets.

VINS DE LIQUEURS.

(La bouteille.)

	fr.	s.
Vin de Madère, sec	7	
Malaga	6	
Alicante	6	
Rota	6	
Muscat de Lunel	5	
Muscat de Frontignan	5	
Xérès	7	
Malvoisie	7	
Le verre de chaque vin de liqueur	»	12
Ceux de Madère, Malvoisie, Xérès	»	15
Eau de Seltz, la bouteille	»	15
La demi-bouteille	»	10

CAFÉ ET LIMONADE.

	fr.	s.
Une tasse de café à la crème	»	14
Demi-tasse à l'eau	»	8
Une tasse de chocolat	»	18
Bavaroise au chocolat	»	18
Bavaroise au lait et à l'eau	»	15
Orgeat et Limonade	»	15
Un thé à l'eau	1	2
Un thé à la crème	1	6
Un thé complet	1	10

PUNCH.

(Le bol.)

Au rhum	5
Au vin de Champagne	5
A l'eau-de-vie	4
Au vin	4

LIQUEURS FINES.

(Le verre.)

	fr.	s.
Extrait d'absynthe		10
Crème d'absynthe		12
Eau-de-vie de Cognac		5
Eau-de-vie d'Andaye		8
Eau-de-vie de Dantzick		12
Marasquin de Zara		12
Rosolio de Turin		12
Anisette de Bordeaux		8
Anisette rouge des Indes		10
Anisette de Hollande		12
Curaçao de Hollande		12
Rhum vieux		10
Noyau de Phalsbourg		8
Kirschenwaser		8
Huile de kirschenwaser		12
Crème de fleur d'orange		8
Crème de framboises		8
Crème des Barbades		8
Crème de Menthe		8
Crème de la Rosière		10

Suite des Liqueurs fines.

(Le verre.)

	fr.	s.
Pékao, liqueur du Japon	1	
Scubac de Lorraine		8
Parfait-Amour		8
Vespetro		8
Huile de girofle		8
Huile de rose		8
Huile de Vénus		8
Cédrat blanc		8
Crème de cannelle		10
Eau de la Côte		10
Genièvre de Hollande		8
Ratafia de Grenoble		8
Crème de thé		12
Liqueur des Braves		10

FRUITS A L'EAU-DE-VIE.

	fr.	s.
Cerises		8
Une prune		8
Un abricot		12
Une pêche	1	»

Imprimerie de [illegible], Passage du Caire, N°. 138.

and the beginning of the nineteenth centuries, we reach the following conclusion: a meal which today costs 100 francs then cost about 20 gold francs. If we compare, we see that 20 gold francs are today worth 45 francs. Against which I set the salary of a cook: in 1790–1800 it was 30 francs a month – today it is 1,000.*

Personally I think prices at that time were distinctly higher than they are today in establishments of identical quality. Increases to date have been very slow, and have kept pace not with the general standard of living but with the stability of money.

In fact, agricultural products have had the most influence on the cost of living, along with the price of bread rather than that of wheat – bread, that eternal symbol. Christ blessed it and made a sacrament of it. Its very whiteness is more than a quality – it is an ideal. Today bread has lost some of its power of suggestion, but though somewhat neglected in favour of steak, is far from being despised. The people of Paris were ready to revolt against what they considered an undue rise in the price of daily bread – now they might be willing to do so again if steak became too expensive.

During the *belle époque* high-class restaurants had regular customers who were charged five francs a meal. Most of the clientele then consisted of regulars. I have heard a restaurateur say 'we do 100 meals a day [for regulars, by implication], plus the casuals.' At that time the price of a meal could be as much as 28 francs if one succumbed to the temptation of expensive wines such as Château Yquem (5 francs château bottled) or Château Margaux (2 francs 50 centimes château bottled). Burgundies and champagnes were relatively less expensive, but Madeira, port and Malaga were much sought after and cost up to 20 francs the half-bottle.

In the same context, the price of very ordinary meals, comparable with those served in workmen's restaurants today, were pretty close to the gold franc. At the beginning of the century my great-grandfather used to serve a 'traveller's' meal for 1 franc 80 centimes. It consisted of a soup, an hors d'oeuvre, an entrée, a sauce, a roast, a vegetable, a salad, cheese, dessert, as

*About £75.

Menu of the Café de Chartres, Paris, eighteenth century

CHAMPEAUX, Restaurateur,

Rue des Filles-St.-Thomas, N°. 13, au coin de celle Vivienne, A PARIS.

PRIX DES METS POUR UNE SEULE PERSONNE.

Les Articles non – chiffrés manquent.

POTAGES.

	liv.	s.
Riz à la purée.		6
Idem, au naturel.		6
Vermicelle au naturel ou à la purée.		6
Potage printanier.		
A la Julienne, 6 s. Aux choux.		6
A la purée, aux croûtons.		8
Consommé.		8

	liv.	s.
Bœuf au nat. 6s. id. sauce hachée.		8
id. sauce tom. 8 s. id. aux cornich.		8
Bœuf aux choux ou à la choucroûte.		8
Choucroûte garnie de saucisses.		
Une saucisse aux truffes.		
Choucroûte garnie de Jambon et saucisson.		
Petit salé aux choux. 10 A la choucroûte.		

HORS-D'ŒUVRE.

	liv.	s.
Huîtres, la douzaine. 18 Un Citron.		6
Anchois aux fines herbes.		12
Melon d'espèce 18. Beurre et radis.		
1 boudin, s. 2 saucisses naturelles.		6
Deux rognons à la brochette.		
Deux œufs frais.		6
Rognons au vin de Champagne.		
Jarret de veau au consommé.		
Andouillette de Troyes.		4
Jambon Cornichons.		
Artichaut à la poivrade.		
Pied de cochon à la Ste.-Menehould.		

ENTRÉES DE BŒUF.

	liv.	s.
Filet de bœuf à la broche.		12
Rotsbiff à l'anglaise.		12
Bifteck aux pom. de t°. ou à l'angl.		12
Idem, au beurre d'anchois.		12
Idem, sauce tomate ou aux choux.		12
Idem, aux cornich. ou au cresson.		12
Entrecôte grillée, sauce hachée.		10
Bœuf à la mode aux racines, etc.		12
Palais de bœuf farci à l'italienne.		
Langue de bœuf, sauce hachée.		
Bifteck aux truffes.		
Filet du bœuf, ou rotsbiff garni		15

ENTRÉES DE MOUTON.

	liv.	s.
Deux côtelettes grillées, panées ou au naturel, 12 s. - A la minute.		14
Une côtelette garnie Laitues.		12
Tendons de mouton aux navets ou aux choux.		10
Poitrine grillée, sauce piquante ou naturel.		8
Gigot de 7 heures dans son jus.		10
Filet en chevreuil.		
Gigot braisé aux haricots, etc.		12
Queue aux navets ou aux racines.		
Langue en papillotte ou à l'ital.		
Potrine grillée à la ciboulette.		8

ENTRÉES DE VEAU.

	liv.	s.
Ris de veau piqué au jus ou à l'oseille.	1	
Id. à la chicorée ou sauce tomate.	1	
Fricandeau au jus ou à l'oseille.		18
Idem, à la chicorée ou sauce tom.		18
Tête de veau au naturel ou frite.		18
Noix de veau à la bourgeoise.		
Oreille aux champ. 15 s. ou frite.		12
Cervelle frite 10 s. au beurre noir.		10
Idem, aux champignons.		12
Idem, à l'italienne.		12
1 Côtelette de veau panée ou grillée.		12
Idem, en papillotte ou sauce tom.		12
Langue glacée à la chicorée ou en papillotte.		12
Foie de veau à la bourgeoise.		
Idem, à la provençale.		
Blanquette de veau aux champig.		
Côtelette de porc frais sauce robert.		
Idem, sauce piquante.		
Tendon de veau garni.		12
Idem, aux champignons.		12
Pied de veau au naturel ou en marinade.		
Fraise de veau au naturel.		
Fricandeau au poin.		18

ENTRÉES DE VOLAILLE.

	liv.	s.
Galantine aux truffes.		
1 Chapon au consom. 5 l. le quart.	1	5
Idem, au riz, 6 l. Le quart.	1	10
1 Poulet au consommé, 3 l. 10 ; le quart.		18
Idem, au riz, 3 l. 10 s. - Le quart.		18
Idem, à la tratare, 3 l. 10 s. Le quart.		18
Idem, en marinade, 3 l. 10 s. le quart.		18
Fricassée de poulet, 4 l. Le quart.		
Fritot de volaille garni d'œufs.	1	4
Canard au navets, 3 l. Le quart. au poin		15
Un pigeon à la crapaudine.		
Perdrix aux choux, la moitié.		
Vol-au-vent garni.		
Civet de lièvre. Salmi de.		
Vol-au-vent de poisson.		
Blanquette de volaille.		
Un aileron de dinde aux navets.		
Demi-poulet à l'estragon.	1	10
Quart de poulet aux champ. etc. au poin		18
poulet Maringo L. Moitié	2	
pigeon au poin 1 - 16 Moitié		18

ENTRÉES DE POISSON.

	liv.	s.
Truite au bleu. ou La Sauce.		18
Saumon sauce aux câpres ou à l'huile.		
Tronçon d'anguille à la tartare ou au bleu.		
Raie aux câpres ou au beurre noir.		18
Morue à la flamande ou mait. d'hôt.		18
Une sole frite 18 au gratin	1	
Un carlet frit idem		
Une carpe frite moitié.		
Un merlan frit ou au gratin.		18
Turbot à l'huile ou sauce aux câpres.		
Moules à la poulette.		
Un grondin au beurre ou à l'huile.		
Matelotte de carpe et d'anguille.		
Cabilleau au beurre ou à l'huile.		
Eperlans frits. écrevisses.		
Goujons frits. Carpeau au bleu.		
Barbue au beurre ou à l'huile.		

ROTS.

	liv.	s.
Poularde au cresson, 6 l. Le quart.	1	10
Poulet gras au cresson, 4 l. Le quart.	1	
1 pigeon, 2 mauviettes.		
Poitrine de veau, Rogn. de veau		
Gigot. Porc frais.		
Dindonneau rôti, le quart.		
Un perdreau rouge la moitié.		
Idem gris. la moitié.		
Levraut piqué à la broche.		
Salade.		10
Demi-poulet nouveau.	1	16
poin à l'anglaise		15

ENTREMETS.

	liv.	s.
Asperges à la sauce, ou à l'huile.		
Idem en petits pois.		
Petits pois au sucre, ou au lard.		12
Haricots verts à l'anglaise		12
Idem, à la poulette.		15
Épinards au jus, Chicorée Id.m.		12
Haricots blancs à la maître-d'hôtel.		12
Truffes au vin de champagne.		
3 œufs brouillés aux truffes.		
Pommes de terre à la maître-d'hôtel.		10
Idem frites au beurre frais.		10
Cardon d'Espagne au jus.		
Céleri au jus. Choux-fleurs.		12
Macaronis, 10 s. glacés.		12
Laitues au jus 10 Navets Id.		12
Beignets de pom. Id de crême.		12
Croquette de riz. Œufs à la neige.		
Charlotte de pommes et confitures.		
Soufflé au pommes de terre.	1	4
3 Œufs brouillés au jus.		12
2 œufs en omelette ou au beurre noir.		8
Un petit pot de crême.		
Omelette soufflée.	1	4
Id. au sucre, 15 s. Id. aux confitures.		15
Salsifis frits ou à la sauce.		
3 œufs frits. Id. pochés au jus.		
Un artichaut à la sauce ou à l'huile.		15
Idem à la barigoule. 18 Idem frit.		15
Deux Œufs à l'oseille.		
Id. à la bechamel.		
omelette au jambon		12
beignets d'abricos.		12

DESSERT.

	liv.	s.
Confitures d'abricots.		15
Idem de groseille.		12
Pruneaux en compote.		
Raisin de Fontainebleau.		
Poire Pomme, abricos		6
Biscuit, 5 s. Fromage de Gruyère, etc.		4
Fromage de Roquefort.		
Mendians Marons.		
Marmelade de pommes.		
Fraises au sucre.		15
Macarons pomme cuite.		
Compotes de cerises.		12
cerise		8

VINS. / LIQUEURS.

VINS.	l.	s.	LIQUEURS.		
Sterne	3		Café, la demi-tasse.		10
Bière.		8	Eau-de-vie de Cognac.		4
Mâcon ordinaire.	1		Scubac.		
Mâcon vieux.	1	5	Kirchenwasser.		8
Chablis.	1	4	Noyau d'Halsbourg.		8
Pouilly.	2		Anisette de Bordeaux.		8
Thorins vieux.	1	10	Fleur d'orange.		8
Bourgogne.	2		Curaçao.		8
Beaune.	3		Vanille.		8
Chambertin.	3	10	Extrait d'absynthe.		8
Pomard.	3	10	Marasquin, le verre.		12
Nuits.	3		Madère sec, le verre.		12
Bordeaux.	4		Alicante, le verre.		12
Champag. mouss.	5		Malaga, le verre.		12
Id. non mouss.	5				
Mulsaut.	2	10			

De l'Impr. de VUEL, rue St.-André-des-Arcs, N°. 33.

La Taverne Pousset, Paris, late nineteenth century

much red wine as one wanted, one glass of white wine (tiny, but it was Sauternes), coffee and a liqueur (tiny, but it was Armagnac about three years old and roughly of the quality of a conventional three-star).

At the same time, a wedding meal or a banquet worked out at 5 francs and for 20 francs the whole wedding-day was catered for, consisting of three meals and including wine and service.

At the start of my career, that is to say in 1927–8, we charged 18 francs for a tourist or 'gastronomic' meal, wine included, with soup or hors d'oeuvre, a fish, an entrée, a roast with vegetables, a salad, cheese, and two sweets. In this case, the entrée was always very elegant: hot foie gras, salmis of larks, hot game

Menu of the Restaurant Champeaux, Paris

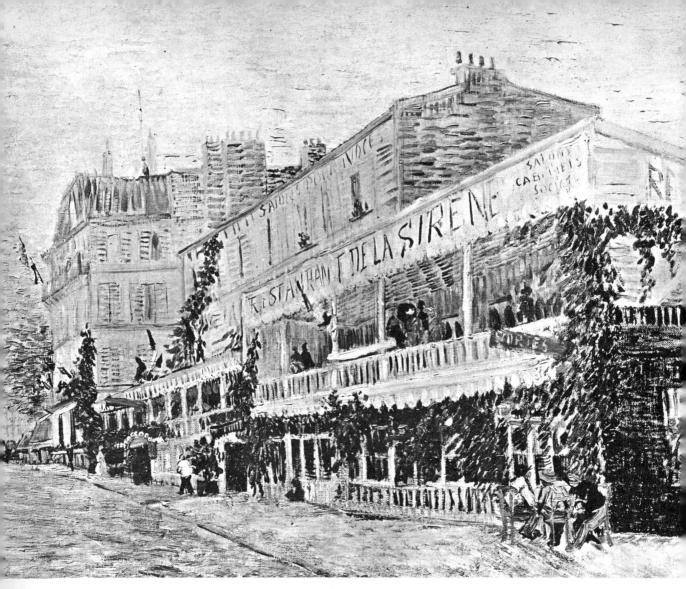

'Restaurant de la Sirène' by Vincent van Gogh, nineteenth century

pâté and so on. This did not bring us in a fortune, but then we virtually ignored general expenses.

The stability of prices in restaurants reflects more or less accurately the evolution of the standard of living. The restaurateur is not (as some of them have us think) an industrialist (the famous hotel industry) but a purveyor of services.

A luxury restaurant employs a minimum of one employee for three customers, but more frequently one for two. If a percentage were not added to the bill for service (at present it covers nearly 30 per cent of salaries) each customer would have to pay for half an employee, say on an average salary of 600 francs, from 12 to 15 francs per meal. So you see that when you are offered a meal at 25 francs all in, there is not much left over for the food and the décor.

One thing has altered immensely – the price charged. For more than a century the price was matched to the customer. There was no harm in this system; the price shown was the maximum, and a regular would obtain a substantial reduction. The fashion lasted until our time and people of my generation have known if not always practised it. Today it is more or less replaced by the credit card system which makes accounting difficulties for the restaurateur. It may have some advantages but I would not subscribe to it myself. The price of an average restaurant is already too high for our way of life. Luxury, to my mind, is now out of the question; commercial travellers do not call on their clients in Rolls Royces and no one holds it against them.

To keep pace with the uninterrupted working day and the ever-increasing traffic difficulties, more and more firms are installing their own canteens. These, which they subsidize fairly heavily, are difficult to run and time will be needed for them to break even even though they are meant to be non-profit-making. Curiously enough, some restaurants include dishes at a very low price representing often no more than the cost of the raw materials, and these may be seen as 'loss leaders', where motives other than profit operate.

Newspapers enjoy themselves publicizing a fabulous meal to be served at 1,000 francs a head; a fantastic idea. But Apicius committed suicide for fear of dying of hunger, for all he had left was the equivalent of a million of today's dollars. Everything is relative; especially in restaurant prices.

Cookery Books

I think I had better start by defining which I call the gastronomic book (or 'gastro' to use the specialist's term) and its collector. Clearly a reference on page so and so to the tenderness of steak and chips or the smell of cooking in the janitor's quarters will not qualify a book to appear on my list.

Collectors have acquired the habit of considering Brillat-Savarin's *Essai sur le duel* as a 'must' because the author wrote *The Physiology of Taste*! An essay on the softening of bones by steam signed by Denis Papin becomes 'gastro' only because the method applies to pig's trotters Sainte Ménehould!

Grimod de la Reynière's letters to Mademoiselle Feuchère (which fetched a pretty price at auction) I found interesting only because the crabbed, spidery writing evoked game and the baskets of oysters for which the *Rocher de Cancale* and Corcelet's shop were famous. The importance of each document varies with the taste of each reader. I remember working for several years on the theme of *bouillabaisse*, only to discover Mistral's manuscript one day when exploring not far from St Sulpice. There are certain financial sacrifices which really *are* necessary.

The correspondence about dining *Chez Magny* which includes the letters of Sainte-Beuve, Dumas and George Sand are of interest not only to a 'gastro' collector, but also to collectors of Romantic literature.

A manuscript can never compare in absolute value with a printed book, for many reasons, of which the most obvious is the law of supply and demand. I have collected a great number of manuscripts because I like the handwriting, not because I want them as an investment. I have equally made a great many mistakes when attempting to date manuscripts, and these have sometimes brought me to despair; it is relatively easy to attribute origins, more difficult to maintain plausibility.

My search for incunabula was for a long time a sort of pursuit of the Holy Grail, a striving for the impossible, but I own some today. Apart from the

Taillevent I prefer certain Gothic works or some from the seventeenth century. To be a 'gastro' collector involves an endless hunt for perfection and the book with a message must mean more to him than printed paper, though I dare say I may change my mind.

'Everything has been said' are the first words in *Les Caractères* by La Bruyère. He says that as men have been thinking for some seven thousand years, there is no subject which is not exhausted. And yet, no period was ever more prolific of cook-books than our own. Apart from the works of certain traditional professionals like myself, the most delightful books appear at every turn. It is likely that vocation plays a leading part in this efflorescence and that writing a cookery book is for some people a form of extroversion.

Although La Bruyère is mistaken about man having been on earth for only seven thousand years, our gastronomic documents go no farther back than that remote period. Taking the first document as a starting point, I shall lead you around my library, and, like Xavier de Maistre, tell you its story.

Dating from 3000 B.C., a Babylonian cuneiform tablet in its velvet-lined case tells us that priests at that time exchanged their prayers for the grain with which they made girdle-cakes. The Phoenicians, as we know, were already cooking *far*.

I have always thought that when deciphering hieroglyphics the Egyptologists took too perfunctory an interest in the gastronomic information they provided. There is certainly a slaughtering scene with which we are all familiar, captioned, alas, in sacred language. In the same way, the unidentified finds of Baalbek or Byblos were lumped together as ritual objects, and it was only later discovered that one of them was a device for peeling beans: a tool, it is true, tending to perpetuate the ritual of the table! The Bible is a mass of gastronomic allusions, and the ritual nature of the daily necessity of eating did not escape the scribes of antiquity. But these are only hypotheses.

The second piece in my collection is a Coptic manuscript of the fifth century A.D. I see no particular connection between these two documents. The Coptic one concerns the despatch of a barrel of wine.

In view of what we know about the Egyptians, it is clear that for many centuries both before and after Christ, eating habits remained virtually unaltered, as I mention in the chapter dealing with ancient gastronomy.

I own manuscripts from the fourteenth century onwards, that is to say, starting with contemporaries of Taillevent. I always hope to penetrate the message contained in a manuscript. For that, I think, one must have recourse to alchemical methods, by which I mean that one must return to them over and over again, to read and re-read, to count the lines and the words, and

Tiers seruice.

poulles pyions lappereaux les lesches gelee
sour ronsel de cresme lesches dorees.

Cy finist le liure de cuysine
nomme Taylleuant lequel
traicte de plusieurs choses
appartenantes a cuysine.

impregnate oneself with the rhythm as well as with the intention or, if necessary, even try to divine the intention. Some great work must surely be born in this search for contact so well defined by the word 'communion'. I have always felt a physical shock on touching a book, and if one lets me down for some reason or other, I feel a sort of pain. I have occasionally enjoyed the

269

quality of something about which I knew nothing or a book I didn't understand at all. It is probable that alchemy found a means of expression in cookery books at a period when its practice was considered reprehensible. In manuscripts and Gothic texts, there is the most exciting research to be undertaken. Some of my copies have later annotations which must have been used as a code or means of communication between lovers or conspirators. Decoding them would be extremely interesting.

But let us return to Taillevent.

His work was known from this book which first appeared at the end of the fifteenth century, but it was not then known who he was. It was Baron Jerome Pichon who discovered his identity: Taillevent was Guillaume Tirel, *queue de bouche* (head cook) to Philippe de Valois, about 1350, and later cook to Charles VI. It is more than likely that a collection of the different versions of Taillevent, from the manuscript reproduced by Baron Pichon (owned by the Vatican Library) to the Gothic editions of 1535, would be the greatest treasure of gastronomic literature. No one is agreed about the number of copies extant. All I know is that the Bibliothèque Nationale has one and I have another, both of which are unquestionably incunabula. Although these two copies resemble each other, they are not identical. Mine is the one which belonged to Baron Pichon, and which, pride of possession quite apart, is without question by far the more beautiful. Apart from its quality, it differs from that in the Bibliothèque Nationale by a letter in the colophon which appears on one copy and not on the other. A very minute difference to be sure, but sufficient in itself. The title in manuscript is different. During the same period, that is before 1500, there were several editions of Platina in Latin of which I have two different copies of fairly good quality.

Still more or less at the same period appeared the famous *Le Ménagier de Paris*. One of the two copies which I own is a tangible illustration of the fate of cookery books. It has been sadly manhandled; rough notes, dog-eared pages, clumsy drawings; it is a wonder it was not thrown on the fire. The other is as fresh as if it had just left the printers.

Although we shall mention this later on, the rarity of certain works is due

Page from the French edition of 'De Honesta Voluptate', Platina of Cremona, Lyon, 1505

ment a la toux antique ꝗ douleur du poulmon.
Et selles sont cuytes ainsi ꝗ dit de Villa noua
en eaue ꝗ mises ensemble leur humidite dessus
les escroelles qꝰt vne iflació dessoubz le mẽ
ton au pres du col les cure ꝗ guerist/ꝗ ainsi pa
reillemẽt fayt les glãdoles ꝗ viẽnẽt cõmune-
mẽt dessoubz les ayselles ꝗ a langle/et toutes
aultres tumeurs ꝗ inflaciõs en ꝗlꝗ ptie ꝗ soyt
au corps. Et pourmieulx curer ces apostemes
dessus dictes/ꝗ pricipalemẽt les faire meurer.
Il dit ꝗ lon doyt faire cuyre lesdictes figues
en eaue ꝗ en ladicte eaue lon doyt mesler vng
peu de vin aigre affin ꝗl ayde a la penetració
de la vertu de la figue/ꝗ la decoctió faicte lon
les doyt piser au mortier ꝗ mesler ensẽble vng
peu deaue ou sont este boulees/ꝗ se cataphas-
me mettre dessus lesdictes apostemes vault
beaucoup/ꝗ y est ppre grãdemẽt. Oultre ce dit
Isidore ꝗ si lon ptinue a mãger les figues seiches gardẽt les gẽs viculx de frõcier. Et dya-
scorides dit ꝗlles nourrissent moult ꝗ engrais-
sent ꝗ engendrẽt gros sang ꝗ pfortent les foy-
bles gens selõ medicine. Et selon de Villa noua cõmouẽt a luxure pource ꝗlles engẽdrẽt vẽ
tosites/sont de grãt supfluite ꝗ augmentẽt le
sperme. Les ptinuer touteffoys grãdement en
gendrẽt poulz ꝗ vermine ꝗ vẽtosites au corps.
Qui veult ꝗ les figues engẽdrẽt bon sang les
doyt mãger auec amãdes ou auec noix/ꝗ va-
lent mieulx a menger a la pmiere table ꝗ a la
secõde ne a la tierce/car lors ont elles plus de
ficace de lascher le vẽtre. Et deues sauoir com
mẽt ꝗ lon les vse/elles sont plus ꝗuenables a
nostre nature ꝗ aultre fruyt. Touteffoys les
pmieres figues fraiches ꝗ grosses sont males
ꝗ pnicieuses pour labõdãce de lumidite ꝗlles
ont que lestomach ne peut seicher aulcũemẽt.
Augustus empereur ayma les figues sur toꝰ
aultres fruitz. Et le grãt Põpee aps la victoy-
re ꝗl eut de mytridates trouua dedans le ccing
dudit mytridates vne ꝓpositió ꝗ recepte escri
pte de sa ppre main/de laquelle quãt il auoyt
prins p tout icelluy iour ne doubtoyt daulcũs
venins ne ifectiõs de lait/ꝗ la ꝓpositió ꝗ re

cepte estoyt telle. Vne noix deux figues/prici
palement seiches vingt fueilles de rue et vng
grain de sel mys ensemble ꝗ pille/ou tout ainsi
menge a iung ꝗ de matin vault merueilleuse-
ment cõtre tout venin ꝗ mauuais air: Les fi
gues fraiches cuillies entierement auec leur
pie si long ꝗ pourras ꝗ mises separees dedãs
du miel se garderõt longuement.

¶Sensuyt le second liure des põmes ꝗ diffe-
rẽces dicelles/huyle/miel/succre lacticie oeufz
chair sallee/vin aigre ꝗ aigrest.

Ceulx ꝗ ont es-
cript de la agri-
culture ont dit
larbre aisi diffe-
rer du fruytier/
cõe le fruytier se
differt des her-
bes. Je appelle
fruytier celuy ꝗ
ne croist pas a la ppre grãdeur dũg arbre/ꝗ est
forment semblable de grãdeur a plusieurs her
bes/mais il ne meurt poit ne seiche cõme lesdi
ctes herbes/ains est lõguemẽt durable/ꝗ de la
noꝰ disons frutifier naistre du fruytier. Et le
fruyt sõt raysins/les grais de ledre du sau des
põmes grãnees. Et y adioustẽt lon auec ceulx
le mourier ꝗ aultres semblables. Et entre les
baques le fruyt du lorier/oliuier/cornier/le lot
ꝗ lon dit feue de surie/le fruyt du myrtte ꝗ aul
tres dõt le Pline les enumere et racõte. A lap
pellació ꝗ nomiació des noix noz anciẽs pde
cesseurs ont pprins tout fruyt ꝗ p dehors a le
scorce dure ꝗ ont dedãs ce quest bõ pour mãger.
Et p le ptraire ont dit a lapellació des põmes
tous fruitz ꝗ ont par dehors ce quest pour men
ger ꝗ dedãs le noyau ou le dur. Dont par ceste
distinction plusieurs ont afferme les pesches
estre compinses a la nomiacion des põmes.

¶Des põmes.

Aintenant fault dire des pommes
et principalement de celles la que
lon mengeue a la premiere table

Le Quadragesimal spiri
tuel/cest assauoir la salade/les feubues frites/les
poys passez/la purree/la lamproye/le saffren/les orê
ges/la biolette de mars/les pruneaulx/les figues/
les alemādes/le miel/le pai/les eschauldez/le bin
blanc z rouge/lypoctas/les iuitez au disner/les cui/
siniers/les seruiteurs a table/les chambrieres ser/
uans de blāches nappes seruiettes potz z baissettes
les graces aps disner/le luc ou harpe/la dragee/pas
ques flories/z les grandes pasques. Puis en fin le
double des lettres du sainct esprit enuoyees aulx da
mes de Paris/beufues/ieunes religieuses/filles z
pucelles/touchāt les boyages de pasques/cest assa/
uoir sainct saulueur/argētuel/nostre dame des ber
tuz/z montmartre.

to their success with professionals and amateurs (who have been far more
numerous than one would think, and often most expert); the books have lain
around in kitchen drawers, next to rolling-pins, pastry cutters and scissors,
large and dangerous neighbours for books. And from outrage to outrage;
some pages were pulled out to be pinned over a work-table, and so on; books

272

have suffered such severe damage that many have been gradually destroyed.

This sort of destruction still goes on and we are in a position to evaluate its progress (in terms, of course, of modern volumes). At the beginning of the sixteenth century, in 1505, French editions of Apicius, and Platina of Cremona (*De Honesta Voluptate*), and *La Nef de Santé* were published. I am the proud

273

possessor of magnificent copies of these. The greatest of rarities, Pierre Pidoux, of which only one copy is known to exist, has a place of honour among my most treasured acquisitions.

There were many treatises on diet, the secrets of longevity, dietetics, and monastery regulations published at the beginning of the sixteenth century. There was also plenty of advice on manners. I have two very rare pieces, of which one is reputed to be unique, and which consists of advice from an old man to a young boy. The first I acquired from the Serrurier Collection at a sale where the city of Brussels was the under-bidder. It is a single printed page, Gothic, with a coloured woodcut initial. The moment I saw it and heard the explanation of the text in Flemish inscribed below, I thought it was a translation of the *Contenances de la Table*. After translation, I learned that these two practically contemporaneous texts on the same subject and written for the same purpose were in fact very different.

I do not want to list titles, authors and texts, nor to tell their history, though it is often fascinating; I would just like to point out those books which have a life of their own so that I may link gastronomy and the philosophy it embodies, thereby underlining its vocation as one of the humanities.

The seventeenth century is very rich in works devoted entirely or partly to good eating.

La Pierre de la Lune was one of the favourite books of Baron Pichon who, as so often, had taken a fancy to the author. It is a famous treatise written by the Duchess of Orléans' *écuyer de cuisine* who also trained pupils. Baron Pichon made pencil notes of his biographical research on the fly-leaf of his copy, which I am now lucky enough to possess.

La Varenne was probably the best-seller of his time. A book like *Le Cuisinier François* was published under several titles such as *L'Ecole des Ragoust* and *Le Chef d'Oeuvre du Cuisinier*.

What befell *Le Patissier François* is worth musing over. This little book was published either with *Le Cuisinier François* or by itself when the Elzevirs of Amsterdam printed it. We do not know how many thousand were printed, but the fact remains that recently there were only ten known to exist, the others having disappeared in pastry shops, probably covered in lard. When bibliophiles began to collect Elzevirs, competition became severe and the

❧ Le grand cui=

sinier de toute cuisine : tresvtille ⁊ prouffitable:
Contenãt la maniere dhabiller toutes viãdes
tant chair que poisson/⁊ de seruir es banquetz ⁊
festes/auec vn memoire pour faire vn escriteau
pour vn banquet. Composez par plusieurs cui-
siniers/reueu ⁊ corrige par Pierre pidoulp: ⁊ con-
tient ledict liure cinq chapitres. vii. f. ⁊ d.

A PARIS
Pour Jean bonfõs libraire demourãt en la rue
neufue nostre dame a lenseigne sainct Nicolas.

Title-page from 'Le Grand Cuisinier, c. 1530

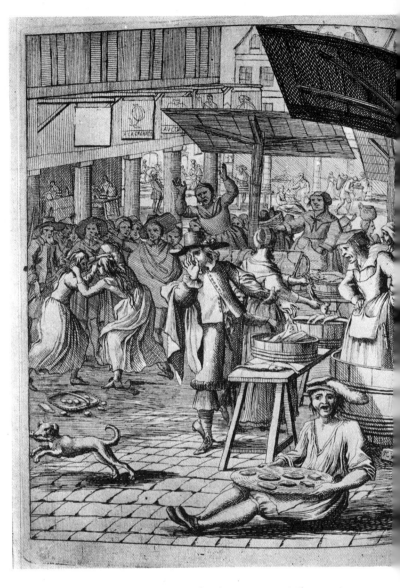

asking price soared; it then became impossible to find a copy. The prices attained since then are fabulous. I do not know how many copies are now in circulation, but the accepted figure now is eleven copies in good condition.

The same period saw the *Ecuyer Tranchant* series of which I have a large collection. They are of different types; woodcuts used as a pattern onto which the text is added by hand in ink. On the opposite page, also in manuscript, are all the instructions. Among my copies there is one said to have belonged

276

PARIS
VRLESQVE.
Par le Sieur BERTHOD.

eſt contenu les Filouteries du Pont-neuf; Les
iſcours de la Gallerie du Palais; L'entretien
le la Grande-Salle; Le deſordre des embarras
euant le Palais; Vne ruë en rumeur contre vn
omme qu'on prend pour vn autre; Le haut
tille des Secretaires de S. Innocent; L'adreſſe
les Seruantes qui ferrent laMulle; L'Inuentai-
e de la Fripperie; L'éloquence des Harange-
es de la Halle, & quantité d'autres choſes de
ette Nature.

A PARIS,
ez la veſue GVILLAVME LOYSON, au Palais, en la gallerie
des Priſonniers, au nom de IESVS.
ET
N-BAPTISTE LOYSON, au Palais, ſur le Perron Royal,
prés la porte de la grande Salle, à la Croix d'Or.
M. DC. LII.
AVEC PRIVILEGE DV ROT.

to Vatel. I have a Jacques Vontet, two Pierre Petits and other copies. It must
be remembered that the art of carving was as much for gentlemen as for
specialists and the popularity of these books is easy to understand.

Although in the seventeenth century the pleasures of Bacchus were widely
celebrated in literature (Saint Amand is the famous example) there are few
works dealing seriously with wines. It is moreover curious that wine which
played so great a part in the development of cookery, should never have

inspired authors to devote themselves to it. Nor until today do we find any reference to our desire to match certain wines with certain dishes.

Drinks were not shown on the menus, bottles did not appear upon the laid tables, and wines were poured by the servants only by request. Louis XIV in true court tradition preferred Champagne to all other wines. As long as Daquin was his medical adviser he drank nothing else, but added water to it, a widespread custom. Although Dom Pérignon was a contemporary of the *Roi Soleil* and had produced the sparkle in Champagne, the King probably never drank anything but still red wine from Ay. When Madame de Maintenon succeeded in replacing Daquin by Fagon, Louis XIV changed to Burgundy of the same colour.

The quarrel over the merits of Burgundy and Champagne at that time was as virulent as the famous quarrel between the 'ancients and the moderns', and made as much ink flow. It was not just a question of which was more delicate or the more excellent in flavour, but of which had the greatest therapeutic powers.

Another aspect of gastronomic literature in the seventeenth century is the popularity of books dealing with the art of organizing the great noble houses both in town and in the country. Audigier's *La Maison Réglée* and *Le Maistre d'Hotel* by Pierre David are good examples. The latter shows twenty-seven different ways of folding a napkin.

Among the books which belonged to Baron Pichon and which are now the pride of my library are two copies of the *Traité des Festins*. Both found their way back to Paris by the most devious and widely divergent routes since the first was purchased in San Francisco and the second in London.

It was the same with *Le Patissier François*, which I bought in Chicago. I remember a detail which will add to what I said about this exceptional book; it was fashionable in the middle òf the nineteenth century and my copy was knocked down to a specialist collector of Elzevirs for 10,000 gold francs. Incidentally, it was the first French cookery book to be published abroad.

Cookery books flourished and multiplied in the eighteenth century. They were no longer the exclusive property of noble households and some of them, like *Cuisinier Royal et Bourgeois* by Massialot became most popular.

One of the best treatises of the early part of the century is *Le Cuisinier*

Moderne by Vincent la Chapelle. This great cook worked for the Earl of Chesterfield, then for the Prince of Orange, and his books were published in London and later at the Hague, but he was French. I have two copies (each in two volumes) in French and in English.

The author of *Le Cuisinier Gascon* which came out in 1740 has remained anonymous. It is one of the most elegant treatises, dedicated to the Prince de Dombes, the great lord who, say the Goncourts, used to stir the *ragoûts* in silver saucepans with Louis XV. The *Festin Joyeux ou la Cuisine en Musique* dated 1738 is a curious book. It is dedicated to the ladies of the court and gives recipes in verses that could be sung: *Pigeonneaux à la lune, Mère Carpe à la Chambord, Poupetons d'Alouettes.*

Marin, majordomo of the famous gourmet Marshal Soubise, wrote one of the best-known books of the second half of the century, *Les Dons de Comus*, but the book which was most often reprinted at that period was *La Cuisinière Bourgeoise* by Menon, which shows how far the democratization of gastronomy had developed at the time.

Science was in the forefront: there was proliferation of works on vine-growing and wine-making. For the first time chemistry was involved. A curious *Dissertation sur les Vins* of 1772 whose author, Plaigne, had worked with wine merchants in France, England and Holland, gives numerous recipes for improving wines by chemical processes and makes no secret of the fact that adulteration of the great vintages was already common.

Until then, the majority of authors were mainly cooks, majordomos, or professionals. In the nineteenth century, amateurs began to wield their pens. The first of these was Grimod de la Reynière, that curious and baffling character; he published between 1803 and 1812 eight volumes of the *Almanach des Gourmands*. His *Manuel des Amphitryons* is a model of the genre which I should have mentioned in my description of the *Ecuyer Tranchant*, because, in a way, it stems from it. I have from his pen not only a fair number of letters, but several scraps of manuscript including an unfinished and obviously un-published short story. And as we know, it was Grimod who paved the way to success for Brillat-Savarin.

There can be no shadow of doubt that *La Physiologie du Gout ou Méditations de Gastronomie Transcendente* was the first gastronomic book to become

'Bunch of Asparagus' by Edouard Manet, nineteenth century

universally popular. The author was born in 1775 in the region of Bugey so well loved by gourmets. He was the mayor of Belley at the time of the Revolution. His book appeared in 1826 just before his death, and I own one of the rare copies he signed for his intimate friends or enemies. I am referring

280

to the Marquis de Cussy. I have the copy which Cussy corrected (saying that in doing so he was following the instructions of Brillat, who was no longer alive to protest). From 1826 on there have been many editions of the *Physiologie*, some of them very *de luxe*.

At the same time, Antonin Carême might be said to be the great figure of the early nineteenth century. He was Talleyrand's cook and was highly thought of by Napoleon (which was indeed exceptional). He later worked for the Emperor of Russia and the Baroness de Rothschild, and during his short life published a number of remarkable treatises. For many cooks he is both a model and a symbol.

Brillat-Savarin, a cultivated man, freed gastronomic literature and raised its social standing. He was followed by Charles Monselet, Alexandre Dumas, Théophile Gautier, Théodore de Banville, Curnonsky, de Pomiane, Paul Reboux, Marcel Rouff and so many others. Illustrators of the calibre of Toulouse-Lautrec, Dufy, Cocteau and Dunoyer de Segonzac have joined with them in work which so charmingly decorates cookery books from the most impressive to the humblest.

I do not want to catalogue books; only to talk of those which I hold especially dear. Books and documents lie side by side; a parchment from Louis XI's wine-butler lies beside Mme Dupin's kitchen account book. *Les Etats de la Table du Roy* or *De la Maison du Roy* are manuscripts in the form of accounts; it is rather touching to know that Marie-Antoinette's brioches were rationed.

I do not think myself exceptional, and without false modesty I cannot but believe that cooks must be interested in this type of literature, and as I quoted La Bruyère at the beginning of this chapter, so I shall quote Montaigne at the end. He mocked the Lombard cooks of the Medicis who discussed cookery as others discuss politics. Cooks, he said, who took themselves for artists! But, Michel Montaigne, they were! They said so boldly and emphatically. Just think what would have happened if Salvador Dali had been a cook?

Banquet given by Louis XIII to the Knights of the Saint Esprit, c. 1625

Recipes of the Past

Here are a few interesting and curious recipes, culled from my library.

HOT ENTRÉES

Le Pot Royal

There are some succulent dishes which have gone out of fashion and are well worth reviving. *Pot Royal* is one of them, and here is the secret as given to me by an old chef who taught me in my apprentice days.

> Line a flat oval casserole with strips of pork fat. On this place 2 carrots, 3 large onions with a clove pressed into each one, a large *bouquet garni*, also a muslin bag with 2 oz. juniper berries. On this mixed bed place 3 lb. fresh white cabbage leaves, and cover with a 2 lb. piece of cooked ham, with the fat trimmed off. Lightly brown 3 stewing partridges in the oven and place them round the ham with a small pork *cervelas*, or saveloy. Cover with 3 lb. more cabbage leaves and cover this in turn completely in goose fat or fresh lard.
>
> Add a half bottle of Champagne *brut* and fill right up to the top with clear chicken stock, very slightly salted. Seal the dish with strips of pork fat and cook for about 5 hours in a slow oven.
>
> Now take out everything from the dish. Replace the cabbage leaves on which you arrange 6 tender young partridges lightly roasted on a spit. Slice the ham and arrange it all round the birds giving the effect of a crown. Serve with a simple gravy made from the liquid in which the birds have been cooking and serve separately 6 slices of bread, fried till crisp in butter and then generously spread with cooked minced wild rabbit.

Eaten in winter, this regal dish will surpass all expectations.

To make a Pastry from Carp or other fish

> Take a fine carp or some other fat fish, and scale it, if it be scaly; and clean it. Some fish, like eel, will have to be skinned.

When the fish is cleaned, you must also take out the gills, that is to say the lungs of the fish.

When the fish is prepared, make deep cuts in the back, then lard the fish with whale fat, or shredded eel flesh, meat; or you may lard it with fat such as would be used for meat.

Do not omit to take out the roes which you will find in the belly of the fish. When your fish is entirely ready, prepare some pastry about as thick as 2 or 3 fingers: if it is a big fish make the pastry sufficiently long and wide, then place at one end of it a bed or layer of butter as long as is the fish: then dust with salt and spices, and place your fish on this bed of butter: dust it inside and out with the salt and spices and put a pat of butter inside and on the top of the fish. Add some bay leaves, lay the roes beside the fish and season them. Salt the pastry carefully, and when it is seasoned, close it up, fold back the open end or knead it up over the fish. Then brush it with a thin coating of beaten egg yolks, if it be in Lent.

Put the pastry in the oven. When it has been in the oven for about half an hour, make a small hole in the crust, then put it back until the cooking be finished.

You must allow 3 good hours to cook one of these fish pasties if it be a large fish: and when you judge it to be cooked draw it out of the oven and gently insert a little stick into the hole in the crust to see if the fish is swimming in its own liquid, with the butter sauce; for if there seems to be too little sauce as often happens, you must melt some butter and add it, by pouring with the aid of a funnel, into the pasty to augment the sauce.

The day after the pasty has been cooked, stop up the hole in the pasty with a little more pastry.

(*Le Patissier François*, 1655)

Canard à la Mantouane (Mantuan Duck)

Vergilius Coquinarius gives some details of the 'Health Diet' followed by the great poet. Among other things will be found the way Virgil's cook prepared duck. I have adapted this recipe to modern taste.

Marinate in a good quality port 24 preserved figs for 36 hours in a china dish with a close fitting lid. Then brown a *Nantais* duckling in butter and cook it in an entrée dish. After 20 minutes, baste it with the wine marinade. Repeat this at intervals, until all the wine is used. Surround the bird with the figs, and pour good veal stock over the dish. Cook in the oven for another 45 minutes, basting often.

Place the bird on a round dish surrounded by the figs. Strain the fat from the gravy and pour the rich, smooth sauce over the duck before serving.
(*L'Heptameron des Gourmets*)

Crespes (Pancakes)

Take flour and blend with eggs, using both yolks and whites. Add salt and wine and beat together for a long time. Put some lard in a little pan, or half butter and half lard, and let it simmer on the fire. Take a ladle pierced with a hole the size of your little finger, pour some of the batter in the ladle and allow it to fall evenly all over the pan. Put the pancake on a plate and sprinkle with sugar. The pan, of iron or of *arain*, should have a capacity of 3 pints. It should be as wide at the top as at the base.
(*Le Menagier de Paris*, 1540)

Cigne revestu en sa pel à toute la plume (Swan redressed in its own fully plumed skin)

Take the swan between the wings and slit down the belly: pull off the skin, with the whole neck severed as low as possible, leaving the legs on the body. Put the bird on the spit, baste and brown. When cooked, dress it again in the skin, and let the neck be stretched out or curved. The flesh should be eaten with yellow pepper.
(*Le Menagier de Paris*, 1540)

Le Grand Cuisinier gives a very much more detailed recipe for a similar preparation of swan. I think I must reproduce it here.

Take a swan, and prepare it and roast it until it is done. Then make a paste with eggs, using both yolks and white, and spread this over the said swan. As it turns on the spit, take heed that neither the wings nor the legs are broken: arrange the swan's neck as if it were swimming on the water: to keep it thus, put a skewer through the head and wings, passing right through them, another nearer the feet and three skewers to each foot to hold the web extended. When the swan is well cooked and the paste a golden colour, take out all the skewers except the one in the neck. Then make a brown dough, thick and soft and strong. Make good borders all round. Let it be two feet across and a foot and a half wide or a little less. Then cook it without boiling and paint it green like a grassy verdant meadow. Let the swan be painted with a skin of silver except for about two fingers' length of the neck, the beak and the feet. These must be gilded. Then

cover with a cover of sandalwood gilded within, and without such armorial bearing as you desire. Around the swan banners, two and a half feet long, and sandalwood pennants, with the same arms as above, and arrange all, and present it to whomsoever you will.
(*Le Grand Cuisinier*, c. 1530)

Brouet Blanc

Take capons, fowls or young chicken, well hung. Use them either whole, halved or quartered; or use veal cut in pieces, and boil them with lard either in water or in wine; when they are cooked drain them, then skin and pound them. Strain the chicken broth until it is quite clear without any dregs or solid matter, and strain it through a tammy cloth. Then take white ginger, peeled or scraped, together with Malaquetta pepper, prepared as above; strain through a fine cloth, and mix with the milk of almonds. And if this is not enough, pour in some meal or boiled rice, and give taste with grape juice and add white sugar to season the broth well. And when all is ready, sprinkle both the spice called crimson coriander and seeds of pomegranate with *dragées* and fried almonds, pricked at each end of the shell.
(*Le Menagier de Paris*, 1540)

Brouet de Canelle (Chicken cinnamon broth)

First joint your chicken or other fowl. Then boil it in water and put in some wine, and simmer; then take some ripe almonds dried and unpeeled, and cinnamon and pound them well; add chicken or beef stock and boil altogether. Then pound ginger, cloves and berries until it is well mixed.

Brouet Georgé, Brouet Houssié

Take a chicken cut into quarters, or veal, or such meat as you would cut in pieces, and boil it with lard: nearby have a pot, with pork fat in which chopped onions are frying. Also have some bread toasted on the grill, let it soak in the stock with wine, and then pound ginger, cinnamon, long peppers, saffron, cloves and berries and the liver of the bird, and pound it well so that all the moisture is taken up: dilute with grape juice and vinegar. And when the spices are taken out of the mortar, crumble and pound your bread, and take away that in which it has been moistened and strain it through a tammy cloth, so that all the liquid in which it has been soaking drains away, and put in spices and parsley stripped of its leaves if so desired, and then fry your grains or berries. The soup should be brown and soft as *soringue*.

Note: The spices must be first pounded. With soup, never run in spices first and afterwards crumble and add the bread. I personally think that wine or vinegar do not become the dish.

Note: It is named *brouet houssié* only when parsley is a part of the broth. Otherwise it is called *frangie de saffron*, so do men call it *houssié*, parsley being therein.

Brouet Rousset is made as the aforesaid *brouet georgé*, except that there is no saffron, nor wine nor vinegar, and in it will be mixed cinnamon, and onions cut in rounds.

Poulets en Chauve Souris (Chicken dressed to resemble bats)

Clean your chickens and truss them with the wings drawn up over the belly, the legs beneath. Beat the birds and break the large bones; put them in a casserole with oil and herbs; season, add a slice of lemon and grill. When they are white they will be cooked. Serve with a sauce of your own choice, or a green one. Partridges, quails, young pheasants and pigeons may be treated in a like fashion.

Nioc à l'Italienne (Gnocchi)

There are several ways in which they may be prepared, either in meat gravies, or plain. For the meat dish, put butter in the casserole, add grated cheese and the soft bread-crumbs, a little flour and whole eggs; use partridges or some other fowl, chopped beef marrow, and a little salt. The plain dish is prepared in precisely the same way, save that there is neither marrow nor meat. You may turn the dish green, if you wish, by putting spinach in it.

Put the pan on the stove with water. When the water boils, cut the *gnocchi* to the thickness of your little finger, and throw them in the water. When they are all in the pan, cover and draw it over the fire. When it is cooked and ready to serve drain, sprinkle with cheese and butter. For the meat dish, boil in the stock, and serve with soup, all well seasoned.

(*Le Cuisinier Gascon*, 1740)

Bourride Bordelaise

Prepare a light *roux*, and stir into it fresh chopped mixed herbs, fennel, bay leaves, thyme, parsley, cress and lemon rind, all finely chopped. Put this into a large pan and add 5 lb. of a mixture of sea fish, all cut in pieces, but do not omit to put in their heads and tails. All or some of these are suitable: conger eel, hake, whiting, red mullet, plaice or flounder, bream, angler fish, red gurnet, salt dried hake and *pelouse*. Season with salt, saffron, black and white pepper corns, cloves and Cayenne pepper. Cover with water and boil until the fish is cooked. When the stock is at boiling point, slip in those fillets of fish which will eventually be taken out and eaten. Turbot, sole, brill, sea-bass, and cod are all suitable.

While the *bourride* is cooking, make the following sauce. Crush 5 or 6 cloves of garlic in a mortar, add salt, the yolk of an egg well beaten, and then beat in drop by drop ½ pint of oil, until it has all been absorbed and you have a thick mayonnaise. Stir this into the stock, strain it, arrange the fillets of fish in a tureen on top of toasted *croûtons* and pour over it the whole hot sauce. Serve it very hot indeed. This should be eaten together with the piece of meat from a *pot-au-feu*. (Recipe from H. de Toulouse-Lautrec, Arcachon, *La Cuisine de Monsieur Momo Célibataire*, 1930)

Rissolles à jour de poisson (Rissoles for fish days)

Take some chestnuts, boil gently and peel them; have ready some hard-boiled eggs, peeled cheese, both finely chopped. Mix with the chestnuts, moisten with white of egg, and season with finely ground salt. Shape the rissoles, and fry them in deep fat and sugar them.

Note that in Lent, use dried salt cod, cut in small pieces, or pike meat or eel with figs and dates all chopped together. On ordinary days, the rissoles are made with figs, raisins, apples and peeled nuts to balance the taste of the spices. Use saffron generously, then fry in oil. Flour and rice may be used for binding if required. Item: lobster meat is good instead of the ones given here.
(*Le Menagier de Paris*, 1540)

Poulets en culottes

Take 2 plump chickens. Lift the tail as you would a pigeon's and arrange the legs and thighs so that they stand away from the body. Beat the breast and rump: stuff with ham, veal, pork fat and a little oil. Roast the birds, drain them and strain off the liquid for gravy. Colour the chicken with the residue of the liquid browned in the pan. Serve with the clear gravy. You may add a green sauce or prawn butter. Or, if you wish, you may prepare any other sort of fowl in the same manner.
(*Le Cuisinier Gascon*, 1740)

Veau en crotte d'âne roulé à la neuteau (veal as donkey droppings)

Take a well hung piece of topside of veal, and prepare as for larding; cut it in 15 or 20 pieces across the fibres. Beat them thoroughly, making each one as long as your hand and as thick as two fingers. Then lay them on a flat board, sprinkle with parsley, chives, shallots, mushrooms and truffles, all chopped very finely together. Season with salt, pepper and moisten with oil. When the meat has taken up the taste roll up the pieces separately, on two skewers, and roast on a spit.

288

When they are cooked serve on the board with a sauce of your own choice, such as a green, an Italian or a shallot sauce, or a reduced clear gravy. You may make this dish from mutton, *Alloyau* fillets, hare or chicken. It is good.

Des Yeux de Veau farcis au gratin (Stuffed calves' eyes *au gratin*)

Soak and then blanch calves' eyes. Take out the pupils and the iris, and replace with a whole small truffle: braise and then arrange on a bed of breadcrumbs on a flat dish with tiny onions and truffles already braised separately and roll the eyeballs on this. Season and serve.

You may also egg and breadcrumb the eyes and fry them, with a clear *espagnole* sauce, or alternatively a green sauce.
(*Le Cuisinier Gascon*, 1740)

Rissoles de tetines de veau (calf's teat rissoles)

Take well blanched and cooked calf's udders. Cut up and put a layer of stuffing between 2 strips of meat, enclose in a light pastry and fry: you may also prepare the rolls on little sticks, egg and breadcrumb, and grill.
(*Le Cuisinier Gascon*, 1740)

CEREAL RECIPES

FAR
A porridge or pudding made from barley or flour.

Far Breton or Farsach du Finistère
A sweet dish, grandfather of the *Pudding Anglaise* (steamed or boiled pudding).

8 oz. flour
5 oz. sugar
4 whole eggs
4 oz. stoned Malaga raisins
A good glassful of rum
Milk

Mix all the dry ingredients except the raisins. Add milk and eggs little by little to avoid lumps and beat until the mixture is smooth and liquid. Butter an ovenproof dish or bowl, and sprinkle all over with the raisins. Gently pour in the batter so as not to disturb or move the raisins, and bake in a hot oven for about half an hour. Dust with caster sugar and serve hot.

(*Recettes et Paysages*, Publications Françaises, 1952)

Far Poitevin

Far Poitevin is a sort of stuffing from Poitou. It is prepared from mixed fresh vegetables, all sliced very small, as in consommé *à la julienne*, such as sorrel, cabbage, beet and lettuce. Mix all these with chopped pork fat, blend with cream and eggs, flavour with mixed herbs and chives, all highly seasoned. This mixture is then wrapped in green cabbage and lettuce leaves, placed in a net, and boiled in a *pot-au-feu*. This *pot-au-feu* can be made with both fresh and salt pork, flavoured with the usual vegetables.

(*Larousse Gastronomique*, 1938)

MILLIASSE OR MILLAS

This is the name given to a sort of maize pudding or cake in the province of Languedoc, prepared either from maize, or a mixture of wheat and maize flour.

The name of this preparation would seem to derive from the word millet, the common name for several members of the grass family grown in the Midi and above all in the Landes region. One of these grasses, called *millette*, a variety of maize with a small grain, was originally used to make these dishes. If *millas* strictly speaking comes from Languedoc, it is made throughout south-east and south-west France. Porridges or puddings or cakes very similar in their nature are made in these parts and are given different names according to the districts where they are known.

So in Guyenne and Gascony the name is *cruchade*. In Béarn it is *broye*, *gaudine* or *yerbilhou*; *las pous* or *rimotes* in Périgord, and *gaudes* in Franche Comté. The *polenta* made in Corsica and also in Provence is very much of the same nature.

The *millas* of Languedoc is a country dish, and is eaten like bread, accompanying such dishes as beef stew, jugged hare, and so on.

Sometimes the cooled *millas* is cut in pieces, either square or rectangular, brushed over with fat, and fried or grilled. In Languedoc it is also used in various ways as a dessert.

Boil salted water in a cauldron, and pour in the maize or maize and wheat flour mixed to make an even consistency. Stir with a wooden spoon and simmer, stirring continuously until the mixture is thick. Add several tablespoonfuls of goose fat. Mix well. Turn this out on a thick linen cloth while it is still hot, and let it run out to a thickness of about one inch. Leave to cool. Cut in squares or rectangles, and adapt to whatever recipe is followed.

Broye

A kind of porridge made from maize flour, either white or roasted, made in Béarn.

Broye made with white, i.e. unbleached flour, is prepared in the same way as ordinary porridge or *bouillie*.

> First boil vegetable stock, seasoned only with salt, and gradually stir in the flour until a solid mass is formed. It must be continually stirred throughout the cooking. Grease the ladle which is used for serving, so that the porridge does not stick to the utensil.
>
> If the flour has been roasted, or *troustado* or *tourado*, the term used in Béarn, it is made with the flour *fontaine*, that is the flour is spread over the bottom of a dish, moistened with the liquid indicated, thoroughly mixed, and then cooked.
>
> When the *broye* is cold, it can be cut in slices, which are then fried in hot fat until nicely brown, and served hot.
>
> (La Cuisine en Béarn, Simon Palay, *Larousse Gastronomique*, 1938)

Cruchade

A kind of porridge, made with milk or water, and maize flour. This porridge, similar to the *milliasse* or millet made in south-west France and also to *polenta* from the south-east and in Italy, is made above all in the Bordeaux region.

> Blend maize flour and milk, cook over a low heat, add a good lump of butter. When the mixture is evenly cooked, turn out on a flat surface and leave to cool.
>
> Cut in pieces in any shape you fancy, and fry in deep fat. Serve, dusted with sugar.
>
> (*L'Art du Bien Manger*, E. Richardin)

Gaudes (*Reseda luteola*): Name given in Burgundy and in Franche Comté to the flour made from this form of maize and to the porridge or pudding made with it, so called because of the yellowish colour of the flour.

This substance is nourishing but rather hard on the digestion for those stomachs not accustomed to it.

Gaudes à la Bourguignonne

Mix the maize flour with water as you would with ordinary flour, the amounts varying according to the quantity and the consistency of porridge desired. Put water in a pan, salt it and bring it to the boil. Pour the flour into this and stir with a wooden spoon so that there are no lumps, and so that the mixture does not stick to the bottom of the pot. Cook for half an hour.

When it is cooked add a lump of fresh butter and serve accompanied by cold milk or cream which will be added according to taste at table. The milk is sometimes replaced by wine, but this mixture is not to everybody's taste.

When the dish is cold it will take the shape of the bowl or dish in which it has been left and will look like a blancmange. This can then be sliced, which has given people the idea of adding sugar.

(*Dictionnaire Universel de Cuisine Pratique*, Joseph Favre)

Miques de Mais (A dish from Périgord)

Make a dough with 8 oz. maize flour, and 8 oz. wheat flour and a good spoonful of pork fat, a pinch of salt and a glass of warm water.

When the dough is well blended, cut it in pieces, each about $3\frac{1}{2}$ oz. in weight, and form into balls. Poach them in boiling salted water. Turn them once or twice during the cooking.

Drain the *miques*, and keep them hot in a cloth. The cooking will take from 25–35 minutes.

These cakes are eaten like bread. In the country districts of Périgord they are always served as an accompaniment to dishes such as salt cabbage, jugged hare or rabbit, etc.

Alternately they can be fried in butter, dusted with sugar and served as a dessert.

Polenta: Maize meal porridge thickened by cooking. Maize plays a very important role among various peoples of the world and lends itself to very many different ways of preparation in cooking. These dishes are known by a great variety of names. I will describe the national Italian dish. Piedmontese cooks disagree over the choice of flour to prepare the best *polenta*. Some prefer a coarse meal, others a very finely milled flour. Whatever the choice, the meal must be freshly ground.

Polenta au fil, so called because it is cut with a string or twine, and not a knife.

    2 lb. maize meal or flour
    5 pints boiling salted water

Boil the water in a saucepan and throw in the maize at boiling point, stirring continuously and cook for 25 minutes. It should then be firm, and will form a single mass coming away from the side of the pan, with the exception of a thin layer which will nearly always stick to the bottom. Turn the whole out on a board and shape into an oblong or rectangle; after leaving it to cool for 10 minutes, cut with string, wire or twine. Serve it quite simply unadorned and smoking hot.

Such is the *polenta* so dear to the Italian workmen, especially in Sardinia and Piedmont. The inhabitants of poor countries eat it like this every day of the year without any other accompaniment. In towns people eat it *bagnata*, that is to say moistened with the sauce from a dish such as rabbit, stew, sausages or cod. It takes the place of bread and vegetables. Masons work for months on a diet of *polenta*, cheese and water.

Beignets de Polenta (a pudding)

    About 7 oz. maize flour
    $3\frac{1}{2}$ oz. sugar
    $3\frac{1}{2}$ oz. butter
    Pinch salt
    4 egg yolks
    $2\frac{1}{2}$ pints milk
    Stick of vanilla

Heat the milk, salt and stick of vanilla. When it has boiled for a few minutes take out the vanilla. Sprinkle the maize flour gradually into the milk, stirring the while. Add the butter and boil for another 15 minutes, stirring right to the bottom of the pan. Take off the heat and blend in the 4 egg yolks. Lay the dough on a damp board and roll it out to about $\frac{1}{2}$ in. thick, then leave to cool. Cut into rings with a pastry cutter, and egg and breadcrumb twice. Fry in deep fat, drain well and dredge with sugar, and serve on a napkin. Serve accompanied by a compote of fresh fruit or zabaglione, or with a fruit sauce.
(*Dictionnaire Universel de Cuisine Pratique*, Joseph Favre)

MILLET

One of the grass family, and also a cereal. Two varieties are recognized – common and grape, or cluster, millet. Common millet has been cultivated in Egypt and the Middle East since ancient times, and grape millet in Japan. It was cultivated in India in prehistoric times. It was used by the Romans as a porridge made with milk. It is still used as dehusked grain by certain African peoples.

Millet au Beurre

Having been scalded with boiling water several times, the millet is cooked in lightly salted water. It is then taken off the fire and strained. Before serving, a good lump of butter is added.

Millet Gratiné

Scald the millet and put in a buttered ovenproof dish. For roughly every 10 oz. of millet allow 2 oz. of cream and about 8 fl. oz. of water and a lump of butter; cook in the oven until it is a light golden brown.
(*Régimes Végétariens*, Mesdames Coquelet and Tissier)

Milliassous (*pâtisserie*)

Put 7 oz. of millet flour, 14 oz. sugar and 8 eggs in an ovenproof dish. Blend the ingredients well, add the finely grated rinds of 2 lemons. Add 2½ pints boiling milk and mix well. Bake for about 20-30 minutes in a hot oven.
(*Larousse Gastronomique*, 1938)

SAUCES

Calimafree or Saulce Paresseuse (Lazy Sauce)

Take some mustard, powdered ginger, a little vinegar and some fat, and the liquid from a carp: boil all together. If you wish to use this sauce for a capon, in place of the fat and carp liquid, use grape juice, vinegar, and chicken fat.

Aulx camelins pour Raye (Uncooked sauce stuffing for Skate)

Mix ginger, garlic and bread soaked in vinegar: or use bread with vinegar: if you add some liver to the mixture it will be better still.

Saulce vert d'espices (Green herb stuffing)

In a mortar pound ginger, cloves, berries, and parsley or *salemonde*, sorrel, marjoram, or two of these four herbs, together with white breadcrumbs soaked in grape juice. Blend and mix them well together and season with vinegar.

Note that it is a good sauce even if it had no bread in it.

Note that many other herbs can be used, but not rosemary.

(*Le Menagier de Paris*, 1540)

SWEETS

Les Noix

Preserved nuts are the longest of all preserves to make. They should be chosen young, before the shell becomes woody, and peeling must be done with a brass knife, as the nuts will be blackened by an iron one. The nuts should be divided lengthwise into three, so that penetration is easier during boiling. Directly the nuts are peeled, they are thrown into tepid water, and are then simmered, in a large quantity of water on hot embers until the next day, when the water is replaced by fresh water, and boiling is repeated. Then take off the fire and drain. Simmer a third time in fresh water, and repeat as often as necessary until the nuts have lost their bitterness.

Finally they are boiled in a good white French wine; for a hundred nuts use a quart of wine and an equal volume of water, adding a nut-sized quantity of saltpetre (potassium nitrate) to facilitate saturation and sweetening of the nuts. If no saltpetre is available, half the quantity of salt should be added. When the nuts are cooked and are tending to break up, drain them thoroughly and dry with a linen cloth. Sprinkle with lemon rind and preserve them as other sweets, adding a little water to dissolve the sugar, with cinnamon and cloves as seasoning. Three-quarters of a pound of sugar is enough for one pound of nuts weighed at the final preserving stage. When the nuts are preserved and the syrup is of the right consistency the nuts are turned out into bowls and left open several days. Add a little ambergris at the end of the cooking. The big nuts of Mauge are the best of all.

(*Le Jardinier François*, 1692)

ALGUES (Seaweed)

Algae marinae species esculentae, Alga coralloides feu agarum coralloides, Acetabulum marinum, Agarum bractualum, Agarum funiculare feu foliatum, Agarum lactucarium feu lactua marina, Agarum cotricosum feu guleola.

As they come from the sea, all *algae* are covered with slimy mucus and are impregnated with salt. They also exude a sea smell and have a salty taste; but if they are marinated and washed in fresh water, most of the mucosity and the saltiness will be washed away. They may then be eaten raw with *Atsjar*. They may also be eaten with lime juice or a little ginger. Or they may be cut up and dried in the sun, before being preserved in vinegar; or may be cooked along with other foods. Be careful not to cook them too long or leave them overlong in the lime juice, because if so, they will lose their goodness.

Algues d'Irlande, algae saccharifera
When Irish *algae* has been exposed for some time to the rays of the sun little salty bubbles, sweet and good to taste, form on the surface. The inhabitants of the coasts of Ireland eat this like sugar. They also gather this plant before it has become covered with this sugar to eat as salad.
(*Manual Alimentaire des Plantes*, M. Buc'hoz, Physician to the late King of Poland, 1771)

Sèvres porcelain, from the set given by Louis XV to the Duchess of Bedford in 1763

8　Historical Menus

Two Royal Meals

'Everything is within everything'. Sparta in its gruel, Rome in Trimalchio's wild boar stuffed with live thrushes. A cookery is a whole civilization, a menu contains an entire reign.

I have a manuscript, illustrated and written by Biron de Sainte Marie, which gives us the details of the supper eaten by Louis XV at the Château de Choisy on 29 September 1755.

THE SOUPS
Two *oilles*
One of large onions
One *à l'espagnole*
Two *potages*
One *de santé*
One of turnip *purée*

THE ENTRÉES
Small pies *à la balaquine*
Rabbit fillets *à la genèvoise*
Filet mignon of mutton with *sauce piquante*
Fillets of pheasant *en matelote*
Quails with bay leaves

Turtle doves *à la venitienne*
Partridges *à l'ancien salmy*
Small garnished pigeons
Blanquette of fowls with truffles
Marinade of *campines*
Fowl wings *en hatelets*
Leg of veal glazed with its own juice
Minced game *à la turque*
Sweetbreads *Ste Ménehould*
Rouen ducklings with orange
Halicot with dark *velouté* sauce

FOUR RELEVÉS
Roast mutton of Choisy
Rump of beef *à l'écarlate*
Sirloin, the fillet minced with chicory
Caux fowls with raw onion

FOUR MAIN ENTREMETS
Pheasant pie
Jambon de perdrouillet
Brioche
Croquante

TWO MEDIUM ENTREMETS – ROASTS
Small chickens
Campines
Ortolans
Thrushes
Guignards
Red-leg partridges
Pheasants
Rouen duckling

'Supper with the Regent' (Philippe, Duc d'Orléans, 1674–1723) by Eugène Lami, 1854

SIXTEEN SMALL ENTREMETS
A coffee cream
Artichokes *à la baligoure*
Cardoons *à l'essence*
Cauliflower with Parmesan
Eggs with partridge gravy
Truffles *à la cendre*
Spinach with gravy
Cocks' crests
Animelles

299

Green beans with verjuice
Ham omelette
Turkey legs *à la duxelles*
Mixed *ragoût*
Chocolate *profiterolles*
Small *jalousies*
Crême à la genest

And so that you may compare this supper of Louis XV at Choisy with a supper given at Trianon for Marie Antoinette, here is the menu of this supper from the imperial archives quoted by *L'Almanach des Gourmands pour 1862* by Charles Monselet. Her Majesty's Dinner, Thursday 24 July 1788 at Trianon:

FOUR SOUPS
Rice soup
Scheiber
Croûtons with lettuce
Croûtons unis pour Madame

TWO MAIN ENTRÉES
Rump of beef with cabbage
Loin of veal on the spit

SIXTEEN ENTRÉES
Spanish pâtés
Grilled mutton cutlets
Rabbits on the skewer
Fowl wings *à la maréchale*
Turkey giblets in *consommé*
Larded breast of mutton with chicory
Fried turkey *à la ravigote*
Sweetbreads *en papillotte*

Calves' heads *sauce pointue*
Chickens *à la tartare*
Spitted sucking pig
Caux fowl with *consommé*
Rouen duckling with orange
Fowl fillets *en casserole* with rice
Cold chicken
Chicken *blanquette* with cucumber

FOUR HORS D'OEUVRE
Fillets of rabbit
Breast of veal on the spit
Shin of veal in *consommé*
Cold turkey

SIX DISHES OF ROASTS
Chickens
Capon fried with eggs and breadcrumbs
Leveret
Young turkey
Partridges
Rabbit

SIXTEEN SMALL ENTREMETS

'And so, *bon appétit*.' Jules de Goncourt.

Vinum.   Vinū uetus.   Vinū rubeum   Vinū citri-   Vinū ace-   Vinum de da-   Vinum Ami-
                          grofsum.   num.   rofum.   ctylis.   gdalinum.

Supper in the theatre at Versailles by Eugène Lami, 1854

Canna mellis.   Candi.   Lutū corafcenū.   Feftuca.   Nucellæ.   Amigdalæ cū fale. Rabes.

Menu for a Dinner of Forty from *Manuel des Amphitryons,* *1808* by Grimod de la Reynière

FOUR SOUPS
A *Julienne*
A *potage à la Condé*
A *garbure au Fromage*
A *potage à la Necker*

TWO RELEVÉS
Rump of beef garnished with sauerkraut
Truffled turkey, braised

TWO TERRINES
One of chipolata
One fricassee *à la marinière* (mussels and shellfish)

SIXTEEN ENTRÉES
Rib of beef, champagne sauce
Saddle of mutton with mashed turnips
Fowl with beans
Partridge cutlets
Sauté with truffles
Game in aspic

The drawings at the head and foot of the following pages are taken from 'Tacuini Sanitatis', *1531*

A hot pâté *à la financière*
Salmon steaks *à l'anglaise*
Veal cutlets *à la singara*
Larded leg of veal with chicory
Quails *à la orly*
Turkey wings *à la villeroy*
A *salmis* of plovers
Fillets of rabbit *en turban*
Vol-au-vent of chicken *blanquette*
Cod *au gratin*

TWO LARGE SWEETS
A baba
Chocolate soufflé

SIX ROAST DISHES
Fowl
Snipe
Small salmon trout
Vineyard quails
Red-leg partridges
Fried smelts

SIXTEEN ENTREMETS
Cardoons *à l'essence*
Spinach with *croûtons*
Suèdoise of apples
Rye rolls
Salad *à l'anglaise*
Truffles served in napkins
Maraschino jelly
Blancmange
Cauliflower with Parmesan
Mashed potatoes

A cake *a la maréchale*
Grilled *choux*
Little rice cakes
Poached eggs
A jelly of Maltese oranges
A caramel cream

Comments★ : We must admit that this menu begins grandly, and that nothing could give a better notion of the first course than those four soups. A well-made *Julienne* is excellent, and only an artist can extract so much wit and charm from carrots, cabbage and turnips. There is nothing nobler than a *potage à la Condé*; it recalls a glorious name which shone on the last reigns of the third dynasty. *Garbure* with cheese successfully unites Languedoc, Spain and Italy; truly a triple alliance in a soup tureen. As for *potage à la Necker* it was probably mockingly or by antithesis that it was given the name for it is excellent, whereas that hypocritical and vain old man, the prime cause of all the ills from which France suffered for fifteen years, could not have fathered anything good. Swollen with pride and self-sufficiency, with insolence and perfidy, he wormed his way up through the literary élite of the day (whom he later repaid, as usual, by ingratitude) to the government of the country, whereas he was fit for no more than being a shop assistant. His presumption destroyed us, and his memory, today ignored (which would be more hateful to him than shame or loathing), hardly survives in this soup which should have been given a more honest name.

The sauerkraut garnish for the rump of beef should come from Strasbourg via Mme Chevet. Hers is one of the best shops in Paris for foie gras, truffles, red-leg partridges, snipe, pike and other great fish, and cooked truffles from Périgord, preserved sardines and so on. The enormous turnover in this tiny shop allows Mme Chevet to renew her stock constantly and to sell at moderate prices. Moreover this charming young mother of fourteen children is extremely pleasant to her customers. (At No. 220 Palais Royal.) Sauerkraut can also be purchased from other first-class food shops. It is even made in Paris, but this is very mediocre stuff as we do not have cabbages suitable for this

★By Grimod.

particular preparation. The garnish will be improved by surrounding it with small chipolata sausages bought from M. Corps (Rue St Antoine) who is from almost every point of view the best pork butcher in Paris. As for the truffled turkey, it should come from Périgord and be bought either at the *Hôtel des Américains*, or at Mme Chevet's, or from M. Catheux, a young man who shows great promise and who has just set up shop on the former premises of the gourmet-bookseller De Senne, at the Palais Royal. (M. Catheux has just left M. Corcelet in whose magnificent shop he worked for ten years to the complete satisfaction of its owner and its customers.) The point is, a really good turkey does not have to be fetched at great expense from Périgord, but its truffles do.

It is a fact that turkeys from that region are drier, less succulent and fat, indeed less delicious than those from the Gâtinais, the Orléanais, and the rich land around the Ile de France. Therefore one need only choose an excellent turkey from one of those happy lands and marry it to the best Périgord truffles – that is the difficulty. Indeed, ten years ago the art of truffling turkeys and other fowls was only known in Périgord whose natives literally held up gourmets of other regions for huge sums like twenty or twenty-five *écus* per bird.

Happily the secret is now in the hands of the great cooks of the capital. They use it daily, for their profit and our pleasure without any loss of sensual satisfaction. They know how to 'truffle'; *truffer* is one of the lucky words which have enriched the French language in the last fifteen years and which has reached out from the cookery dictionary into the vocabulary of modern French *salons*, though the Academy, or its representatives, for better or for worse, have not yet given it its patents of *bourgeoisie*. It means, literally, to

Afsum.   Iudep de pane.   Iudep de Chatay.   Iudep de papauere.   Iudep de Melonibus.   Iudep de dactylis.   Coriandrum.

306

give something the scent of truffle. We have seen in the Sixth Year of the *Almanach des Gourmands* that maraschino can be truffled just as well as turkeys. Yes, they now truffle Orléanais and Gâtinais turkeys so perfectly that our palates respond to them with the same delight as to the real Périgourdines, but at considerably less expense.

Indeed, seven-eighths of the truffled turkeys sold today in Paris under the name of Périgord turkeys have never been closer than sixty leagues to the department of the Dordogne. However, people buy them as such, and the dupes pay for them as such (a real Périgord turkey, stuffed with truffles and very large, sells in Paris for up to 60 *livres* and transport charges account for a great deal of this enormous price; whereas one can buy an excellent *Orléanaise* as beautiful and even fatter and stuffed with the same truffles for half this sum). But the gourmets who eat know quite well what they are doing though they make no difference in their choice.

This parenthesis has led us rather far from our subject: the menu. The chipolata and the *marinière* fricassee will adorn the two terrines (which should come from the admirable workshops of M. Henri Auguste, the finest gold-smith in Paris) far better today than when they were included in the banquet given by the First President d'Aligre for the Paris Parlement.

Among the entrées we shall only draw attention to the *sauté* of truffles, the game in aspic, the salmon steaks *à l'anglaise*, the plover *salmis*, the quails *à la orly*. (One has seen in many other menus a number of *ragoûts à la orly*. We have searched in vain for the etymology of this name; all we have been able to ascertain is that there is, near Pontoise, some very rich game-land which today belongs to M. de Lameth who played such an important part during the finer days of the Revolution), the turkey wings *à la villeroy*, and the rabbit

Vinum.   Vinū uetus.   Vinū rubeum   Vinū citri-   Vinū ace-   Vinum de da-   Vinum Ami-
                          grofsum.   nutn.   rofum.   ctylis.   gdalinum.

fillets *en turban*, all very refined dishes with which the chef must take particular care. The six roasts offer three kinds of first class game which must be bought from Mme Chevet; plus the little salmon trout from Strasbourg which should be no larger than the sprats which counterbalance them, and which are none-the less divine fare. The sixteen *entremets* provide a happy assortment of vegetables and pleasing sweets. Among the latter we note particularly the *suèdoise* of apples, the little rye rolls, the little rice cakes and the cake *à la maréchale*; the truffles in napkins (so called because they are cooked in an excellent court-bouillon with white wine, and then served in a folded napkin like boiled eggs or Lyon chestnuts) must be huge and heavily scented. There must be at least one per guest, and it is rare for them to be eaten at the table: one may put them in one's pocket and the ladies set the example. It is the finest of aphrodisiacs, but one of the most costly *entremets* in the world, for a dish of truffles in napkins for a table of forty guests like this cannot cost less than two *louis*.

Eggs poached *au naturel*, that is to say in the best mutton juice, must be very fresh, very soft, and eaten very hot with a pinch of mignonette; as aphrodisiacs they are worthy to accompany the truffles in napkins.

The two jellies of Maltese oranges and Maraschino, the caramel cream, and the blancmange (so much superior to other creams when it is properly made) complete this *entremets* in the most distinguished fashion.

Sèvres porcelain, from the set given by Louis XV to the Duchess of Bedford in 1763

Canna mellis.   Candi,   Lutū corascenū.   Festuca.   Nucellæ.   Amigdalæ cū sale.   Rabes.

Dinner for a Meat Day, of Thirty-One Dishes in Six Plates from *Le Ménagier de Paris, 1540*

FIRST PLATE
Garnache and *tostées*
Veal pies
Pinparneaux pies
Black puddings
Sausages

SECOND PLATE
Jugged hare and cutlets
Pease pudding
Salt meat
Large joint
Soringue of eels and other fish

THIRD PLATE: Roast
Rabbits
Partridges
Capons
Pike
Sea-perch
Carp
Potage *escartelé*

FOURTH PLATE
River birds *sauce Dodine*
Rice *engoulé*
Bourrée with hot sauce
Eels *renversés*

FIFTH PLATE
Aloes pasties
Rissoles
Lait lardé
Sugared *flaonnes*

SIXTH PLATE
Pears
Sugared almonds
Medlars
Peeled walnuts
Hippocras
Le mestier

Garnache: Grenache wine. See Legrand d'Aussy, Vol. III, p. 48.
Mestier: Thin type of waffle made of flour, water, white wine and sugar and cooked in a waffle-iron.

Myrtus.   Rofa.   Ocimū origanatū. Violæ.   Lilia.   Citra.   Fruct̃ Mãdragoræ.

Aqua fon- Aqua plu- Nix & Gla- A qua Niui Aqua calida. Aqua falfa. Aqua fluminofa.
tium.   uialis.   cies.   mixta.

Another Dinner of Twenty-Four Dishes in Three Plates
from *Le Ménagier de Paris, 1540*

FIRST DISH

Pease pudding

Salt eels

Herring

Leeks with almonds

Large joint of meat

Yellow broth

A *salemine*

Sea-fish

Jugged *oï tres*

SECOND DISH

Roast

Freshwater fish

Sea-fish

A Savoy broth

A larded broth of eels *renversées*

THIRD DISH

Roast of bream

Galantine

Swan

311

Zuccharum.　Mel.　Feludichi.　Catayf cū nucibus.　Chabis.　Chaloe cū nucib.　Cuskabenchi.

Pilgrim capons
Jelly
Blancmange *parti*
Plaice *en l'eau*
Turbot *à la soucie*
Cream *darioles*
Lampreys with hot sauce
Doreures
Rice *engoulé*

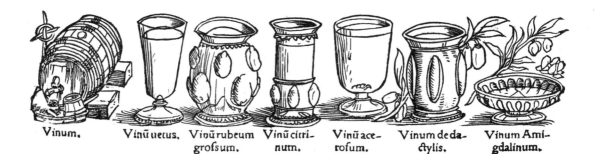

Vinum.　Vinū uetus.　Vinū rubeum grofsum.　Vinū citrinum.　Vinū acerofum.　Vinum de dactylis.　Vinum Amigdalinum.

Afsum. Iudep de pane. Iudep de   Iudep de pa-   Iudep de Melo-   Iudep de da-   Corian-
                        Chatay.   pauere.   nibus.   ctylis.   drum.

Fish Dinners for Lent from *Le Ménagier de Paris, 1540*

FIRST DISH AND PLATE

Baked apples

Large Provençal figs roasted under bay leaves

Cress and sorrel with vinegar

Pease pudding

Salt eels

White herring

Gravé of whitebait

Small freshwater fish, fried

SECOND DISH

Carp

Pike

Soles

Red mullet

Salmon

Eels

Præparatoria   Maheleb,   Aqua Cam-   Vfuem. Ciperi.   Sandalus albus,   Rofæ.
Dentium.   phoræ.   &rubeus.

Præpararoria Dencium.   Maheleb,   Aqua Cam- phoræ.   Vſuem.   Ciperi.   Sandalus albus, & rubeus.   Roſæ.

Banquet for François I offered by the Town of Harfleur in August 1520 from *Les Classiques de la Table, 1855* by Justin Améro

The following document drawn from the *Memorial de Chronologie* (Paris, Verdière, 1830), p. 1001, may give some idea of the dishes which then constituted a ceremonial feast. Some interesting conclusions may also be drawn from it regarding the monetary value of basic foodstuffs at the beginning of the sixteenth century. It is a statement of costs for the entertainment, as mentioned in the title:

	Livre	*Sous*
15 dozen loaves	1	10
Partridges, ducks, cocks' kidneys, plovers, capons	1	15
Two sheep	1	12
Four legs of mutton	1	10
Six tarts	1	18
8 lb. lard	1	16
A dozen stem glasses	1	9
57 gallons of wine at *2 sous 6 deniers* a pot	14	5
A puncheon of Orléans claret	8	–
Total for having had the honour to please the King and his suite	35	15
Plus for the quartermaster	8	–
The King's lackey	6	–
Total expenditure	49	15

314

Canna mellis.   Candi.   Lutū corafcenū.   Feftuca.   Nucellæ.   Amigdalæ cū fale.   Rabes.

The King's Meat (*Louis XIV*)

Three hundred and twenty-four people were exclusively employed on preparing the toothless monarch's food. This army was lodged in the Grand Commun, now the Hôpital Militaire.

At meal-times, the 'meat', that is to say, all the dishes shown on the menu, was borne in solemn procession, led by the First *Maître d'Hotel*, himself accompanied by thirty-six serving gentlemen and twelve Masters bearing as a sign of seniority a silver-gilt baton, from the kitchens across the road into the palace, through a maze of galleries and corridors and finally to the King's table which was usually laid in his bedroom. Louis XIV generally ate alone, except when away from Versailles; he seldom if ever entertained another man and only admitted his family to his board on rare occasions when the Princes of the Blood wore their hats and he remained bareheaded, no doubt in order to convey that he was the host and at home, whereas the others were no more than transient guests.

On rising, for his breakfast he took only a *bouillon* or a cup of sage tea, so that by the ten o'clock meal his appetite was keen and the matter serious; the following meal was prepared for one person.

SOUPS
Of the two old capons, four partridges with cabbage, six pigeons for a *bisque*, one of cocks' crests and *béatilles*

HORS D'OEUVRE
One of capons, partridges

ENTRÉES
A quarter of veal with the rump, the whole of 28 lb. 12 pigeons for pie

SMALL ENTRÉES
Six fricasseed chickens, two minced partridges, three young partridges in gravy, six ember cooked pies, two young grilled turkeys, three fat chickens with truffles

ROASTS
Two fat capons, 9 chickens, 9 pigeons, 2 *pétendeaux*, 6 partridges, 4 tarts

DESSERTS
Two bowls of fruit, 2 of dried preserves, 4 of stewed fruit, or liquid jams

It was a bold trencherman who could confront a 28 lb. quarter of veal, 69 fowls and so many pies all on his table at once! But this did not affect the supper served at 6 p.m.: 2 old capons, 12 pigeons, 1 partridge with Parmesan, 4 other pigeons, 6 chickens, 8 lb. veal, 3 fat chickens, 1 pheasant, 3 partridges, 2 fat hens, 4 *pétendeaux*, 8 chickens, 9 pigeons, 4 tarts.

And the King seems to have considered he was being put on short commons, for there is a note added to the effect that four partridges *sauce espagnole* and two fat chickens roast in pastry were to be added to the menu.

The roast was also flanked by two small dishes; one of a capon, two snipe and two teal, and the other consisting simply of five partridges.

The hors d'oeuvre are not mentioned, but they were not tiny dainties but solid stuff: sausage, white *boudin*, truffled pasties and warmed up beef in gravy.

However, during Lent, the King rested and allowed his royal stomach to benefit by abstinence. It must however be noted that a totally meatless meal, for fear that he might be too debilitated on fast-days, usually began with a soup made of a capon, 4 lb. beef, 4 lb. veal and 4 lb. mutton. This purely hygienic precaution taken, abstinence began: a carp, a hundred crayfish, a milk soup, a herb soup, two turtle soups, a sole, a large pike, four medium soles, two perch, a sole, a hundred oysters, six sting-fish, and as a roast half a salmon and six soles. So much for dinner.

316

And for supper: two foot-long carp, two soups, a pike a foot and a half long, three perch, three soles, a trout a foot and a half long, half a large salmon, a large carp. All the King had then to do was retire to bed, but for fear of his collapsing from night starvation a tiny snack was put at his door – a mere nothing – a bottle of water, three loaves and two bottles of wine.

Zuccharum.   Mel.   Feludichi.   Catayf cū nucibus.   Chabis.   Chaloe cū nucib.   Cuskabenchi.

Aqua fon- | Aqua plu- | Nix & Gla- | Aqua Niui | Aqua calida. | Aqua falfa. | Aqua fluminofa.
tium. | uialis. | cies. | mixta.

Maréchal de Richelieu: Menu of an Entirely Beef Supper
from *Les Classiques de la Table, 1844*

DORMANT (centrepiece)

The big silver-gilt tray with the equestrian portrait of the King. The statues of Du Guesclin, Dunois, Bayard and Turenne.

My silver-gilt plate with the arms in enamelled relief.

FIRST SERVICE
An *oille à la garbure* with beef *consommé*

FOUR HORS D'OEUVRE
Our own beef *à la Ste Ménehould*
Small minced beef pies with chives
Beef kidneys with fried onions
Tripe *à la poulette* with lemon juice

RELEVÉ DE POTAGE
The rump of beef garnished with root vegetables
(Cut these into grotesque shapes for the sake of the Germans)

SIX ENTRÉES
The oxtail with chestnut purée
The tongue, jugged, *à la bourguignonne*
Stuffed fillets of beef with preserved nasturtiums

318

The beef breast braised with celery
Beef rissoles with walnut purée
Roasted *croûtes* with our beef-marrow (Army biscuit will do as well as any
other bread)

SECOND SERVICE
The sirloin, roasted (baste with melted marrow)
Chicory salad with ox tongue
Beef *à la mode* in clear jelly mixed with pistachios
Cold beef loaf with blood and Jurançon wine (make sure you get it right)

SIX ENTREMETS
Glazed turnips with the juice of the roast beef
Beef-marrow pie with breadcrumbs and candy sugar
Aspic, beef essence with lemon rind browned in sugar
Purée of artichoke bottoms with juice and almond milk
Beef-brain fritters marinated in bitter orange juice
Beef jelly with Alicante wine and Mirabelle plums from Verdun
Then all my remaining jams or preserves

'Should this meal by some unfortunate mishap not be very good indeed, I
shall impose a fine of one hundred *pistoles* on the wages of Maret and Roque-
lere. Go, and doubt no more.' Richelieu

Præparatoria Dentium.   Maheleb.   Aqua Cam- phoræ.   Vfuem.   Ciperi.   Sandalus albus, & rubeus.   Rofæ.

'The First Meal' by Vagnier, c. 1920

Conclusion

Throughout every chapter of this book I have tried to combine as much information as possible with one or two theories of my own. Boileau Despréaux used to say: 'Ignorance is better than affected knowledge.'

Alas, I am an ignoramus who is perfectly aware of the fact.

At no time have I wished to impose an opinion or categorically state the truth of a fact. History reaches us conditioned by gossip, embellished or tarnished by courtiers. Our trade, which is our art, is mostly a manual one. Intelligence has nothing to do with culture, and indeed, much has only reached us by oral and corrupt tradition.

I have not wanted to set up idols or restore legends. It matters little to me that Vatel was a majordomo and not a cook or that Dunand was absent from the battle of Marengo. What has sustained me throughout is love for my work and for those who do it for love of their neighbours. Christ said blessed are the meek. The humble had to be protected and given the strength to carry on. Have you ever thought at your restaurant table or at that of your friend of all the effort which has gone into your meal, precisely from those you do not even see?

Have you never congratulated the chef or the *patron* on a meal which gave you pleasure? You know of course that they all have heavy responsibilities, but how many times have you asked the chef to come up and be congratulated? It is to ask the chef up on your behalf that I have written this book, as much as to recapture the past.

Index

An entry in capital letters represents a recipe given in full
rather than mentioned incidentally to illustrate a point